Coach U's Essential Coaching Tools

Coach U's Essential Coaching Tools: Your Complete Practice Resource

Coach U, Inc.

WILEY

John Wiley & Sons, Inc.

ISBN 0-471-71172-1

Printed in the United States of America

10

Contents

Acknowledgments

In 1992, the original curriculum for Coach U was authored by Thomas J. Leonard, the person recognized as the founder of the coaching profession. Since its inception, we have remained committed to regularly updating and improving our materials to remain the leading accredited coach-training organization in the world. There are literally hundreds of seasoned coaches to thank for contributing to the quality of our training materials. One particular individual who deserves recognition is Jodi Jan Shafer, the training director for CoachInc.com. This book would not have been possible without her ongoing focus and dedication.

Each year, we receive many calls and e-mails from our students and graduates, who graciously and generously provide us with input on how to further improve our body of knowledge. Today, our materials truly embody the concept of collective wisdom at its very best. This book is a synergistic product of many minds coming together in collaboration. Although we cannot thank each contributor individually, we sincerely appreciate all of the support that you have given us throughout the years. The comments, suggestions, class facilitation and participation, and coaching experiences that you have shared with us have made a difference. We hope that you are proud of the role that you have played and the contributions that you have made.

Finally, we would like to acknowledge you for considering this book. We know that if you are reading this book, you have an interest in supporting others in their personal and professional development or supporting the growth of organizations. Our vision has always been to have all individuals and organizations on the planet take a coach approach in all forms of communication, whether at home or at work.

We have come a long way since 1996, when we started working together—there were fewer than 500 coaches worldwide. Now, it delights us to know that you, our readers, understand that coaching isn't found just in sports and that coaching is changing the world, one person at a time.

Sandy Vilas
Owner and CEO of CoachInc.com

Jennifer Corbin
Coach U and Corporate Coach U President

Preface

I began my journey in the coaching profession in 1989, when I took a course offered by Thomas Leonard and became certified as a life planner.

Over the next five years, I wrote a book, led workshops, and spoke to groups all over the country. During that time, Thomas started Coach U (along with being my own personal coach). I was using my coaching skills at every opportunity, and in 1994 I enrolled in Coach U and became a full-time coach. At that time, most people had no idea what coaching was or how it worked. With the support of my coach, I was coaching 80 people a week at the end of my first year.

I was having more fun, was making more money, and was deeply imbued with a sense of peace, fulfillment, and satisfaction that I had never before experienced. I had clearly found my passion and mission in life; or, rather, it found me because I had done the work and was ready. Two years later, Thomas was ready to sell Coach U, and a week later I was the owner, amidst a great deal of excitement, mixed with a heavy dose of fear. The journey since has been full of lessons, satisfaction, and joy!

Today we have 27 staff members working out of their homes in four countries, and they are the most dedicated, hard-working, and creative people I've ever worked with. We have over 100 faculty members that are highly skilled at delivering our training and love giving back to this profession. We have over 11,000 students and graduates from 51 countries that are making a difference one client at a time.

I attribute my success as a coach to excellent training in the skills, language, and distinctions available in the book, as well as the brilliant coaching I received, and as a result I developed a strong desire to support others in their success. One way to realize this goal is to give new coaches the benefit of not only my experience but also the expertise of the many coaches, graduates, staff members, and faculty members of CoachInc.com. Part of this is to give our students the many forms and tools we have developed over the years. There's no need to reinvent the wheel; by understanding and using these tools provided, you will have the opportunity not only to spend time on your own self-awareness and development but also to support your coachees in having a great life.

As the reader of this book, you are beginning your journey and learning skills that will support you in any endeavor you choose to undertake. You may be a professional manager, entrepreneur, or consultant, or you may have a desire to become a full-time coach. Whatever motivation brought you to this book, I encourage you to immediately put the principles to work in your life. I hope it brings you the fulfillment so many others have attained as a result.

Sandy Vilas
Owner and CEO of CoachInc.com

Introduction

This book is designed to be a complete resources containing everything a coach needs to begin and maintain a successful coaching practice. These materials are intended to make the road to success easier so that you don't have to begin from scratch and reinvent the wheel. Whether you are developing a coaching business or positioning yourself as an internal coach, you will find materials to support your success.

Throughout your professional career, you may encounter a coaching situation you are not sure how to handle. You may also find new and unfamiliar challenges with your position or in developing your business. This book provides resources that can help you through these situations. You will often find the just-in-time resource that makes your work more effective.

Our intention is not that you read this resource cover to cover. From time to time you will go directly to a specific resource to address a particular situation. At other times you will explore the different areas and find the resources that resonate with your style and best serve your coaching niche.

The resources are divided into three different types of documents:

Forms

Forms are designed with open space you can use to record information. Forms for the coach provide practice or position documentation. Forms for the coachees can provide valuable information for you and also give the coachee information to refer to at a later date. The forms are available in word format on the CD-rom so you can modify them to include your personal coaching practice or position information. It is not necessary to include the CoachInc.com attribution when you manipulate the forms.

Programs

We offer numerous programs that develop awareness and provide information to you and your coachees. Several programs are building blocks in handling major life or business challenges used in the CoachInc.com curriculum. The programs are only provided in PDF format and are not to be altered in any manner.

7. Personal Foundation

Your personal foundation is much like the foundation of a building. The deeper and stronger the foundation, the taller the structure can be built. You want your coachees to build a strong foundation for their lives in order to have lives of authenticity, which are aligned with their values, and to have their needs met, once and for all. With a strong personal foundation, your coachees will be able to deal with life on life's terms.

This chapter includes list of information, tracking forms, and in-depth programs that will strengthen your coachees' foundation. It is designed to walk them through the core structure that forms the base from where they live their lives.

8. Attraction

This chapter covers the laws of attraction. You attract that which you put out to the universe. The concept of attraction is to naturally pull things toward you rather then pushing them toward you—in other words, floating downstream instead of fighting the current. Applying these concepts, you will struggle less and life will become effortless. You and your coachees will benefit tremendously from becoming attractive.

Included in this chapter are the main principles of attraction, changes to make, step-by-step programs, enhancement programs, and purpose worksheets.

9. Perfect Life

In this chapter we will explore the concept of having a perfect life. Can this be done? We believe so. This is about your coachee taking his or her life to the next level and creating the life he or she truly desires. By taking everything up a notch, your coachees will raise the bar on the quality of their lives.

You will find information on improving and perfecting their lives along with concepts and programs that will enhance their development in this area. By implementing the concepts presented they can dramatically improve their lives.

10. Personal Evolution

This chapter will continue your coachees' personal evolution and take everything they have learned up to this point to the next level. It will continue their growth and development as individuals.

Included is information that defines evolving, explores ways to evolve, and explains how to know you are evolving. There are lists, assessments, and programs to support the coachee in this continued growth.

11. Business Coaching Page 459

This chapter targets the business world from sole proprietors to corporations and includes information, forms, and programs relating to businesses or organizations. They can be used for your client's business or internal coaches within corporations. Not all information will be applicable to all situations; however, you can adapt it to suit your needs.

The information is laid out so that it provides introductory material, programs to work through for skill awareness and growth, and business forms, tracking sheets, and checklists to use. Many of these forms can be passed on to your coachees to use.

Please feel free to forward your questions or comments to me at Trainingdirector@coachinc.com.

Jodi Jan Shafer, Master Certified Coach
Training director, CoachInc.com

www.coachinc.com

Part 1
Practice Support

Chapter 1

About Coaching and Being a Coach

This chapter is designed to provide information for both the coach and the coachee on the profession. It will provide information on the profession in general, the coaching relationships, focus areas and specialties. Learn about what coaching is, the benefits of coaching, who hires a coach, customs, and foci along with basics of the relationship and coachee situations.

You will find general and specific information, key points, charts, lists, and assessments to guide you.

The following sections are included in this chapter:

1. Client Q&A about Business and Personal Coaching
2. Coachee Q&A about Business and Personal Coaching
3. Benefits of Being a Professional Coach
4. All about Coaching: 100 Key Points about Coaching and the Coaching Process
5. Coaching Customs
6. Primary Foci of Coaching
7. Coaching Focus Areas
8. The Professional Coach Is . . .
9. Basics of the Coaching Relationship
10. Things People Want Most
11. Coachee Situations
12. Should You Be a Coach?

Client Q&A about Business and Personal Coaching

What is coaching?

Coaching is a new profession that has synthesized the best from psychology, business, evolution, philosophy, spirituality, and finance to benefit the entrepreneur, professional, and business owner.

Why does coaching work?

Coaching works because of three unique features:

Synergy: Client and coach become a team, focusing on the client's goals and needs to accomplish more than the client would alone.

Structure: With a coach, a client takes more action, thinks bigger, and gets the job done, thanks to the accountability the coach provides.

Expertise: The coach knows how to help entrepreneurs make more money, make better decisions, set the best goals, and restructure their professional and personal lives for maximum productivity.

Who works with a coach?

Entrepreneurs, business owners, professionals, and people in transition use a coach to fix, solve, create, or plan something, personally or professionally.

What is worked on?

Here is what the client and coach work on together:

- Business planning, budgeting, and goal setting
- Integrating business and personal life for balance
- Turning around a difficult situation
- Achieving maximum work performance
- Handling business or personal problems
- Making key decisions and designing strategies
- Prioritizing actions and projects
- Catching up and getting ahead of the business
- Increasing sales substantially or filling a practice

But how does a coach do this?

Coaching is delivered during regular, weekly sessions by telephone or in person whichever is more convenient. Clients bring an agenda of items to the call or meeting. The coach helps them solve problems and make the most of opportunities. When they are taking on a large goal, we help them design the project and provide the support and structure needed to make sure it gets done. We bring out each client's best by offering advice, expecting a lot, helping them strategize and celebrating their wins. A practice can be national, with clients in every area of the country, from big cities to small towns; clients can range from small business owners to CEOs; and coaching can focus on either business goals or personal goals.

What should I look for in a coach?

The right coach brings out your best, consistently. To do this, the coach you select should pass the following three tests: (1) Does this coach have a track record of helping someone like me accomplish the goals I want? (2) Do I feel good and motivated to act when with this coach? (3) Will this coach keep up with me—and stay ahead of me—as I grow? That's it. You can always check references and try out the coach for a month to see if he or she is really the right one for you. I work well with three types of clients: (1) entrepreneurs and small-office professionals who are smart, quick, and ready to do what it takes to reach blockbuster goals; (2) individuals who are making substantial changes in their personal and professional lives; and (3) individuals who are working on an important project.

How much does it cost?

The fee for most entrepreneur and professional clients ranges from $200 to $500 per month for a weekly meeting or coaching call. For example, monthly coaching fees may be $250 for a weekly half-hour call or $500 for a weekly one-hour call, using an 800 number. There are no other charges, and clients may call in between calls for additional assistance, if needed. For projects, they may be billed at $125 per hour. For presentations, facilitating, or training, the fee is $1,500 per day, plus expenses.

How would I get started?

If you feel that this type of relationship could work for you, call and let's talk. Coaching is not something we sell; it is something you buy because you want it.

Where do I start with a coach?

Most coaches begin with a special client meeting to get to know each other. The coach wants to hear about the client's goals, needs, and problems. The client wants to get comfortable with the coach. During this meeting, both parties design a list of goals and a game plan to reach these goals. Prior to this meeting, the client will have received a welcome package containing checklists and assessment materials to make the most of the meeting. Some coaches spend extra time (gratis) with new clients getting to know them and coaching them to set the best goals for themselves, and together they design the best way to work together as a team to accomplish the goals.

Coachee Q&A about Business and Personal Coaching

What is coaching?

Coaching is a new profession that has synthesized the best from psychology, business, evolution, philosophy, spirituality, and finance to benefit the entrepreneur, professional, and business owner.

Why does coaching work?

Coaching works because of three unique features:

Synergy: Coachee and coach become a team, focusing on the coachee's goals and needs to accomplish more than the coachee would alone.

Structure: With a coach, a coachee takes more action, thinks bigger, and gets the job done, thanks to the accountability the coach provides.

Expertise: The coach knows how to help entrepreneurs make more money, make better decisions, set the best goals, and restructure their professional and personal lives for maximum productivity.

Who works with a coach?

Entrepreneurs, business owners, professionals, and people in transition use a coach to fix, solve, create, or plan something, personally or professionally.

What is worked on?

Here is what the coachee and coach work on together:

- Business planning, budgeting, and goal setting
- Integrating business and personal life for balance
- Turning around a difficult situation
- Achieving maximum work performance
- Handling business or personal problems
- Making key decisions and designing strategies

- Prioritizing actions and projects
- Catching up and getting ahead of the business
- Increasing sales substantially or filling a practice

But how does a coach do this?

Coaching is delivered during regular, weekly sessions by telephone or in person whichever is more convenient. Coaches bring an agenda of items to the call or meeting. The coach helps them solve problems and make the most of opportunities. When they are taking on a large goal, we help them design the project and provide the support and structure needed to make sure it gets done. We bring out each coachee's best by offering advice, expecting a lot, helping them strategize and celebrating their wins. A practice can be national, with coachees in every area of the country, from big cities to small towns; coachees can range from small business owners to CEOs; and coaching can focus on either business goals or personal goals.

What should I look for in a coach?

The right coach brings out your best, consistently. To do this, the coach you select should pass the following three tests: (1) Does this coach have a track record of helping someone like me accomplish the goals I want? (2) Do I feel good and motivated to act when with this coach? (3) Will this coach keep up with me—and stay ahead of me—as I grow? That's it. You can always check references and try out the coach for a month to see if he or she is really the right one for you. I work well with three types of coachees: (1) entrepreneurs and small-office professionals who are smart, quick, and ready to do what it takes to reach blockbuster goals; (2) individuals who are making substantial changes in their personal and professional lives; and (3) individuals who are working on an important project.

How much does it cost?

The fee for most entrepreneur and professional coachees ranges from $200 to $500 per month for a weekly meeting or coaching call. For example, monthly coaching fees may be $250 for a weekly half-hour call or $500 for a weekly one-hour call, using an 800 number. There are no other charges and coachees may call in between calls for additional assistance, if needed. For projects, they may be billed at $125 per hour. For presentations, facilitating, or training, the fee is $1,500 per day, plus expenses.

How would I get started?

If you feel that this type of relationship could work for you, call and let's talk. Coaching is not something we sell; it is something you buy because you want it.

Where do I start with a coach?

Most coaches begin with a special coachee meeting to get to know each other. The coach wants to hear about the coachee's goals, needs, and problems. The coachee wants to get comfortable with the coach. During this meeting, both parties design a list of goals and a game plan to reach these goals. Prior to this meeting, the coachee will have received a welcome package containing checklists and assessment materials to make the most of the meeting. Some coaches spend extra time (gratis) with new coachees getting to know them and coaching them to set the best goals for themselves, and together they design the best way to work together as a team to accomplish the goals.

Benefits of Being a Professional Coach

The professional coach benefits in six special ways, given the level of commitment it takes to become one. This article describes these benefits unique to our profession.

Benefit #1: You double your rate of personal development.

One of the fastest ways for a person to grow is to coach others. When you are accountable for results, share distinctions, and give advice, you learn, learn, and learn. In fact, you'll learn 80 percent of what you need to know directly from your clients. (A mentor coach or coach-training program gives you the critical 20 percent, but you should consider your clients as your real trainers. You spend a lot of time with them and learn much about yourself in the process.)

Benefit #2: You can make an extraordinary living.

Coaches earn between $25,000 and $200,000 per year. A few earn even more. Hourly fees range from $25 to $225. It takes a lot of training and experience to earn the higher numbers. After about five years, you can start making that kind of money if you are extraordinary, if you attract entrepreneurial or corporate clients, and if coaching is the right profession for you. If $50,000 a year is the right income for you, that can take between one and three years to reach.

The point is that with proper training, having the gift of coaching, and being part of a strong network, coaching can be a well-paying profession.

Benefit #3: You build close friendships and empowering relationships that will last a lifetime.

People who coach and clients who want to be coached are special people because they understand and value the power of synergy and partnership. They are at a place in life where being a lone ranger is not effective and not fun.

There is nothing wrong or unethical with having a client be your friend, assuming both of you are up to it. Clients become your partners in life, because they are contributing to you just as you

9

are contributing to them. (Be careful, though; some clients need all the focus on them right now, particularly if they are going through a transition or challenging time. Be selective.) Notice that new clients usually are preoccupied with themselves and their issues. If a friendship occurs, it will develop over time.

Benefit #4: You become a master of life.

A full-time coach is on a path of development that leads to mastery. If you've learned the distinctions of coaching, managed a full practice for several years, and taken care of your own life accordingly, chances are you'll be extraordinary. (Having clients and keeping them straight and in integrity will send you to the funny farm if you don't honor yourself and your life accordingly.)

Benefit #5: You are well positioned for the next opportunity.

Some coaches are built to coach for a lifetime. Others love the profession but will move on after four or five years. The profession is full of opportunities—many of which are not yet revealed.

The skills you learn, the growth you experience, and the great group of people you meet (colleagues, clients, and friends) set you up to notice, participate in, and benefit from opportunities such as:

- Pursuing new business opportunities
- Getting involved in national issues
- Writing, speaking, and more

Benefit #6: You get to give your gift.

We all have a special gift—a set of skills, a unique ability, a natural passion. Most coaches have a strong desire to empower others and contribute to them. Being a professional coach gives you license to do just that, full-time; what could be better? And you learn how to share your gift without hurting, depleting, or costing you—while you make a living.

Benefit #7: You will be appreciated.

Coaching another person is a contribution—and many clients will love you for it. Coaches shouldn't coach to get love, but you will get it. So enjoy!

All About Coaching: 100 Key Points about Coaching and the Coaching Process

This section should come in handy for anyone preparing a brochure, presentation, or story on coaching. It lists the key elements that comprise the coaching process and describes the purpose and focus of coaching. Obviously, each point can—and should—be a course of its own; however, you can use this as a helpful summary.

1. Why Coaching Works
What makes the process effective?

○ Creative synergy/spark

○ Emotional support/caring

○ Type of questions asked/discussion

○ Intellectual challenging/evocation

○ Outside influence/objectivity

○ Interdevelopmentalism/exchange

○ Complete confidentiality/safety

○ Continual/immediate access

○ Frequency of interaction

○ Convenience/accessibility

2. Who Hires a Coach
What are the primary markets?

○ Entrepreneurs/business owners

○ Consultants/trainers/coaches

○ Coaches from other disciplines

○ Psychologists/counselors

○ CEOs/executives/human resources departments

○ Managers/supervisors

○ Professionals (legal, financial, sales)

○ Career changers/transitioners

○ Creative types (writers/artists)

○ Project managers

3. Driving Demand

Why is coaching becoming so popular?

- ○ Entrepreneurism/self-employment
- ○ Increased selfishness/hedonism
- ○ Lifestyle preferences/dreams
- ○ Self-determination/individualism
- ○ Wanting it all now, with no delay
- ○ Desire for self-expression
- ○ Rapidly changing world
- ○ Competitive advantage
- ○ Hipness of having a coach
- ○ Increased isolation

4. How to Fill a Practice

What are your keys to becoming a successful coach?

- ○ Building a strong network
- ○ Marketing letters
- ○ Electronic newsletters
- ○ Web site/web presence
- ○ Apprenticeship/skill sets
- ○ Coach/coachee referrals
- ○ Public relations/media
- ○ Specialties/reputation
- ○ Teleclasses/workshops
- ○ Writing books/tapes/programs

5. Key Coaching Skills

What types of skills work the best?

- ○ Listening/hearing
- ○ Clarifying/prioritizing
- ○ Truth telling/integrating
- ○ Messaging/languaging
- ○ Gapping/distinctions
- ○ Correcting/educating
- ○ Challenging/evoking
- ○ Directing/guiding
- ○ Caring/supporting
- ○ Training/demonstrating

6. Coaching Foci/Goals

Where do clients want to focus?

- ○ Revenue/profitability
- ○ Marketing/promotion
- ○ Communication/thinking skills
- ○ Personal foundation/development
- ○ Management/organizational skills
- ○ Home/family life
- ○ Integration/prioritization
- ○ Personal lifestyle/freedom
- ○ Financial independence
- ○ Problem solving/tolerations

7. Benefits of Coaching

Why is coaching worthwhile?

- ○ Better, more rewarding goals
- ○ Faster, easier results, advancement
- ○ Rapid personal evolution/development
- ○ Clearer, sharper thinking
- ○ More money, security
- ○ Meaningful accomplishments
- ○ Happier, more fulfilling life
- ○ Far fewer problems
- ○ Higher profits and profitability
- ○ Better optimization of ideas

8. Future of Coaching

What is on the horizon?

- ○ Group/common-interest coaching
- ○ On-call/as-needed coaching
- ○ Annual-fee coach-training packages
- ○ Web/e-mail/QuickCam coaching
- ○ Teach via TeleClasses
- ○ Specialty coaching/experts
- ○ Niche markets
- ○ Hosting virtual communities
- ○ International/global coaching
- ○ Multiple-coach/single-coachee coaching

9. Client Priorities

What will coachees want more of?

Willingness/optimism

Openness/flexibility

Love/energy

Creativity/experimentation

Commitment/dedication

Communication/relating

Effectiveness/efficiency

Integrity/responsibility

Integration/balance

Organization/space

10. Source of Coaching

Where do coaching principles come from?

Business/management theories

The sciences/nature/life

Psychology/self-help practices

Common sense/proven wisdom

Education/teaching skills

Sports and teamwork skills

Awareness/eastern philosophy

Parenting/community skills

Communication/relating skills

Motivation/inspiration techniques

Coaching Customs

Every profession has distinct ways of operating, and coaching is no different. Described here are the emerging customs of the professional coach. Not every coach follows every custom, but most coaches have experimented with most of these standards, procedures, policies, and ways of doing business. Some are business oriented and others reflect who the coach is and how they profoundly affect others. If you enjoy a custom, please write and let us add it to this list, so that all coaches and clients can benefit.

We work weekly.
Professional coaches work weekly, or more often, with our clients. We believe an ongoing, nurturing, and developing relationship works best for the client and coach and encourage all clients to see us regularly. We offer three to four sessions per month.

We gift coaching to clients.
Professional coaches work with up to five special clients who need the coach's services yet cannot pay full fare. We are in business, yet we recognize helping others is a way to show our gratitude.

The client's needs come first.
Professional coaches place people with the coach who can help that person the most. We don't keep clients we cannot do a great job for.

We share our community.
Professional coaches are a resource for our clients, and we do our best to put our clients in touch with people in our community for mutual benefit.

We are paid in advance.
Professional coaches are paid monthly, in advance, for individual coaching. We don't bill for each session.

We have our own coach.
Professional coaches always have a coach of their own. We believe that to be a developing coach, one must have a coach.

We walk our talk.
Professional coaches walk their talk. We maintain high scores (over 90th percentile) on Clean Sweep and related programs. We ask our clients to grow as we do.

We maintain a full practice.
Professional coaches maintain a practice that is 50% greater than needed to pay business and personal expenses. We believe in maintaining a healthy reserve so that we can give straight, empowering advice.

We practice coaching, not therapy.
Professional coaches work only with clients who can use us well. We are not therapists, parents, caretakers or financial planners. We refer clients to the best available professionals for their psychological, health and financial concerns. We help clients reach goals.

We live a balanced life.
Professional coaches are models for their clients. We live a great life!

We are completely confidential.
Professional coaches don't talk about their clients to anyone. We protect everything our clients tell us.

We have a national practice.
Many clients work with us on the telephone—from next door, across the state, and around the country. Generally, clients use the coach's 800 number.

We know many other coaches.
We've gotten to know at least 20 other coaches for mutual support, cross-referring, and professional development. Some coaches are members of the International Coach Federation (www.coachfederation.org).

We are on a path of mastery.
We understand that the technology of coaching is growing rapidly, and we keep ourselves continuously growing, personally and professionally. Some of us are preparing to be Professional Certified Coaches (PCC) or Master Certified Coaches (MCC).

We have money in the bank.
Professional coaches maintain an emergency savings account of at least $10,000 so that money concerns do not interfere with coaching our clients.

We are available.
We recognize the importance of the relationship we have with our clients and strive to keep ourselves emotionally, physically, mentally, and spiritually available, so we can assist our clients fully.

We protect relationships.
Coaches complement the work of other professionals. We do not knowingly interfere with other professional relationships the client has. If a client is changing coaches, all parties are in full communication.

Primary Foci of Coaching

You will pass on three things to your coachees:

Become internally motivated versus externally prompted.

You've heard of Pavlov and his dogs? Well, we're all a lot like that, and most of us don't even realize it. One of the benefits of good coaching is that the coachee becomes self-generative and motivated, rather than relying on outside influences or circumstances to get and keep him or her going. Major areas to work on that provide this shift are:

- Trusting one's own intuition (self), even in the face of disagreement, circumstances, or reality.
- Becoming fully responsible for one's self, life, and problems, because responsibility permits choice.
- Accepting what is so, telling the truth, and knowing that everything is exactly as it should be right now.
- Placing one's emotional and physical balance as the number one focus.

Take all of the necessary actions effortlessly versus just talking and struggling about it all.

No pain, no gain? Sorry, that's an old paradigm sponsored by the aspirin companies. No pain, more gain is closer to how it really works, and without the angst of side effects. Your coach motivates you to take courageous actions but not suffer about them. Working on the following areas helps make taking actions much easier and lets them turn into results faster.

- Make a simple plan with little steps with many opportunities to win. Don't make it hard.
- Get all unfinished business or integrity items out of the way, so miracles can happen.
- Design goals that mirror or express your Tru Values rather than shoulds, coulds, or oughtas.
- Keep enjoying your personal life in the midst of major projects. You're worth it.

Develop an extraordinary community versus just knowing people.

The one with the biggest Rolodex may get a bigger bank account or ego, but the one who has developed key relationships and gone seven layers deep with these finds that success can come. Areas to develop include:

- Build an effective network of 100 colleagues, key coachees, centers of influence, close friends.
- Strengthen personal boundaries and honor high personal standards to feel good about yourself.
- Attract people who wish to interdevelop with you, rather than folks who just need a lot.

Coaching Focus Areas

What would you like to work on?

Personal Foci	Coaching Foci	Business Foci
Financial stress/problems	Increase awareness	Revenue growth
Personal organization	Personal polish	Profit growth
Happier/more fulfilled	Creativity/innovation skills	Value added for customers
Communication skills	Legacy identification	Productivity/effectiveness
Personal evolution track	Acceptance of events	New business start-up
Relationship problems	Acceptance of others	Marketing plan
Relationship enhancement	Higher learning rate	Internet marketing
Life purpose clarification	Stronger boundaries	Team/collaboration
Salary/income increase	Higher standards	Project management
Stress reduction	Grace/style development	Product quality
Personal life plan design	Compassion/empathy	Negotiation skills
Blocks/limits removal	Reserves/security increase	Professional network
Spiritual development	Confidence/the edge	Selling skills training
Time management	Ease/effortlessness	Vision/mission
Internet/cyber skills	Integrity improvement	Internet/cyber skills
Decision making	Fear/resistance reduction	Management skills
Adrenaline reduction	Life simplification	Reputation development
Motivation/inspiration	Character development	Employee retention
Structure/support	Relating skills	New economy orientation
Finding Mr./Ms. Right	Strengths identification	New client acquisition
Problem resolution	Passion identification	Leadership skills
Balance improvement	Peace/harmony	Improve staff morale
Career change/transition	Selfishness/pleasure	Improve company culture
Career advancement	Receptiveness/flexibility	Improve intangibles
Goals identification	Self-awareness	_____
Setting priorities	Attraction approach	_____
Personal foundation	Bandwidth expansion	_____
Values clarification	Life makeover	_____
Needs identification	Personal turnaround	_____
Needs satisfaction	_____	_____
Toleration reduction	_____	_____
Postrecovery track	_____	_____
Self-care skills	_____	_____
Truth identification	_____	_____
Family communication	_____	_____

The Professional Coach Is ...

The professional coach is all of the following:

○ **Your partner** in achieving business and personal goals

○ **Your champion** during a turnaround

○ **Your trainer** in communication and life skills

○ **Your sounding board** when making choices

○ **Your motivation** when strong actions are called for

○ **Your unconditional support** when you take a hit

○ **Your mentor** in personal development

○ **Your codesigner** when creating an extraordinary project

○ **Your beacon** during stormy times

○ **Your wake-up call** if you don't hear your own

and most important ...

○ **Your partner** in helping you have all of what matters most to you

Basics of the Coaching Relationship

The trained coach is able to do so much with the client that both parties sometimes forget what they are there together to accomplish. Here is our view of the coaching relationship.

Who	The coach works with a client who is up to something and who is willing to include another party in the design, implementation, and success of it.
What	**The coach works with each client to:** 1. Become fully self-generative by being whole and well. 2. Take the smart actions rather than just be busy. 3. Build a sustaining community for love, resources, and support.
Why	**The coach is hired by a client in order to:** 1. Accomplish something specific, whether personal or professional. 2. Restore their heart, soul, and quality of life. 3. Contribute well by discerning, developing, and sharing their gifts.

How	**The coach coaches, using the following methods:**
	1. Sharing information
	   a. Drawing distinctions
	   b. Teaching principles
	   c. Offering perspective
	2. Providing structure
	   a. Asking for a lot
	   b. Expecting the client's best
	   c. Being unconditionally constructive
	3. Training
	   a. Being a model for the client
	   b. Walking the client through the growth steps
	   c. Giving specialized instruction

Where	**The process of coaching occurs daily, regardless of how often the sessions are held:** Coaching conversations Scheduled calls Emergency calls Success calls Client support structures Buddy system Seminars led by coach Social events hosted by coach Homework Making promise of actions to take Increasing scores on program like Clean Sweep Reading and studying

Things People Want Most

Individuals

Make and Keep More Money

- Start saving or investing 10 to 30 percent of income
- Get a handle on spending, lifestyle, and habits
- Increase income by 20 to 200 percent
- Handle debt, financial problems, and crises
- Stabilize cash flow

Get More Done in Less Time

- Get focused on what you most want to have
- Simplify your life, responsibilities, projects
- Automate systems for peak efficiency
- Permanently eliminate inventory of to-do's
- Reduce the shoulds, coulds, and oughtas in life

Communicate Much More Effectively

- Say everything you need to; withhold nothing
- Motivate others better (by speaking in messages)
- Respond better in the moment (by hearing it all)
- Be able to ask more for what you want
- Ask the right questions

Feel Better Physically and Emotionally

- Get your home, office, and car in perfect order
- Recognize and eliminate any high hidden "life costs"
- Establish a reserve of time, energy, money, and love
- Redesign eating and lifestyle habits
- Get personal needs met

Substantially Increase Quality of Life

- Establish the perfect balance between home, work, play
- Increase personal standards
- Strengthen professional network and personal community
- Have a whole lot more fun

Become Closer with Others

- Attract and deepen relationships with quality people
- Become more intimate with spouse and family
- Learn to enjoy people more
- Develop adult-adult relationships, nothing less
- Know what you want for others

Eliminate the Hassles of Life

- Stop suffering, tolerating, waiting, hoping
- Stop having problems (really)
- Calm down, eliminate adrenaline, stress, procrastination
- Complete unresolved matters, unfinished business
- Extend boundaries

Get on a Path

- Develop your spirituality
- Discover personal mission, purpose, vision
- Reorient life exclusively around values
- Develop stronger relationship with self or God
- Be internally peaceful

Business

Have a Successful Small Business

- Start a new business
- Increase profitability by 20 to 500 percent
- Increase sales by 50 to 1,000 percent
- Develop a strategy and an action plan
- Strengthen the internal management systems

Corporate Work

- Build cooperative culture of self-managing teams
- Establish 5 to 20-year vision, mission, and strategies
- Train nonsales staff to sell, too (and enjoy it)
- Strategic repositioning in markets/industry
- Double firm's sales volume and profitability

Professionals

- Develop a full, successful practice
- Develop a strong reputation; be known as a model
- Manage clients better
- Increase sales and profitability
- Recognize and eliminate high hidden delivery costs

Coaches

- Get trained and master the craft of coaching
- Develop a full, successful practice
- Grow through resistance, blocks, the unknowns
- Achieve coach certification
- Develop a strong reputation; be known as a model

Benefits of Having a Coach

- You'll reach for much, much more because of the support and structure the coach provides.
- You'll start making and keeping more money and get on the path to financial independence.
- You'll make better decisions because you can run your ideas by an objective listener.

Coachee Situations

Read the following list of coachee situations, foci, and goals.

○	Personal foci
○	Financial stress/problems reduction
○	Personal/paper organization
○	Happiness/fulfillment
○	Communication skill development
○	Personal evolution
○	Relationship problems/enhancement
○	Life purpose clarification
○	Salary/income increase
○	Stress reduction
○	Personal life plan design
○	Blocks/limits removal
○	Spiritual development
○	Time management improvement
○	Internet/cyber skills
○	Decision making
○	Adrenaline reduction
○	Motivation/inspiration
○	Structure/support
○	Finding Mr./Ms. Right
○	Problem resolution
○	Balance improvement
○	Career change/transition
○	Career promotion/advancement
○	Personal goals identification/prioritization
○	Personal foundation strengthening
○	Values clarification

○	Needs identification/satisfaction
○	Toleration identification/elimination
○	Postrecovery track
○	Self-care skills
○	Truth identification/reorientation
○	Family communication/relationships
○	Awareness/contextual improvement
○	Personal polish/professionalism
○	Creativity/innovation skills
○	Legacy identification/creation
○	Acceptance/endorsement of events/others
○	Assimilation/learning rate increase
○	Generosity/bigness increase
○	Boundaries extension/management
○	Standards setting/management
○	Requirements identification/management
○	Grace/style development
○	Compassion/empathy development
○	Reserves/security increase
○	Confidence/edge
○	Ease/effortlessness
○	Events/resources integration
○	Integrity improvement
○	Fear/resistance reduction
○	Life simplification
○	Character development
○	Relating skills/effect on others
○	Strengths identification/development
○	Passion identification/expression
○	Peace/harmony improvement
○	Selfishness/pleasure

○	Receptiveness/flexibility
○	Self-awareness/understanding
○	Attraction approach/methodology
○	Bandwidth expansion
○	Life makeover/personal turnarounds
○	Business foci
○	Revenue growth
○	Profit growth
○	Value added for customers
○	Productivity/effectiveness improvement
○	New business start-up
○	Marketing plan
○	Internet marketing
○	Team/collaborative environment
○	Project management
○	Product quality improvement
○	Negotiation skills
○	Professional network expansion
○	Selling skills training
○	Vision/mission development
○	Internet savviness
○	Performance enhancement
○	Management skills
○	Reputation development
○	Employee retention increase
○	New economy reorientation
○	New coachee acquisition/development
○	Leadership skills
○	Staff/morale problems/conflict
○	Company culture improvement

Should You Be a Coach?

Coaching is not for everyone, but it may be for you. Coaching is becoming a popular profession. Business consultants, therapists, teachers, entrepreneurs, trainers, and other advisors find the quality of work and clientele appealing enough to invest in the training and time required to become a coach. It will take about five years to become a master coach, but a number of entrants earn six figures by the end of year two, so they must be doing something right! But take this little quiz to see if coaching is the right profession for you. (If not, perhaps you will enjoy it as a hobby or an opportunity to contribute to others.)

Check the box that most applies. Then score yourself using the key at the end of the test.

Yes	Umm	No	Statement
☐	☐	☐	I truly enjoy people just as they are.
☐	☐	☐	I am not afraid of anyone.
☐	☐	☐	Folks have been coming to me for counsel for a long time.
☐	☐	☐	I love to help and am willing to relearn how to do it right.
☐	☐	☐	I don't mind the ups and downs of being self-employed.
☐	☐	☐	I am truly fine just the way I am, but I like to grow, too.
☐	☐	☐	As far as I am concerned, people do not need fixing.
☐	☐	☐	I am on a rewarding spiritual or self-awareness path.
☐	☐	☐	I have a good grasp on how life works effortlessly.
☐	☐	☐	People consistently listen and respond to me.
☐	☐	☐	I can easily charge a lot of money for my coaching.
☐	☐	☐	I could *tell* people to work with me; I don't mind selling.
☐	☐	☐	I am well connected with a strong network.
☐	☐	☐	I'll do whatever it takes to get a full practice in one year.
☐	☐	☐	I can invest $1,000 to $5,000 in the first year for training and expenses.
			Totals for Yes, Umm, and No boxes

Yes	Umm	No	Statement
x 3	x 1		
			Points for Yes and Umm answers (no points for No answers)
			Total of Yes and Umm points

SCORING KEY

Yes	3 points
Umm	1 point
No	0 points

Minimum score to seriously consider becoming a professional coach is 30 points (maximum is 45).

Chapter 2

About the Prospective Coachee

Included in this chapter is information on prospective coachees and situations relating to prospects. Learn the questions to ask, the objections that may be raised, and the sellable features of coaching. Be prepared when talking with prospects to improve your closing ratio.

Included are lists of questions to ask prospects, benefits of working with a coach, forms, information on how you coach for prospects, and an assessment. With these tools you will be well on your way to articulating the benefits of the coaching relationship.

The following sections are included in this chapter:

1. Top Questions to Ask a Potential Client
2. Potential Coachee Selling Questions
3. Top Sellable Personal Features of the Coaching Service
4. Benefits of Working with a Coach
5. Top Five Objections Potential Clients Raise
6. Client Lead Form
7. How I Coach
8. How I Coach Clients
9. How I Coach Coachees
10. Coachability Index
11. Complimentary or First Session Agenda
12. Referral Thank You Letter

Top Questions to Ask a Potential Client

There are dozens of excellent questions to ask a prospective client. Here are the top five.

- What's the biggest change you'd like to make in your life, assuming you had enough support to do it right?

- What's the first thing we would work on together if you hired me as your coach?

- What's the hesitation about getting started?

- How do you define success for yourself at this stage of your life?

- What are the three biggest challenges you are facing right now in your business?

Potential Coachee Selling Questions

- What are the three challenges you are facing right now?
- What financial opportunity are you missing out on because you are too busy dealing with problems?
- What outcome would make coaching worthwhile?
- What can I say that would interest you in having your own coach?
- What's the most exciting thing about your job?
- What do you feel passionate about? What gets you out of bed in the morning?
- What do you have some of that you'd like a lot more of?
- What is it about coaching that sounds most interesting?
- How would you benefit from partnering with a coach?
- What would be different if you worked with a coach?
- If you wanted to make your job more impactful, what are two or three things you would do differently?
- Rather than me talking about coaching, would it be okay with you if you share what's most on your mind?
- What would have you start working on that right now?
- There's so much more I'd like to learn about you and what you're doing—and to tell you more about what I do—and I know we are pressed for time. Are you available to speak on Monday afternoon?
- Would you be interested in knowing the kind of people that I coach?
- Would you like to know what a coach does?
- Is there something you would like some help with right now?
- Would you be interested in my coaching you in one of the areas you have mentioned to me?
- Would having some support with that be helpful?
- May I be so bold as to ask when you would like to start?
- If you want to improve _____, why not begin by hiring me?
- How's your foundation—your personal foundation?
- Have you considered using the attraction principles to reach that goal?
- How are you solving that?
- If there were a perfect solution, what would it be?
- Have you set your life up to take full advantage of that opportunity?
- How ready are you for that?
- Have you worked with a coach before?
- Who's around to keep you stretching the vision you have for your company?
- Have you considered the possibility of having a *perfect* life?
- What do I need to say so that you might say yes to giving coaching a try?
- What do you really want in your personal life that you've never told anyone?
- Why wait for that? Why not start working on that right now?
- What gift or skill do you want to use more often?
- Would you let me help you with that?

- What consumes your time that isn't making you any money?
- What are you putting up with (tolerating)?
- Are you living *your* life or just working for a lifestyle?
- How much profit *should* your business be making?
- What motivates you at this point of your life?
- What's something that you really, really want?
- Where do you hold yourself back?
- On a scale of 1 to 10, with 10 being highest, where, honestly, would you rate your personal quality of life right now?
- What are you doing that makes no sense at all?
- If you did hire a coach, where would you start?
- How much would it be worth to you to solve those problems?
- What's in the way of your having a perfect life?
- Have you ever considered having your own coach?
- How is business this year compared to last year?
- What are three changes you could make in your life to significantly improve it within a week?
- What is holding you back?
- What can't you do for yourself that perhaps a partner like a coach could help you do?
- Am I the first professional coach you've met?
- I'd love to spend some time with you to find out more about that. Can we speak on Monday morning?
- May I tell you who I work with?
- May I tell you how I work?
- If you could have any type—or amount—of support with that, what would it include?
- Would it make sense to bring in whatever support is needed to get that problem solved?
- What questions do you have about coaching?
- May I tell you a little bit about a client I've worked with who was facing something similar?
- How I can help?
- What would be the perfect solution for that?
- What are the strategies you are considering using to accomplish that most quickly?
- Do you have everything you want in your personal life?
- Has your company brought in a professional coach yet?
- Would it help to talk to a coach about that?
- Who coaches you?
- How long has that been the case?
- When would you like to start working together?
- May I introduce you to one of my clients who might be able to help?
- What is the vision you have for your company?
- What is that costing you?
- Is that problem solvable?
- If not now, when?
- Would you like a referral to someone who I trust?

Top Sellable Personal Features of the Coaching Service

Like any other professional service, coaching has features and benefits. Here are some of the easiest-to-sell personal features of coaching.

Your Presence and Dedication

Your being there is worth at least 50% of your fee. And the more sophisticated your coachee, the higher the percentage in their eyes. Finding a professional who is there with them is a challenge for anyone looking for professional services.

What is "there"? Caring, listening, focusing on, being honest with, standing in the shoes of, challenging, thinking of the coachee between sessions, coming up with ideas for the coachee on your own and without prompting, and so on. You know, "there."

Selling this feature: "One of the things you will get by working with me is that I am there—intellectually, emotionally, and spiritually. You will feel this—it's palpable. Especially between our calls—when the going gets rough. You can always call me!"

Your Set of Related Experiences and Knowledge

We all have experiences and knowledge, but are you sharing the specifics of these so that the potential coachee has reason to believe in you?

Bad form: "I have been coaching for 25 years" (vague, quantity- vs. quality-oriented).

Good form: "Based on what you have said, I have worked with three coachees with similar opportunities. Would you be interested in hearing how they leveraged these similar opportunities?"

Moral of the story. Show—don't tell.

A Creative and Collaborative Environment

The best coachees want someone who can help them come up with clever strategies, solutions, and approaches to their goals and problems. It is important to educate the potential coachee that this creative environment is part of what you offer as a coach.

Here is a way to weave this in to a conversation with a potential coachee:

"How creative are you going to have to be in order to solve that problem?" (Person answers ... segue ...) "Part of what you will be getting from a coach is a fresh, but experienced, set of eyes and ears. That contributes to the creative exchange between us. Creativity and collaboration are the best solution to most problems. Either we will find the solution together, or we will create the solution together."

The Basic Structure of the Coaching Relationship Service

It's one of those life truisms: "With the perfect amount of support and structure, a person can do just about anything."

Benefits of Working with a Coach

Coaching is proven to work when these two factors are present: The client is willing to grow, and there is a gap between where they are now and where they want to be. That is all that is necessary for you and your coach to solve problems, create a new life, turn a business around, double sales and profitability, and design and implement a plan of action, or create whatever else is called for to ensure that you have what you need to get more of what you want.

With a Coach, You Will:

Take More, Better, and Smarter Actions Because You Set the Goals You Really Want

Ultimately, humans do what they really want to do anyway. Finding out exactly what you *really* want for yourself and your business is our first task together. I help you to distinguish between what you "coulda," "shoulda," "oughta," and have-to want from what you, in your heart of hearts, *really* want for yourself. Once you create the ideal goal, you're much more likely to naturally and consistently take actions to reach it.

Have a Balanced Life that Works Well Because You Designed It "Selfishly"

Sorry, but having it all means starting with a balanced life. And you know what *that* means—it's time to be very, very selfish. Not egotistical, but Selfish. With a capital S. I'll show you how to be selfish yet responsible. And how to get your needs met and still have people like you! This process is called establishing your personal foundation. You'll *love* building your foundation because you know you're worth it. You need this base if you are to be yourself.

Make and Keep More Money. You Are Worth More Than You're Making

Money, money, money! You must have it and have a lot more of it than you think. You know you can make and keep more money, so why don't you? I'll help you increase your business, fill your practice, pay off old bills, set up a financial plan and future, and help design a strategy for you to earn more from your professional efforts. Yes, you can!

Reach for More, Much More, and Not Be Consumed in the Process

When people have a partner they trust, they will always reach for more because they can *afford* to.

Make Better Decisions for Yourself and Your Business Because Your Focus Is Clear

Every single client of mine is smart, smart, and smart. Yet they still use me. Why? Because they know the value of sharing ideas with someone who understands them and is subjective enough to want a lot for them, yet objective enough not to be biased or self-serving. Just talking about your options with someone who can listen is often enough to have it all become very clear. You'll always get my honest, constructive views.

Have a Lot More Sustainable Energy—No More Chugging Along

When you're happy, productive, and free from tolerations and problems, you're going to *feel* better!

Top Five Objections Potential Clients Raise

Most potential clients want to work with a coach. But potential clients often have objections to starting. Usually, these objections are not real; they are simply perceived. So your job is to help them get through or over these, without being too pushy. Remember, your prospective clients do want to work with you; they are simply afraid, slow, or unclear on the focus. You can help them make a great buying decision. Remember, the first "No" is just the beginning of a wonderful relationship. Here are some ideas.

Objection: "I don't have time to work with a coach."

Possible responses:
- "Why are you that busy?"
- "And how healthy is the stress your busy schedule is causing you?"
- "Perfect! I only work with clients who are way too busy to work with me."
- "Perfect! Let's spend 30 days getting you ahead of your busy schedule."

Objection: "I can't afford the coaching fee."

Possible responses:
- "We all have the money we need for what we really want. What's the goal you'd set for yourself that you really want?"
- "Are you living that close to the financial edge?"
- "Perfect! Let's first start working on getting you a financial reserve!"
- "No problem. Let me discount it for you for the first 90 days. How much do you feel is both fair and affordable for you, to get started?"
- "Are you sure?"

Objection: "I'm not sure what I would work on with a coach."

Possible responses:
- "Yes, that's pretty typical. We usually spend a couple of sessions to sort out the various priorities you have. That itself is coaching."

- "What are the three biggest challenges you are facing right now?"
- "What is draining you or zapping your energy most?"
- "What is the opportunity that will pass you by if you don't act on it?"

Objection: "I'm not sure that a coach can help."

Possible responses:

- "Really. How come?"
- "Is the problem overwhelming?"
- "Would this be your first time working with a coach?"
- "What part don't you think a coach could help with?"

Objection: "I've already got a mentor."

Possible responses:

- "What aren't you working on with him or her that you would still like some strategic support with?"
- "Do you have a personal goal or problem that would benefit from immediate, dedicated attention?"
- "Wonderful! What sort of things do you two focus on?" (Then listen for what else you could offer.)

Client Lead Form

HOT LEAD?

Name		Title/occupation/company	
Address	City	State	Zip
Day phone	Evening phone	Fax	

Call Back Date _____

Source
- Referral from _____
- Workshop/speech _____
- _____

Interest Level
- Immediate start
- Very interested
- Interested
- Curious

Action Taken
- Scheduled meeting
- Sent materials
- Called, left message
- Discussed coaching
- _____

Waiting For
- Decision
- Timing
- _____

Considerations

- Time
- Money
- Timing
- Value
- Partner: Okay
- _____

Focus Areas

- Money
- Work
- Relationship
- Problem-solve
- Change
- Health
- Balance
- _____

I Want For _____

_____

_____

Notes _____

_____

_____

_____

_____

_____

_____

_____

_____

How I Coach

Because each professional coach has his or her own style of coaching clients, I thought that you would be interested in knowing how I coach, what I expect of my clients, and what my clients can expect of me.

My clients are great.

I am blessed with the privilege of choosing you, my clients; I want and enjoy each one of you. You are all growing, successful, and well, and I am assisting you to further your personal, spiritual, and professional lives.

I expect your best.

If you are hiring me, then you're probably ready to do and be your best. And if you aren't doing your best, I'll ask you to. If you can't do that at the moment, I'll understand and do what you need to be heard, loved, and helped back onto your path.

I make direct requests.

From time to time, I'll make a binding inquiry, like *"Will you accomplish X by the end of the month?"* You may say yes, say no, or offer another solution. I'll make you right whichever way you respond.

I give straight advice.

If I am sure of the situation, and if you're open to it, I'll make specific suggestions on how to handle a problem or go for an opportunity. If I am not sure, I'll say so. Honesty is one of my values—I am straight and expect the same from you. Regardless, use the best of what I say and use your own judgment.

I don't step over much.

When I hear a funny tone in your voice or notice something amiss, I'll ask you about it. Often, it is these small moments that offer the chance to resolve something. However, I don't confront or push; I'll merely invite you to look at something.

I give lots of homework.

I usually ask that the client come up with two or three goals, actions, or shifts to have between one call and the next. If it is too much, say so. If you want more, just ask.

You are expected to use me, not depend on me.

As your coach, I am a resource for you to use to your best advantage: I have an almost unlimited amount of love, compassion, forgiveness, and strength for you, and I can share many principles that will increase your success and add to the quality of your life. I ask that my clients use me as this resource and the friend that I am, but not to let themselves get into the position of needing me (or coaching) as a dependency thing or a fix.

I am here.

I want to hear it all. If you have a personal problem, are disturbed with something (even me or the coaching), are just starting to realize something big, or can't wait to share a shift or win, call or e-mail me. Any time.

How I Coach Clients

Every coach has his or her own coaching style. Here is a brief description of my approach.

I commiserate with and agree with my clients. I make my clients feel good, show them that I care, and help them to believe in themselves (because I do!).

I share what I'm sensing from my clients. I intuit, point stuff out, and tell the truth if it needs to be looked at.

I ask the obvious questions. I want facts, feelings, and preferences, and I want my clients to know these as well.

I step back, look for the whole picture, and discover how their situation or problem is perfect. In other words, they've gotten themselves where they are for some reason. I want to know that reason, because it provides the context I need to have a clear perspective.

I talk about the state my clients want, the most perfect place for them to be, or the most ideal result they want. Most clients have never had someone do this with them to this extent.

I tell my clients what I think is going on. I provide words for what I see going on. I help them to label these things, so they can see the events, situation, or problem objectively.

I ask my clients what they need or want from me right then. I want them to use me as they want to. I need to know their needs and my role.

I present, and we discuss, several strategies or solutions—often unconventional. I like to offer simple advice that fits perfectly and is tailored to their personality, priorities, and resources. Sometimes my advice is counterintuitive, but it usually works.

I sense and share the next evolutionary step for my clients. I listen for missing distinctions and for shifts that the client is ready to make. I look for the next step of an Evolutionary Progression.

I ask my clients to do more than they would do on their own. I like to stretch them when the timing is right.

How I Coach Coachees

Every coach has his or her own coaching style. Here is a brief description of one approach.

I commiserate with and agree with my coachees. I make my coachees feel good, show them that I care, and help them to believe in themselves (because I do!).

I share what I'm sensing from my coachees. I intuit, point stuff out, and tell the truth if it needs to be looked at.

I ask the obvious questions. I want facts, feelings, and preferences, and I want my coachees to know these as well.

I step back, look for the whole picture, and discover how their situation or problem is perfect. In other words, they've gotten themselves where they are for some reason. I want to know that reason, because it provides the context I need to have a clear perspective.

I talk about the state my coachees want, the most perfect place for them to be, or the most ideal result they want. Most coachees have never had someone do this with them to this extent.

I tell my coachees what I think is going on. I provide words for what I see going on. I help them to label these things, so they can see the events, situation, or problem objectively.

I ask my coachees what they need or want from me right then. I want them to use me as they want to. I need to know their needs and my role.

I present, and we discuss, several strategies or solutions—often unconventional. I like to offer simple advice that fits perfectly and is tailored to their personality, priorities, and resources. Sometimes my advice is counterintuitive, but it usually works.

I sense and share the next evolutionary step for my coachees. I listen for missing distinctions and for shifts that the client is ready to make. I look for the next step of an Evolutionary Progression.

I ask my coachees to do more than they would do on their own. I like to stretch them when the timing is right.

Coachability Index

Circle the number that comes closest to representing how true the statement is for you right now. Then, score yourself, using the key provided. Your coach needs you to be at the place in life where you are coachable. This test helps your coach—and you—discover how coachable you are, right now. How coachable are you?

Less time		More time			Statement
1	2	3	4	5	I can be relied upon to be on time for all calls and appointments.
1	2	3	4	5	This is the right time for me to accept coaching.
1	2	3	4	5	I am fully willing to do the work and let the coach do the coaching.
1	2	3	4	5	I keep my word without struggling or sabotaging.
1	2	3	4	5	I'll give the coach the benefit of the doubt and "try on" new concepts or different ways of doing things.
1	2	3	4	5	I will speak straight (tell what's really true) to the coach.
1	2	3	4	5	If I feel that I am not getting what I need or expect from the coach, I will share this as soon as I sense it and ask that I get what I want and need from the relationship.
1	2	3	4	5	I am willing to eliminate or modify the self-defeating behaviors that limit my success.
1	2	3	4	5	I have adequate funds to pay for coaching and will not regret or suffer about the fee. I see coaching as a worthwhile investment in my life.
1	2	3	4	5	I am someone who can share the credit for my success with the coach.
					TOTAL SCORE (add up all numbers)

SCORING KEY

10–20   Not coachable right now.

21–30   Coachable, but make sure ground rules are honored!

31–40   Coachable.

41–50   Very coachable; ask the coach to ask a lot from you!

Complimentary or First Session Agenda

Your logo here.

Client		Session No.		Follow-up	
Date		Time		Format	

Before the Session

Get clear of the previous session or activity I was involved with.

Review any notes taken on prospect previously.

Starting the Session

"Hi, how are you? Thanks for your interest in coaching."

"So, tell me a little about yourself."

"What's your greatest challenge right now?"

"What motivates you in life right now?"

"What are you tolerating (physically in the home or office)?"

"What are you willing to do in the next 30 days?"

Toward the end of the Session

Give one great insight, tip, tool, or action—use my intuition.

Ask prospect if they would like to proceed with coaching for next X months.

YES   NO

If not, why not?

"We have about five minutes left; let's review your Action Items."

"What's one thing you have gotten out of today's session?"

Confirm next session date, time, and format.

After the Call

Send fieldwork via e-mail and file this form.

Referral Thank You Letter

[Date]

[Name]

[Address]

[City, State, Zip]

Dear [Name],

Thank you very much for referring _____ to us for coaching. We really appreciate your ongoing support of our business and also your continual support and enthusiasm for the coaching profession.

Your support of our coaching services certainly is contributing to making our vision a reality. We sincerely thank you.

As a small gesture of our thanks, please enjoy the enclosed Thank You Gift. I strongly encourage you to take the time to go to the movies and relax for a couple of hours.

[Name], it is such a pleasure to be your coach.

Kind regards,

[Signature]

[Title]

Encl.

Chapter 3

For the New Client/Coachee

This chapter will provide you with a starting point for the new client/coachee. You will have all the paperwork and forms you need to get started. It will support you in the administration and processes for your practice. Having clarity in this area will promote the professionalism of your business and provide you with peace of mind.

Provided are forms for credit cards, client/coachee data, client/coachee direction, agreements, letters, information, charts, questions, and evaluations. All these tools will get you off to a strong start with both your practice and your client/coachee.

The following sections are included in this chapter:

1. Agreement
2. Credit Card Authorization
3. Welcome
4. Coachee Profile
5. How to Get the Most Out of Your Coaching
6. Focus and Scope of Work
7. Client Data Sheet
8. Coachee Data Sheet
9. Welcome to Clients
10. Welcome to Coachees
11. Preparing for Coaching
12. Top 10 Ways to Get the Most Out of Coaching
13. What to Talk about with Your Coach
14. Comprehensive Assessment Chart
15. Welcome to Coaching: Client Welcome Letter
16. Coachee History
17. I Believe in You: The Coach's Credo
18. Assessment Summary
19. Goals List

Agreement

Please review, adjust as necessary, sign where indicated, and return to the coach. Putting this in writing strengthens one's dedication.

Name:	
Initial term	_____ months, from _____ Through _____
Fee	$_____ per hour $_____ per month $_____ for the project
Payment	Fees to be received in the office by the _____ of the month
Bonus agreement	
Session day	☐ Mon ☐ Tue ☐ Wed ☐ Thu ☐ Fri ☐ Sat ☐ Sun
Session time	☐ AM ☐ PM ☐ Pacific ☐ Mountain ☐ Central ☐ Eastern
Duration	_____ minutes
Call procedure	
Services provided	
Focus of work	
Ground rules	Client calls the coach at scheduled time Client pays coaching fees in advance ☐ Client ☐ Coach pays for long distance charges, if any

Other terms
Above agreed to on
Client signature
Coach signature

Credit Card Authorization

This authorization is valid for use for the following services or products:

Name of coaching program _____

@ $_____ per month for _____ months

Once at _____ or _____ recurring for _____ months

Visa

MasterCard

Bankcard

Card number: _____

Expiration date: _____

Name as it appears
on card: _____

Signature: _____

Welcome

I am pleased to welcome you as a client. I look forward to helping you achieve greatness. Please complete the items checked and return to me the documents indicated.

☐ Send your check for $_____ today, for the month of _____, if you haven't done so already.

☐ Please complete the enclosed tests and forms, then make and send me a copy of them. Put your originals in a file folder marked "Coaching."

☐ Read the enclosed client articles so you'll know how best to use me.

☐ _____

☐ _____

☐ _____

Our calls are scheduled for:

Day

Date

From _____ to _____ P M C E time

Call me at (   ) _____ - _____

I look forward to speaking with you at that time.

Warmest regards,

Coachee Profile

Read and complete the following.

Life Purpose

What do you want for yourself, for others, and for life, personally? What is truly most important to you? Use the worksheet to assist you.

_____

_____

_____

_____

Business Mission

What do you want, professionally, for your clients and others? Why do you do what you do? What do you offer that turns you on? Use the enclosed worksheet.

_____

_____

_____

_____

Personal Needs

Please take the NeedLess test and complete the following list of your top four needs.
Test score: ____

_____ satisfied by _____

_____ satisfied by _____

_____ satisfied by _____

_____ satisfied by _____

Core Values

Please take the TruValues test and complete the following list of your top four values.
Test score: ____

_____ satisfied by _____

_____ satisfied by _____

_____ satisfied by _____

_____ satisfied by _____

Personal and Professional Strengths

Evaluate your strengths on the Strengths Inventory and list the top five here.

_____

_____

_____

_____

_____

Primary Attachments

Please take the Attachment Index test. List your three primary attachments here.
Test score: ___

_____

_____

_____

False Assumption/Lie

Is there a false assumption (something you've been holding to be true, but maybe isn't) that it's time to take another look at? Is there a basic lie that it is time to admit?

_____

_____

_____

_____

Other Test Scores				
	Scores as of			
	Now			

Clean Sweep Program (# of TRUE responses)				
	Scores as of			
	Now			
Physical				
Wellness				
Money				
Relationships				
TOTAL TRUE				

You and your coach will complete this section at a later time. Keep the enclosed personal profile until that time.

Areas of Life				
	Scores as of			
	Now			
Health				
Career				
Relationships				
Personal development				
Fun/pleasure				
Money				
1 = Low quality → 10 = High quality				

10 Daily Habits

Clients who take great care of themselves are able to achieve more with less cost. Make a list of the 10 daily habits that will keep you well. Use the daily habits tracking sheet if desired.

1. _____

2. _____

3. _____

4. _____

5. _____

6. _____

7. _____

8. _____

9. _____

10. _____

Lighten Up!

Most of us have a couple of extra undertakings, promises, or projects that we'd do well to suspend for six months to give us the freedom and space to have the current ones be effortless and more enjoyable. List yours here.

1. _____

2. _____

3. _____

Personal Goals

Please complete the goals/skills checklist and summarize the higher-priority ones here.

Health and Emotional Balance

1. _____

2. _____

Career/Business

1. _____

2. _____

Relationships/Family

1. _____

2. _____

Personal Development/New Skills

1. _____

2. _____

Fun/Pleasure

1. _____

2. _____

Money

1. _____

2. _____

Business Goals

Use the business problem checklist and/or the Biz Whiz assessment test to prompt ideas for business or company goals. List the top three here.

1. _____

2. _____

3. _____

Current Challenges

What are you facing right now that needs immediate focus or resolution?

1. _____

2. _____

3. _____

Personal Shift

Coaching helps you shift your perspective and where you come from in life to a perspective that really empowers you and lets you accomplish your goals with ease. What kind of shift do you now want?

What else do you want your coach to know?

Any concerns? Fears? Past problems? Requests that your coach interact with you in a special way?

How to Get the Most
Out of Your Coaching

I want you to benefit greatly from the time we have together each week and also during the time in between our calls. This brief guide is what most of my clients do to maximize the value from their coaching with me.

Make a list of what you really want in life.

Coaching works best when you have clear goals that are based on your needs and values. Included in your Welcome Packet is a list of popular goals and a form on which to list these. If you're not sure what your goals should be, we can discuss them during our call.

Keep focused on your Clean Sweep Program.

The Clean Sweep program is an essential element in a strong personal foundation, and all of my clients work this program. If you haven't yet, take the assessment test of 100 questions and start handling at least one item per week. Keep me posted on your current score. The Clean Sweep program is in the Welcome Packet.

Get to know yourself in a new way.

Working with a sensitive and empathic coach is a healthy way to grow. Most clients hire a coach to accomplish several specific goals, and much of the time and focus is spent on these goals. Yet, with coaching don't be surprised if you discover new parts of yourself and then find your goals adjusting to who you really are. This discovery process is natural, so you needn't rush it; just realize it will likely happen. Accelerated personal and professional growth is the hallmark of being coached. Get to know yourself more by completing the NeedLess and Tru Values programs. These pinpoint what you need and what really fulfills you. Feel free to discuss this with me when you wish. Please take both tests now and let me know your scores.

Double your level of willingness.

Part of working with me as your coach is that I will ask a lot of you. Not too much, I hope, but certainly more than you may have been asked recently. I need you to be willing to experiment with fresh approaches and be open to redesigning the parts of your life that you are able to right now. This will help you more easily reach your goals and live an integrated and fulfilled personal and professional life, using the gifts you have and enjoying life as it was meant to be enjoyed. And let me tell you what I need you to be willing to do. Please be willing to:

- Change your behavior, a lot
- Examine the assumptions and decisions you've made
- Experiment and try new things
- Start telling what's really true, regardless of the consequences
- Remove all sources of stress
- Eradicate all triggers of adrenaline
- Redesign how you spend your time
- Get the support you need to handle a problem
- Set goals that are much bigger than before
- Raise your personal standards to be very, very high
- Start treating people much better
- Stop tolerating or suffering about your life

Come to the coaching call prepared, with an agenda.

We have 30 minutes together, and you'll want to have a written list of things for you to share and us to discuss. On this list, include things like:

- Success and wins that you've had that week
- Report on the homework
- Problems you faced and how you handled them
- Advice you want about a situation
- What you're currently working on and how it's going
- New skills you want to develop
- Insights, "aha's," and new awarenesses
- Strategies you wish to develop

Having this agenda helps you get what you want from the call. Several examples are included in the Welcome Packet.

Enjoy our call.

We have work to do together, clearly, but feel free to enjoy the call with me. After several sessions, you may find that we take a little time to catch up on those parts of your life that mean a lot to you, or you may want to share something personal and confidential. And after several months, perhaps sooner, you may find that we even laugh a lot during the call—at life, how you've grown, how things happen. Coaching calls aren't gabfests, but they are enjoyable, for both of us. What I mean to say is that they needn't be intense or demand an effort for you to produce the miracles you know are possible. But feel free to set the tone of the calls, and I will respect what you need in this area.

Work the other programs of your choice.

You are invited to work any of the programs I have for my clients:

- NeedLess
- Full Practice
- Time Peace
- Irresistible Attraction
- Tru Values
- Master Coach
- Stress Index
- Power Networking
- Biz Whiz
- Reserve Index
- 100 Smiles

These programs are included in your Welcome Packet. Select one or two that most appeal to you, and let's work on these together.

Keep yourself well between our sessions.

Coaching can require energy: emotionally, intellectually and physically. Given this, I want you to take extraordinary care of your health and emotional balance while being coached. Only you know what this looks like, but I suggest you go much further than you ever have in this regard. The place to start is to develop a list of 10 daily habits that keep you well. Some of the habits my clients have developed into a routine are:

- Walk or take other exercise
- Reduce fat intake
- Read
- Listen to great music

- Floss
- Eat more vegetables
- Meditate
- Underpromise, don't offer
- Handle unresolved matters
- Consume no caffeine, nicotine, or alcohol
- Start being early
- Don't abuse sugar
- Take vitamins
- Write in your journal

Included in the Welcome Packet is a chart for you to record your 10 daily habits. Please fill this out and start using it now.

Do your homework each week.

This is not homework like in grade school. These are tasks, actions, results, or changes you are committing to do your best to complete before our next call. You must apply yourself and use the homework to help you achieve your personal and business goals.

Focus and Scope of Work

Please complete this and return to the coach. Be sure to include target dates for reaching each goal or objective. What are we going to work on together?

Personal goals	By

Business/professional objectives	By

Life skills	By

Communication skills	By

Other goals, distinctions, and conditions to have	By

Client Data Sheet

Complete the following data sheet.

Date prepared:
Name:
Company:
Address:
City and state:
Zip/postal code:
Day phone:
Evening phone:
Voice mail:
E-mail address:
Fax number:
Date of birth:
Occupation:
Nature of business/position:
Referred by:
Initial term month(s):
Start date:
Renewal date:
Rate: $_____ per _____
Additional time: $_____ per _____

Bonus agreement:
Payment due on _____ of month
Call day and time: M   T   W   Th   F   Sa   Su _____   P M C E   time for _____ minutes
Call instructions:
Ground rules:
1. Client calls and pays in advance.
2. Coach has permission to be direct, though unconditionally constructive.
Other terms:
Above agreed to on:
Client signature:
Coach signature:

Coachee Data Sheet

Complete the following data sheet.

Date prepared:
Name:
Company:
Address:
City and state:
Zip/postal code:
Day phone:
Evening phone:
Voice mail:
E-mail address:
Fax number:
Date of birth:
Occupation:
Nature of business/position:
Referred by:
Initial term month(s):
Start date:
Renewal date:
Rate: $_____ per _____
Additional time: $_____ per _____

Bonus agreement:
Payment due on _____ of month
Call day and time: M   T   W   Th   F   Sa   Su   _____ P M C E time for _____ minutes
Call instructions:
Ground rules: 1. Client calls and pays in advance. 2. Coach has permission to be direct, though unconditionally constructive.
Other terms:
Above agreed to on:
Client signature:
Coach signature:

Welcome to Clients

You have chosen to use me as your coach. I appreciate the opportunity to work with you. I have prepared the following Coaching Q&A and the enclosed materials to assist you to get the most from your time and out of our relationship.

What is coaching?

Coaching is a unique and distinct profession. A coach helps you and/or your firm to:

- Solve problems
- Reach goals
- Design a plan of action
- Make decisions

In addition to these areas, the coach "stays with" (coaches) the client to:

- Implement the plan of action, working through the inevitable changes and any obstacles
- Maintain a healthy balance between your personal and professional life
- Keep looking ahead to take advantage of opportunities that are just now formulating
- Bring out your personal best, keeping focused on your needs, values, and vision

What type of goals can a coach help me achieve?

Every coach has several specialties. That is, they are trained and experienced in helping clients reach several types of goals. All told, there are countless specialties. I work with the following people:

Entrepreneurs who are at one of the following places with their business:

- Wanting to double sales or profits. Ready to blow the roof off? Fully committed but needing a specific plan of action? Want strategic planning to make the most of the resources you have?
- In trouble. Can't meet the payroll? Sales declining? Problems with key staff? Having personal conflicts or problems? Too much stress? Business too successful, too fast? Time and prioritizing problems? Ready to go bankrupt?
- Making changes. Adding a new product or service? Starting a new business? Wanting to shift your focus from one area to another?

Professionals like stockbrokers, real estate agents, trainers, therapists, sales representatives, consultants, and health professionals such as physicians, chiropractors, and others who:

- Want a full practice. Ready to be full? Upgrade your clientele? Become irresistibly attractive rather than promotion-based? Find and develop a high-level referral network?
- Are ready to be leaders. I work with professionals who want to be number one in their firm, be recognized as a master in their field, and/or develop a model reputation.
- Are committed to being financially independent, sooner. Professionals and entrepreneurs are uniquely positioned to make a lot of money. My job is to help you make more and keep much more.

Managers and executives responsible for the success of a sales team, branch, or division, who need to:

- Reach high targets and quotas. Accomplishing this consistently requires a manager who also coaches the team to work together to reach unreasonable goals. I coach managers and executives and show them how to coach their people to reach these targets.
- Pull off large projects. These can include successfully completing projects and implementing programs such as enhanced customer service and customer relationship development. Having your own coach can make the process easier. It helps to have someone to speak with as you face this type of challenge.
- Substantially increase productivity. No longer merely an option, substantially increasing productivity is a primary focus for many firms. A coach advises on how to upgrade the company culture, develop teamwork based on values, align departmental goals with the company's mission, and shift the firm to be innovative and profit driven, not just the gung-ho more-is-better work-harder-and-we'll-all-make-it approach, which is simply not effective in today's market.

Why does coaching work?

Coaching works because it brings out your best. A coach believes you can create your own best answers and is trained to support you in that process.

Specifically, this is what I do with you during our coaching sessions:

- *Listen.* I listen fully. You are the focus. I listen to what you say, what you are trying to say, and what you are not saying.
- *Share.* After you have fully communicated, I share with you my advice, ideas, comments, and views on your situation, dilemma, or opportunity.
- *Endorse.* Anyone who's up to something—an entrepreneur, a manager with an extraordinary objective, a professional filling the practice—needs, yes, *needs*, an outside voice full of endorsement, compassion, and acknowledgement. Not a yes-type person, but someone who knows what it takes to achieve.

- *Suggest.* I want a lot for you. I want you to be healthy, happy, and successful. I want you to be on a strong financial track. I want you to enjoy your family and friends. I want you to have a life that inspires others—and yourself. Part of my job is to be at least three steps ahead of you, yet be with you. As such, I make requests and suggestions. And you are the client.

What is the fee?

I charge $150 per hour.

How do you work?

I work mostly on the telephone: This is called telecoaching. You call me at a local or toll-free number at a prescheduled time. Most clients call me once per week at the same time each week. Calls last 25 or 55 minutes. The monthly fee, payable in advance, for the 25-minute call is $300; for the 55-minute call, $500. Additional time is billed at $150 per hour. Clients may meet with me, but most find the telephone to be more efficient (and practical, since all of my clients live outside my hometown).

What other services do you offer?

In addition to coaching and telecoaching, I offer the following services:

- I lead workshops and trainings: Referrals Right Now, Values/Goals Alignment, PowerSource, and other programs.
- I deliver presentations and keynote speeches: Coaching Employees for Productivity, Entrepreneurial Success, Goal Setting for the Best Year Ever, From Transition to On-Track, and others.
- I assist with proposals: loan packages, business plans, corporate sales proposals, project outlines, and others.
- I write seminars and programs: public seminars, corporate training programs, and others.

What credentials do you have in order to coach?

The primary credential of any coach is the assessable success of his or her clients. Additionally, I have:

- Practiced for 10 years as an accountant and Certified Financial Planner
- Led full-day workshops for over 8,000 participants
- Coached over 200 clients since starting my practice

References are available upon request.

What else should I know about how you work?

There are several administrative guidelines that you should know:

1. Fees are paid in advance, due on the first day of each month.
2. Your time slot is your time slot. Please don't try to reschedule. In an emergency, however, we can make our time together a priority. If you are going on vacation or can't make a call one week, we will make up the time before you leave or after you return. You may call me at the toll-free number: _____. From time to time when you call, you may get my voice mail asking that you call another number to reach me. This number will be a local call or the toll-free number.
3. The monthly fee covers four sessions per month. Every three months, there's an extra week on the calendar. I take that time off to restore, and there is no coaching call.

What do you expect of your clients?

I ask that you grant our relationship enough room so that you can reach your goals quickly. What that means is that you be willing to tell me everything you are thinking and feeling and that you're willing to listen to what I have to say. You should also take the time you want to develop the trust you need between us.

Please read the articles and materials that accompany your Welcome Packet.

What can I expect from you, as the coach?

You can expect me to be:

- *Unconditionally constructive.* No matter what happens during our call, you can expect me to say only those things that further your life and your goals. If you are disturbed, I do understand. If you are stuck, I will be patient. If you can't wait to share a victory, I will celebrate with you. I will not put you in the wrong, criticize you, complain to you, or gossip about you.

- *Straightforward.* Yes, one can be unconditionally constructive and still speak straight. From time to time, I will ask you to begin, end, or modify something. And I will honor your right to refuse.

About Confidentiality

A coach doesn't gossip. That means that what you are doing, how you are doing, what you have accomplished, and your personal secrets and confidences are not discussed or hinted at by me to anyone else. From time to time, the person who referred you to me may ask how you are doing. My stock answer: He or she is doing just fine. Period.

My client list is confidential. People may know you are working with me, but that information won't come from me.

Speaking of Referrals ...

My practice fills by referrals. If you are benefiting from our relationship, I expect you to suggest that appropriate colleagues and friends of yours speak with me.

I know many full-time coaches. I will be happy to speak with anyone you send me, and I will introduce them to the coach who I think is qualified and right for their needs, whether it is me or another coach.

Thanks!

Thanks for giving me the chance to serve you. Please fill out the Welcome Packet and return it to me ASAP.

Welcome to Coachees

You have chosen to use me as your coach. I appreciate the opportunity to work with you. I have prepared the following Coaching Q&A and the enclosed materials to assist you to get the most from your time and out of our relationship.

What is coaching?

Coaching is a unique and distinct profession. A coach helps you and/or your firm to:

- Solve problems
- Reach goals
- Design a plan of action
- Make decisions

In addition to these areas, the coach "stays with" (coaches) the coachee to:

- Implement the plan of action, working through the inevitable changes and any obstacles
- Maintain a healthy balance between your personal and professional life
- Keep looking ahead to take advantage of opportunities that are just now formulating
- Bring out your personal best, keeping focused on your needs, values, and vision

What type of goals can a coach help me achieve?

Every coach has several specialties. That is, they are trained and experienced in helping coachees reach several types of goals. All told, there are countless specialties. I work with the following people:

Entrepreneurs who are at one of the following places with their business:

- *Wanting to double sales or profits.* Ready to blow the roof off? Fully committed but needing a specific plan of action? Want strategic planning to make the most of the resources you have?
- *In trouble.* Can't meet the payroll? Sales declining? Problems with key staff? Having personal conflicts or problems? Too much stress? Business too successful, too fast? Time and prioritizing problems? Ready to go bankrupt?
- *Making changes.* Adding a new product or service? Starting a new business? Wanting to shift your focus from one area to another?

Professionals like stockbrokers, real estate agents, trainers, therapists, sales representatives, consultants, and health professionals such as physicians, chiropractors, and others who:

- *Want a full practice.* Ready to be full? Upgrade your clientele? Become irresistibly attractive rather than promotion-based? Find and develop a high-level referral network?
- *Are ready to be leaders.* I work with professionals who want to be number one in their firm, be recognized as a master in their field, and/or develop a model reputation.
- *Are committed to being financially independent, sooner.* Professionals and entrepreneurs are uniquely positioned to make a lot of money. My job is to help you make more and keep much more.

Managers and executives responsible for the success of a sales team, branch, or division, who need to:

- *Reach high targets and quotas.* Accomplishing this consistently requires a manager who also coaches the team to work together to reach unreasonable goals. I coach managers and executives and show them how to coach their people to reach these targets.
- *Pull off large projects.* These can include successfully completing projects and implementing programs such as enhanced customer-service and customer relationship development. Having your own coach can make the process easier. It helps to have someone to speak with as you face this type of challenge.
- *Substantially increase productivity.* No longer merely an option, substantially increasing productivity is a primary focus for many firms. A coach advises on how to upgrade the company culture, develop teamwork based on values, align departmental goals with the company's mission, and shift the firm to be innovative and profit driven, not just the gung-ho more-is-better work-harder-and-we'll-all-make-it approach, which is simply not effective in today's market.

Why does coaching work?

Coaching works because it brings out your best. A coach believes you can create your own best answers and is trained to support you in that process.

Specifically, this is what I do with you during our coaching sessions:

- *Listen.* I listen fully. You are the focus. I listen to what you say, what you are trying to say, and what you are not saying.
- *Share.* After you have fully communicated, I share with you my advice, ideas, comments, and views on your situation, dilemma, or opportunity.
- *Endorse.* Anyone who's up to something—an entrepreneur, a manager with an extraordinary objective, a professional filling the practice—needs, yes, *needs,* an outside voice full of endorsement, compassion, and acknowledgement. Not a yes-type person, but someone who knows what it takes to achieve.

- *Suggest.* I want a lot for you. I want you to be healthy, happy, and successful. I want you to be on a strong financial track. I want you to enjoy your family and friends. I want you to have a life that inspires others—and yourself. Part of my job is to be at least three steps ahead of you, yet be with you. As such, I make requests and suggestions. And you are the coachee.

What is the fee?

I charge $150 per hour.

How do you work?

I work mostly on the telephone: This is called telecoaching. You call me at a local or toll-free number at a prescheduled time. Most coachees call me once per week at the same time each week. Calls last 25 or 55 minutes. The monthly fee, payable in advance, for the 25-minute call is $300; for the 55-minute call, $500. Additional time is billed at $150 per hour. Coachees may meet with me, but most find the telephone to be more efficient (and practical, since all of my coachees live outside my hometown).

What other services do you offer?

In addition to coaching and telecoaching, I offer the following services:

- I lead workshops and trainings: Referrals Right Now, Values/Goals Alignment, PowerSource, and other programs.
- I deliver presentations and keynote speeches: Coaching Employees for Productivity, Entrepreneurial Success, Goal Setting for the Best Year Ever, From Transition to On-Track, and others.
- I assist with proposals: loan packages, business plans, corporate sales proposals, project outlines, and others.
- I write seminars and programs: public seminars, corporate training programs, and others.

What credentials do you have in order to coach?

The primary credential of any coach is the assessable success of his or her coachees. Additionally, I have:

- Practiced for 10 years as an accountant and Certified Financial Planner
- Led full-day workshops for over 8,000 participants
- Coached over 200 coachees since starting my practice

References are available upon request.

What else should I know about how you work?

There are several administrative guidelines that you should know:

1. Fees are paid in advance, due on the first day of each month.
2. Your time slot is your time slot. Please don't try to reschedule. In an emergency, however, we can make our time together a priority. If you are going on vacation or can't make a call one week, we will make up the time before you leave or after you return. You may call me at the toll-free number: _____. From time to time when you call, you may get my voice mail asking that you call another number to reach me. This number will be a local call or the toll-free number.
3. The monthly fee covers four sessions per month. Every three months, there's an extra week on the calendar. I take that time off to restore, and there is no coaching call.

What do you expect of your coachees?

I ask that you grant our relationship enough room so that you can reach your goals quickly. What that means is that you be willing to tell me everything you are thinking and feeling and that you're willing to listen to what I have to say. You should also take the time you want to develop the trust you need between us.

Please read the articles and materials that accompany your Welcome Packet.

What can I expect from you, as the coach?

You can expect me to be:

- *Unconditionally constructive.* No matter what happens during our call, you can expect me to say only those things that further your life and your goals. If you are disturbed, I do understand. If you are stuck, I will be patient. If you can't wait to share a victory, I will celebrate with you. I will not put you in the wrong, criticize you, complain to you, or gossip about you.

- *Straightforward*. Yes, one can be unconditionally constructive and still speak straight. From time to time, I will ask you to begin, end, or modify something. And I will honor your right to refuse.

About Confidentiality

A coach doesn't gossip. That means that what you are doing, how you are doing, what you have accomplished, and your personal secrets and confidences are not discussed or hinted at by me to anyone else. From time to time, the person who referred you to me may ask how you are doing. My stock answer: He or she is doing just fine. Period.

My coachee list is confidential. People may know you are working with me, but that information won't come from me.

Speaking of Referrals ...

My practice fills by referrals. If you are benefiting from our relationship, I expect you to suggest that appropriate colleagues and friends of yours speak with me.

I know many full-time coaches. I will be happy to speak with anyone you send me, and I will introduce them to the coach who I think is qualified and right for their needs, whether it is me or another coach.

Thanks!

Thanks for giving me the chance to serve you. Please fill out the Welcome Packet and return it to me ASAP.

Preparing for Coaching

Read and understand the following.

Introduction

You may come to your first coaching call without preparing, if you wish. Coaching can be equally effective with or without preparation, but many clients enjoy getting ready for coaching, so I encourage you to prepare if you would like to. The steps and suggestions here should help. Please feel free to e-mail me whatever you prepare so I that can come to quickly understand you and what you most want, both out of life and out of our coaching together.

Write down a list of at least 20 things you are tolerating.

Most clients want to get busy on their goals right away, but I often recommend they first start (or concurrently work on) what they are putting up with. In my experience, it is hard to create new stuff when you are being drained by stuff (i.e., tolerations).

Make a list of the five outcomes you want to enjoy within the next 90 days.

What do you most want to have happen in your personal and professional life within 90 days? What is going to make the biggest difference to you? What would make your coaching worthwhile? Please be as specific and measurable as possible, and please select outcomes that are doable and that do not depend on others to occur.

Identify one or more of the 100-point checklists to focus on.

Most clients like working on one or more of the Client Programs, such as Clean Sweep, Personal Foundation, Attraction, or New Business Start-Up. Some of these programs will strengthen you and your life (Personal Foundation); others will guide and direct you (New Business Checklist); others will train you (Communication Skills). Pick one or several of these Client Programs—they will provide a focus and support structure between your coaching sessions. Then take the test(s) and let me know your current score(s).

Write down three fundamental changes you need to make in order to become more successful.

You probably already know these, and it is good to articulate them. Please share them with me.

Ask your friends and family what they feel you could or should work on with your coach.

I ask that you do this for two reasons. First, your family and friends know you and have an objective perspective on you, so it's very valuable to know what they think about your work and life. Second, I find it to be extremely helpful to tell people you have a coach and are being coached. Some clients want to keep this a secret (and I can understand why), but I have found that clients progress faster when they share with others what they are working on, changing, improving, and creating, and this includes having a coach. Sharing creates synergy and support. Secrets keep the energy restricted.

Top 10 Ways to Get the Most Out of Your Coaching

Just by having a coach and chatting with him or her on a regular basis, you will get plenty of value—you don't have to work hard at it—for the benefits of coaching to occur. This is because the synergy that occurs in a coaching relationship is what makes the biggest difference to any well-motivated coachee.

But if you do want to maximize the value of the coaching relationship, here are 10 ways that work very, very well. If some of the ideas are new to you, we can talk about them as part of our first several sessions.

○ **Focus on how you feel and want to feel, not just on what you want to produce.** Sometimes coachees feel the need to focus the coaching time on how to produce more tangible or financial results. But do not forget the intangibles, such as feeling happier, more peaceful, and more inspired. Results are very important, but the feelings you experience during your day are equally important. Think of a brick wall; the bricks are the results, the mortar is the feelings. Enjoy having both.

○ **Talk about what matters most to you.** You may talk about anything you want during the coaching session. This includes your goals, your life, your needs, what you want to improve, what's bothering you, an idea you have, a problem you are dealing with, even stuff that may not appear to be all that useful to talk about. It's surprising what a difference it makes in the long run when you focus on what you most selfishly want to talk about during coaching, not what you feel you should talk about during the session.

○ **Sensitize yourself so that you see and experience things earlier than before.** As you know, time is collapsing, meaning that things are happening faster and faster and that the pace of change continues to increase. For some, this causes stress because they feel both the pressure to keep up and the fear of getting left behind. But others recognize this phenomenon as a chance to seize opportunities at the moment instead of seeing them too late. You do this by reducing whatever is clouding your ability to see or numbing your ability to sense; we call this process *sensitizing yourself*. The more you can feel, the faster you can respond to events and opportunities. You sensitize yourself by reducing or eliminating alcohol, television, adrenaline, stress, and caffeine.

○ **Feel coached during the 10,000 minutes of your week, not just the 30 minutes of your session.** There are 10,080 minutes in a week. Coaching is occurring all during your week, not just during your coaching session, which is the power of coaching and the coaching relationship. What you and your coach talk about during your sessions will resonate with you during your week, and some of the seeds or ideas that you have discussed will grow between sessions. All you have to do is to fully live your life between coaching sessions and be open to seeing what you and your coach talked about.

○ **Reduce the drain and strain in your life.** Coaching works because it focuses you on two life areas: first, you will be helped to stretch yourself further, take more actions than you would on your own, and devise or implement effective strategies to get what you want. At the same time, you will also be identifying and reducing things that drain and strain you, such as tolerations, stressful situations, difficult relationships, pressured environments, and recurring problems. So don't just hoist a bigger sail: Make sure there are no cracks or barnacles on your hull.

○ **Get more space, not just time, in your life.** Coaching needs room in order to work. If you are too busy, rushed, adrenaline charged, or burdened, you will be using coaching to push yourself harder instead of to become more effective. We strongly suggest that you put some projects on hold, reduce your roles, simplify your day, reduce your goals, streamline your work, install personal management systems, and so on, before or immediately after starting with a coach. Simplification gets you space. Space is needed to learn and evolve yourself beyond where you are today.

○ **Become incredibly selfish.** Coaching is about you and what you most want. Thus, you will probably need to start putting yourself first if you haven't done so already. At the very least, you will want to become selfish, in the sense that you are what matters most. When you are happy and doing well, others will benefit as well.

○ **Be open to seeing things differently.** In coaching, you will be working with your goals (called the "What") and your strategies to reach these goals (called the "How"). But you will also be working on you (the "Who"). In other words, you will get more out of coaching if you are willing to reassess some of your assumptions, ways of thinking, expectations, beliefs, reactions, and approaches to success. There are always newly developed concepts, principles, distinctions, and evolutionary steps to learn. You will not be forced or even encouraged to make these changes, given that they are so personal, but we do ask that you at least consider different approaches and ways of thinking and try them out to see if they work for you.

○ **Be willing to evolve yourself, not just develop yourself.** Coaching is both a developmental process and an evolutionary one. In other words, you will be learning how to accomplish more with less effort—let's call this the developmental aspect of coaching. But you will also be thinking differently and expanding yourself and your world, which we call evolving. Perhaps surprisingly, evolving is a skill, and it is worth learning because life itself is evolving, not just developing.

○ **Design and strengthen your personal and business environments.** The value of coaching can be extended if you use part of your coaching time to design the perfect environment in which to live and work. Where you live and how you live are key to your success. Who you spend time with and are inspired by can make the difference between success and failure. Be willing to invest some time—and money—in improving your environment so that you feel supported to be your best.

What to Talk about with Your Coach

Because the coaching relationship is unique, it helps to know what is best to talk about during our call or meeting, and what not to talk about!

How are you?

- How you are feeling about yourself—good stuff and bad stuff
- How you are looking at your life
- How you are feeling about others

What has happened since the last session?

- What has occurred to you since the last call
- Shifts, wins, and insights
- Any new choices or decisions made
- Personal news

What are you working on?

- Progress report on your goals, projects, and activities
- What you've done that you are proud of
- What you are coming up against

How can I help?

- Where you are stuck
- Where you are wondering about something
- A distinction
- A plan of action
- A strategy or advice

What is next?

- The next goal or project to take on
- The next goal or distinction to understand
- What you want for yourself next

Comprehensive Assessment Chart

Score yourself in the assessment tests listed at the bottom of each bar, then fill in your current score for each. Add to the bar chart as you increase your points in each program. Update monthly. Track progress in 1 to 10 aspects of your life.

Your name _____

										100 %
										90
										80
										70
										60
										50
										40
										30
										20
										10

Clean Sweep	Need- Less	Tru Value	Reserve Index	Irresist. Attract.	Time Peace	Biz Whiz	___	___	___

Welcome to Coaching: Client Welcome Letter

Dear Client:

I am pleased to welcome you as my client, and I look forward to collaborating with you over the coming months and, hopefully, years.

Your coaching calls are scheduled for:

Day: _____

Date: _____

Time: From _____ to _____

Eastern   Central   Mountain   Pacific   Other: _____

We have agreed to initially work together for at least ___ months at a rate of $___ per month.

I will be calling you at (_____) ____ - _____.

You will be calling me at (_____) ____ - _____.

I would like for you to complete the enclosed forms, based upon what you are seeking to accomplish during coaching.

_____

_____

_____

_____

_____

Thank you for the privilege of serving you.

Warmest regards,

Coachee History

Every coachee has a history—you need to know it.

○ **What** have been your three most fulfilling accomplishments in life, thus far?

○ **What** was the biggest thing you have had to overcome?

○ **How** strong/powerful/healthy have your past personal or business role models been?

○ **How** have you failed, and how has that affected the way you think and act today?

○ **Have** you worked with a coach before? What worked? What did not work?

○ **How** have your attitudes about people and life changed over the past 10 years?

○ **What** has made you the most successful or powerful?

○ **Are you** mostly past, present, or future oriented?

○ **What** should I know about your professional background or history?

○ **What** should I know about your personal background or family history?

I Believe in You:
The Coach's Credo

○ I believe that you have a unique gift to offer in this lifetime, which will bring you joy.

○ I believe that you are willing to be honest with yourself and with me.

○ I believe that you can solve any problem you encounter.

○ I believe that you are capable of far more success than you know.

○ I believe that you are willing to learn what others are not.

○ I believe that you are able to commit yourself to mastering your craft.

○ I believe that you are coachable.

○ I believe in you.

○ I believe.

Assessment Summary

This form records detailed scoring information. Fill in scores from the assessment tests under "Start." Then update quarterly using the additional three columns.

Start Score:			
1st Quarter Score	2nd Quarter Score	3rd Quarter Score	4th Quarter Score
Clean Sweep			
Environment			
Health and emotional balance			
Money			
Relationships			
TOTAL (Maximum 100)			

Start Score:			
1st Quarter Score	2nd Quarter Score	3rd Quarter Score	4th Quarter Score
NeedLess			
Need 1 _____			
Need 2 _____			
Need 3 _____			
Need 4 _____			
TOTAL (Maximum 100)			

Start Score:			
1st Quarter Score	2nd Quarter Score	3rd Quarter Score	4th Quarter Score
Tru Values			
Value 1 _____			
Value 2 _____			
Value 3 _____			
Value 4 _____			
TOTAL (Maximum 100)			

Start Score:			
1st Quarter Score	2nd Quarter Score	3rd Quarter Score	4th Quarter Score
Reserve Index			
Time			
Love			
Money			
Energy			
Opportunity			
Source			
TOTAL (Maximum 100)			

Start Score:			
1st Quarter Score	2nd Quarter Score	3rd Quarter Score	4th Quarter Score
Master Coach Profile			
_____			
_____			
_____			
_____			
TOTAL (Maximum 100)			

Start Score:			
1st Quarter Score	2nd Quarter Score	3rd Quarter Score	4th Quarter Score
Biz Whiz Index			
_____			
_____			
_____			
_____			
TOTAL (Maximum 100)			

Start Score:			
1st Quarter Score	2nd Quarter Score	3rd Quarter Score	4th Quarter Score

Stress Index

Start Score:			
1st Quarter Score	2nd Quarter Score	3rd Quarter Score	4th Quarter Score

Client Coachability Index

Start Score:			
1st Quarter Score	2nd Quarter Score	3rd Quarter Score	4th Quarter Score

Spending Questionnaire

Start Score:			
1st Quarter Score	2nd Quarter Score	3rd Quarter Score	4th Quarter Score

Attachment Index

Goals List

Please mark the goals you most want to work on during the first year of coaching. Here's a list of popular goals to achieve, using the services of a coach.

Health and Emotional Balance		
Reduce stress	Begin exercising	Achieve more vim and vigor
Reduce sugar/fat intake	Look better	Handle body problem
Reduce alcohol/nicotine intake	Lose weight	
Sleep better	Take responsibility	
Financial		
Face a money problem	Start saving	Buy a home
Go through bankruptcy	Begin investing	Build financial reserve
Set up/follow a budget	Stop overspending	Learn about money
Pay off debts/credit cards	Create lifetime money plan	Review insurance
Earn more/make more	Moonlight	
Design financial independence plan	Plan pre- or postretirement finances	
Career		
Upgrade profession	Get a raise/promotion	Start own business
Find a new career	Get a job/better job	Be more productive
Reduce stress on the job	Undergo job training	
Design a career track	Do a better job	
Relationships		
Get one/find Mr. or Ms. Right	Resolve past experiences	
Redesign to get needs met	Attract better people	
Socialize more	Get closer to family	
Get closer to spouse	Feel more loved	

Transition		
Divorce recovery	Retirement planning	One- to five-year life plan
Recovery from trauma	Loss of loved one	Medical challenge
New job	Gain of large monies	
Big loss/failure	Big opportunity	

Special		
Have a lot more fun	Get some hope	Become more patient
Complete special project	Address sexual concern	Grow the heck up
Undergo mediation	Design vision, purpose	Become more responsible
Clean up something	Handle all needs	Wake the heck up
Discover core values	Start spiritual path	
Begin path of recovery	Make big life changes	
Be mentored	Learn distinctions	
Be listened to fully	Awaken creative juices	

Promise Log

Write down the promises you make to yourself and your coach.

Date Made	Date Due	OK	Specific Promise or Goal

Possibility

Open some windows for the coachee.

○ If you had all the money you needed, where and how would you live?

○ If you had the answers to your problems, how long would it take to solve them?

○ Do you have a personal or professional vision?

○ If so, what is it?

○ What is probably *not* possible for you to achieve in this lifetime that you wish you could?

○ On a scale of 1 to 10, with 10 being the highest, how would you rate the quality of your life today?

○ Using the same scale, how high will that number likely rise during your lifetime?

○ What is a dream or goal that you've given up on?

○ What part of you have you given up on?

○ What goal or part of your life have you put on the back burner because the time isn't right? What part of you is just waiting for the right person or opportunity to catalyze it?

Priorities

Most coachees appreciate support to identify and focus on their most important goals.

○ **What** is your most urgent personal problem?

○ **What** is your most urgent business problem?

○ **What** problems feel unsolvable right now?

○ **What** are the three biggest changes you wish to make in your life over the next 90 days?

○ **What** are the three biggest changes you will need to make in your life over the next three years?

○ **What** are the three biggest opportunities you have right now that you are not making the most of?

○ **What** feeling is most important for you to have a lot more of, and quickly?

○ **What** goal or outcome do you have that you are pining for or are really, really ready to achieve?

○ **What** is the single focus for our coaching that will help you reach multiple goals?

○ **What** is most pressing on your mind today that you are willing to share with me?

Work, Career, or Business Environment

Help the coachee to perfect his or her work or business environment.

○ **What** five things do you spend most of your time doing during your business day?

○ **How** much more money could you make if you focused and were properly inspired and supported?

○ **Where** is the stress coming from in your work?

○ **Are you** working with the right people? the best people?

○ **What** conflicts are you having at work?

○ **What** is the most fulfilling aspect of your work?

○ **What** is the most difficult or stressful part of your work?

○ **What** is the most exciting aspect of your work?

○ **What** strengths or skills do you have that are immediately marketable?

○ **What** resources are missing that you feel are necessary for your success?

Money

Almost all coaching has a financial aspect to it.

○ **How** is your financial situation?

○ **How** stable is your income stream?

○ **Do you** live within, at, or beyond your means?

○ **Are you** a natural saver or a habitual spender?

○ **How** much credit card debt are you carrying?

○ **How** much money is enough for you?

○ **What** actions could you take that would double your current salary or profit?

○ **What** mistakes do you seem to make with money?

○ **How** much of a priority is making more money?

○ **What** holds you back financially?

Improvements to Make

These questions prompt the coachee to think of things to achieve in areas of their life they might not have thought of otherwise.

○ **What** are the improvements you wish to make in your family or home life?

○ **What** are the improvements you wish to make in your financial situation?

○ **What** are the improvements you wish to make in your job, career, or work?

○ **What** are the improvements you wish to make in your personal character?

○ **What** are the improvements you wish to make in your business?

○ **What** are the improvements you wish to make in your professional skills?

○ **What** are the improvements you wish to make in your communication skills?

○ **What** are the improvements you wish to make in the quality of your life?

○ **What** are the improvements you wish to make in your love life?

○ **What** are the improvements you wish to make on the inside?

101 Things to Work on with Your Coach

Your name_____   Coach's name_____

Date _____   Coach's fax/e-mail_____

Section 1: Business or Career Success

Priority Level
Low → High

○○○○○ 1. I see the importance of providing even more value to my clients or customers than they receive currently.

○○○○○ 2. I need to make a change or advancement in my *career or profession.*

○○○○○ 3. It's important to learn how to *better prepare my staff, customers, or colleagues for change.*

○○○○○ 4. I need to put together a budget, pro forma plan, and/or strategic *plan for my business project.*

○○○○○ 5. I need to become *more effective and/or efficient* in how I do my work or run my business.

○○○○○ 6. I see the need to deliver work or services at a *higher level of excellence and standards,* even perfection.

○○○○○ 7. I want to easily and *more powerfully influence* my staff, vendors, and colleagues.

○○○○○ 8. I feel the need to *invest more time and money* into my business or professional skill set.

○○○○○ 9. I definitely need to feel, think, and *act like a stronger leader* than I do now.

○○○○○ 10. It's important to me to *build and leave a legacy* in this lifetime.

○○○○○ 11. I could *better leverage my assets, resources, connections, and talents.*

○○○○○ 12. I see the need to become a *stronger, more effective manager* of people, projects, and results.

○○○○○ 13. I am ready to *totally master what I do* professionally. I want to be the best at what I do.

○○○○○ 14. I wish to learn *key negotiating skills* that will help me get what I want and create win-win situations.

○○○○○ 15. I need to increase the size, scope, and depth of my *professional network and community.*

○○○○○ 16. I see the need to *increase my personal or company's productivity* significantly.

○○○○○ 17. I want to feel like a real pro and be *regarded as a real pro* by my customers and colleagues.

○○○○○ 18. I definitely want to *increase the profits* of my business.

○○○○○ 19. I have an *important project* that would probably progress more smoothly if I had a coach for support.

○○○○○ 20. I need to learn and really *master selling skills* so I can increase revenue immediately.

○○○○○ 21. I need to develop a *marketing plan* or create unique ways to market my product or service.

○○○○○ 22. I need to *install administrative, selling, or management systems* in my business or work.

○○○○○ 23. I want to learn *effective team-building skills* and management techniques to bring out the best of my group.

○○○○○ 24. I want to *improve my timing, synergy, and synchronicity* so I don't miss out on opportunities.

○○○○○ 25. I need to properly *articulate my business or professional vision* so it is compelling.

Section 2: Life Enhancement

Priority Level
Low → High

○○○○○ 26. I recognize the need to become someone who *accepts things more readily and with less resistance.*

○○○○○ 27. I want to *quickly assimilate what I notice, experience, or learn,* and apply it immediately.

○○○○○ 28. I see the need to *become a bigger, more magnanimous person,* and I'm ready to change.

○○○○○ 29. I need to set *much stronger boundaries* so I am not taken advantage of, or disrespected, by others.

○○○○○ 30. I need to become a much more compassionate and patient person with others.

○○○○○ 31. I have important projects, situations, or *problems I haven't finished* but need to.

○○○○○ 32. I need to gain a *broader perspective or context* about life, myself, my life, and/or my work.

○○○○○ 33. My life is "expensive" to my body, heart, and/or spirit, and I need to *reduce these stress costs.*

○○○○○ 34. I would be more effective and successful if I had *more of an edge* or more inner confidence.

○○○○○ 35. I believe I can get a lot more done with a lot less effort. I want *life to be effortless.*

○○○○○ 36. I have noticed others who are *very graceful in how they deal with life,* and I want to be that way as well.

○○○○○ 37. I would like to be *more grateful* for what I do have, instead of always needing more.

○○○○○ 38. I am ready to *take a lot more initiative* in certain parts of my personal and business life.

○○○○○ 39. I need to *more fully integrate* the various elements of my personal and work life.

○○○○○ 40. I need to *increase the level of integrity* in my life; I currently feel out of integrity in at least one area of my life.

○○○○○ 41. I would like to *better prioritize* my goals, responsibilities, roles, and projects so that I don't fall behind.

○○○○○ 42. I feel overwhelmed or am in a swirl, and I feel the need to get back on more *solid footing that is based in reality*.

○○○○○ 43. I find myself slowed down by either *resistance or fear*, or both, and I am ready to work through this.

○○○○○ 44. I wish to become a person who *responds quickly and fully* to both opportunities and problems as they occur.

○○○○○ 45. I don't feel as *physically or financially safe* as I want to feel, and I am ready to do something about it.

○○○○○ 46. I feel the need to *simplify my life*, dramatically.

○○○○○ 47. I am ready to *raise my standards* of behavior, expectations, relationships, and lifestyle.

○○○○○ 48. I want to learn to *deal with difficult people* in a more constructive, yet powerful, way.

○○○○○ 49. I need to *manage my time* better in order to get the most out of each day yet have enough time for myself.

○○○○○ 50. I am *tolerating more than I know is good for me*, and I would like to work on this.

Section 3: Who I Am

Priority Level
Low → High

○○○○○ 51. I would like to *improve my physical appearance and presentation* so that I am delighted with how I look.

○○○○○ 52. It's time to *change some of the assumptions* I have made about myself and upgrade my paradigm.

○○○○○ 53. I am interested in *identifying and focusing on selected attainments*.

○○○○○ 54. I feel out of balance, like I am juggling parts of my life. I'd like to *get back in balance*.

○○○○○ 55. I want to *make significant changes to my body* in terms of weight, tone, and/or strength.

○○○○○ 56. I would like to *strengthen or perfect my character*.

○○○○○ 57. I need to *have more confidence* in how I present myself; I'm ready to develop this part of myself.

○○○○○ 58. I want to have more of a *positive effect on others*, without trying to rule or control them.

○○○○○ 59. I feel the need to improve the quality of my physical and/or spiritual *energy*.

○○○○○ 60. I want to improve the communication, cooperation, and love within *my family*.

○○○○○ 61. I feel I have a special gift, but I would like to *better identify and orient my life around my gift.*

○○○○○ 62. I would like to be *much happier* than I am right now.

○○○○○ 63. I would like to *develop my mind and intellect* more than I have. I need a challenge.

○○○○○ 64. I would like to accurately identify and once and for all *satisfy my personal needs.*

○○○○○ 65. I would like to be *more consistently enthusiastic* about my life and/or my work.

○○○○○ 66. I feel the need to *be more at peace* with myself, life, and/or others.

○○○○○ 67. I need to develop or *improve my personality*, my attitude, and how I come across.

○○○○○ 68. I am ready to enjoy my life a lot more and *experience more pleasure.*

○○○○○ 69. I am intrigued about the idea of becoming a *problem-free zone.*

○○○○○ 70. I want to become a lot *more receptive to new ideas, approaches, and views.*

○○○○○ 71. I see the value in *building significant reserves* in all areas of my life: time, money, love, and opportunity.

○○○○○ 72. I need to *take much better care of myself*: body, mind, and spirit.

○○○○○ 73. I want to get to know and *understand myself better*, and to know what makes me tick and motivates me.

○○○○○ 74. I feel the need for significant spiritual development and/or to *embark on a spiritual path* that fits me.

○○○○○ 75. I want to *develop a stronger personal style* and be able to express myself fully.

Section 4: Personal Success

Priority Level
Low → High

○○○○○ 76. I would like to learn how to *attract success* to me instead of pushing so hard for it.

○○○○○ 77. I know that I need to *become aware more quickly* of what's occurring to and around me.

○○○○○ 78. I see the need to *increase my bandwidth*—my ability to quickly receive and process lots of information.

○○○○○ 79. I need to *deliberately cause (meaning to create) my life and success*, instead of waiting for it to happen.

○○○○○ 80. I recognize the need to be a lot *more coachable and flexible to input* from others.

○○○○○ 81. I would like to *learn key coaching skills* so I can be more effective with others.

○○○○○ 82. I need to *improve my communication and speaking skills* so that I am better heard and understood.

○○○○○ 83. I'd like to *contribute more to others* without feeling I am wasting my time or resources.

○○○○○ 84. I'd like to become *much more creative* in my life and unblock what gets in the way of my creativity.

○○○○○ 85. I would like to *develop a formal schooling/education plan* or strategy for my life and career.

○○○○○ 86. I have *several important goals* I would probably reach sooner if I had support and advice from a coach.

○○○○○ 87. I have *great ideas,* but I need to develop them into something that is financially and personally rewarding.

○○○○○ 88. I want to learn how to *be interdevelopmental* with everyone, meaning to work in a collaborative partnership.

○○○○○ 89. I need to *develop my intuition* so it's finely tuned and to fully respect and immediately respond to it.

○○○○○ 90. I need to increase my vocabulary and learn how to *communicate and phrase my thoughts better.*

○○○○○ 91. I would like to create a coordinated and *comprehensive life plan* for the next five years.

○○○○○ 92. I am ready to become a *much better listener*; I want to really hear what others are saying or trying to say.

○○○○○ 93. I need an *entire life makeover,* starting from the ground up.

○○○○○ 94. I need help in becoming *much better organized* with paperwork, bill paying, or other tasks.

○○○○○ 95. I want to *develop a customized personal reading program* to better educate myself or expand my thinking.

○○○○○ 96. I need help to either *resolve a relationship problem* or improve a key relationship.

○○○○○ 97. I would like to *get to know all the parts of myself better* so I can make better decisions and be happier.

○○○○○ 98. I want to start saving or *increase the amount I'm saving* each year.

○○○○○ 99. I need to *quickly turn around* a very important part of my life.

○○○○○ 100. I see the value of getting online and understanding the Internet and web; *I want to get wired!*

And, finally,

○○○○○ 101. I want to learn more about what love is, how it works, and how to become *more loving to everyone.*

Goals to Work on with Your Coach

Here's a master list of things to work on with your coach.

- Expand my thinking beyond what I am conditioned to conceive of
- Delegate more effectively so that I have more time to work on what matters most
- Lose weight without orienting my life around it
- Develop a financial plan to become financially independent at age____
- Change my relationship with food from comfort to sustenance
- Change my approach from selling to telling and from telling to modeling
- Learn how to set up a web site that showcases myself and my services or company
- Become proficient with sending and receiving all forms of e-mail
- Improve the quality of my home life
- Take much more time for me instead of living too much for others
- Take charge of my life instead of letting other people run it for me
- Become unconditionally constructive in everything I say
- Design a lifestyle that makes me incredibly happy
- Dramatically improve the profitability of my company
- Expand my network to include the finest professionals in 100 different fields
- Stop pushing for sales and start investing in relationships
- Goof off without feeling guilty
- Communicate so well that people respond immediately
- Turn my time into an asset—1,440 assets a day
- Eliminate or reduce adrenaline in my life so I don't burn myself and others up
- Redesign my life so that it's oriented around vacations, not work
- Increase my ability to process more information without getting overwhelmed
- Accelerate my personal evolution
- Feel a lot better about my family and myself
- Reduce the amount of conflict in my life so that I can relax
- Increase the amount of money I have in savings
- Start a new business and avoid the common learning curve
- Identify the triggers that cause adrenaline, before they get me wired
- Start reading books that will help me evolve instead of merely develop
- Design my path of personal development
- Reduce what I am tolerating at work
- Clean out the clutter in my closets, drawers, and garage

○ Learn how to ask the right questions in any selling situation
○ Create a buying environment instead of a selling environment
○ Learn how to make more money in the new economy
○ Discover what is causing dissonance in my life
○ Become cyber and Internet literate
○ Endorse my worst weakness as my biggest strength
○ See opportunities in problems without wearing rose-colored glasses
○ Have more patience, especially when I have none
○ Walk my talk without strutting
○ Become a toleration-free zone
○ Strengthen my personal foundation so that the underpinnings of my life are rock solid
○ Add value to my customers and clients, just for the joy of it
○ Identify the unique skills and talents that I know are waiting to be leveraged
○ Eliminate delay, so I don't miss opportunities
○ Stop procrastinating and be inventory free
○ Toss out my to-do list (or plan to create one)
○ Expand my vocabulary so that I can better express myself in any situation
○ Stop whining and start winning
○ Find a career that works
○ Play with my kids every day, instead of just when I have time
○ Identify every source of stress in my life and either reduce or eliminate it
○ Put my family first without putting myself second
○ Learn how to give people what they want, without its costing me anything
○ Change my thinking from win-lose to win-win
○ Design values-based goals instead of whim-based goals
○ Stop taking life so darn seriously
○ Give others the experience of being heard, instead of just being listened to
○ Increase my bandwidth in order to handle more input
○ React less and respond more
○ Clean up my life and start clean
○ Start over
○ Discover my personal values and orient my life around them
○ Identify and eliminate 10 tolerations in the next 10 days
○ Create a perfect life
○ Become self-actualized
○ Write a book without pain
○ Develop a life plan and start living it
○ Make the personal changes I have been unable to make on my own
○ Get focused
○ Blow up the blocks standing in my path to success
○ Start taking the path of least resistance instead of working against life
○ Increase the momentum in life so that I am carried forward instead of pushing myself
○ Find a better way to motivate myself
○ Stop watching Jay Leno and get to bed earlier
○ Throw out my television set
○ Move to the country because I want to
○ Make a significant personal decision
○ Create a business plan without taking three months to do so

○ Get in the habit of flossing daily
○ Get the support I need to visit the dentist
○ Get the nudge I need to hire a housecleaner so I don't have to do the cleaning
○ Improve my attitude so I'm always positive, naturally
○ Take more chances
○ Change my relationship with risk
○ Develop a reserve of time during my day
○ Get out of a rut
○ Do a personal makeover
○ Improve what I see in the mirror
○ Stay on track using Nautilus three times per week
○ Better identify the people who are really good for me and those who are not
○ Extend my boundaries without setting up walls
○ Strengthen my character so I am really proud of who I am
○ Become more sensitive with people who need that from me
○ Stop micromanaging people
○ Bring in five new clients a month
○ Make a million dollars next year
○ Become a saver and start saving because I enjoy it
○ Reduce my credit card debt faster than I currently am
○ Get control over my spending
○ Build a team with my area managers
○ Spend more time in the garden
○ Spend more time at the beach
○ Spend more time
○ Learn how to practice extreme self-care
○ Increase my havingness so I can maintain my success
○ Simplify everything
○ Get back to exercising: 40 sit-ups and 20 push-ups per day
○ Be able to meet men and women and not get anxious about it
○ Book at least five selling appointments in the next 10 days
○ Identify my unique selling proposition and my label
○ Close 10 new clients in next 90 days
○ Start an e-mail-based weekly newsletter to expand my network
○ Easily ask for what I want
○ Become a very direct and confident communicator
○ Tell the truth instead of what people want to hear
○ Increase my awareness
○ Slow down to enjoy the weather and take in the wonder of everyday life
○ Spend less time in the future and more time enjoying the present
○ Design my winning formula
○ Reduce business expenses by $20,000
○ Increase business by 20% without spending more on advertising
○ Identify three specific goals that light me up for next year
○ Get clear on my values and align my goals with them
○ Create an inspiring project through which I will touch at least 100 people per month
○ Launch a national organization
○ Become a better team leader so employees love their jobs
○ Create a sales program for a new niche

○ Let go of the people in my life who drain my energy
○ Create a personal health plan that includes exercise
○ Take more days off
○ Plan three wonderful vacations for next year
○ Set clear boundaries and train those around me to treat me with respect
○ Begin a financial independence plan
○ Save $100,000 next year
○ Take a day every week to renew and rejuvenate
○ Develop a national reputation for what I do well
○ Brainstorm and prioritize the best ideas to use in my business
○ Work 25 percent fewer hours without making less
○ Become a person who smiles almost all of the time
○ Write to someone with whom I have unfinished business
○ Apologize to someone, even if it is very difficult
○ Ask my partner to give three hours of time per week to release me to do something I really enjoy
○ Discover what makes me tick
○ Bring balance to work, home, community, and personal time over a three-month period
○ Start running each morning
○ Decrease body fat percentage by 10 percent within six months
○ Upgrade all computer programs within three months
○ Stop smoking completely within three months
○ Stop overpromising and making commitments
○ Complete a tough project on time
○ Pay off car loan one year early
○ Buy a new car within six months
○ Buy a house within one year
○ Quit my job to work from home within two years
○ Become a telecommuter
○ Go half-time at work
○ Redecorate house in six months
○ Negotiate a 10 percent raise next evaluation.
○ Learn five skills to better communicate with my children
○ Learn five skills to better communicate with my spouse
○ Establish one delicious habit and do it every day
○ Rebuild my life after a loss
○ Bring romance back into my marriage within 90 days
○ Discover my life purpose and begin setting goals to live it within 90 days
○ Become more efficient without becoming a machine
○ Return to school to pursue a graduate degree
○ Get married within five years
○ Expand business to sell products over the Internet
○ Take a trip to Europe
○ Go on a safari
○ Own a boat
○ Stop fibbing and lying completely within three months
○ Build meditation and yoga into daily schedule
○ Achieve assigned sales numbers one week prior to end of month to avoid rushing for sales the last week

- Spend 10 percent less money monthly
- Identify 101 things I love to do, and do one each day
- Decrease time spent paying bills
- Increase personal time by four hours a week within one month
- Enroll in a cooking class
- Take scuba lessons and go on a Caribbean dive
- Discard unnecessary household and personal items within three months
- Discard items cluttering office and desk within one month
- Establish three things I am passionate about as priorities in my life within six months
- Drop three clothing sizes within six months
- Fit into those 32-inch-waist Levi's within six months
- Go on a guilt-free shopping spree
- Pay back money owed to friends within six months
- Stop complaining within 14 days
- Shift or release a sabotaging belief within 60 days
- Reconcile credit report within six months
- Establish and enforce boundaries within a relationship
- Reduce number of credit cards to three in 18 months
- Move into a larger apartment within nine months
- Visit grandparents out of state within the year
- Design a class or TeleClass and market it within six months
- Allow one day out of each month to do something I really want to do
- Organize my pension, will, life insurance, and mortgage papers within 60 days
- Meet with a financial advisor twice a year to keep finances updated to set goals on a weekly basis
- Genuinely thank people who help me, daily
- Reestablish a lost relationship
- Call up one member of my family per week, just to say hi
- Pay off mortgage within five years
- Be prepared for a holiday season (e.g., Christmas) at least one month before the holiday begins
- Train a pet to consistently perform a desired action on command
- Reorient personal and professional life completely around values (not wants and needs) within three years
- Join Toastmasters and complete first 10 speeches within six months
- Develop two new profit centers in my business within one month
- Trash 100 megabytes of stuff I don't need on my computer
- Clean out or purge all home and work files this month
- Get my hair cut and styled the way I really want it and the way that is most attractive for me
- Say no five times this week
- Keep the gas tank in my vehicle at least half full at all times
- Join and participate in those networking groups that will assist in business and personal life
- Disentangle myself from those organizations that do not add value to business or personal life within one month
- Develop a sense of style
- Take a world tour
- Improve my reputation among my colleagues

○ Attract the mate of my dreams
○ Become Ms. Right instead of searching for Mr. Right
○ Turn my ideas into revenue streams
○ Clean up where I get my energy from
○ Reduce the friction in my life by finding the right lubricant
○ Develop a reserve of opportunities so I don't have to look for them
○ Build a personal support network of people with similar interests
○ Learn how to attract business instead of constantly marketing for it
○ Design a personal development plan for my children
○ Deepen my relationships with my friends
○ Delight my customers, not just please them
○ Become more respectful of other people's ways
○ Keep my word
○ Be accountable for results
○ Enjoy responsibility instead of trying to avoid it
○ Clarify my professional commitments
○ Become an adult in every sense of the word
○ Learn how to say no without turning people off
○ Make it clear to people what I require of them
○ Reorganize my office and work environment
○ Automate and delegate almost every aspect of my personal tasks and chores
○ Get more done, but slow the pace at which I'm working
○ Increase my self-esteem
○ Balance my personal, family, and business lives
○ Better integrate what I already have
○ Reduce the roles I fill for others
○ Become a lot more creative in what I do
○ Prioritize my time so that I don't feel rushed and exhausted
○ Trust my inklings more
○ Turn my intuition into my primary decision-making system
○ Develop a marketing strategy for my business
○ Build my personal brand
○ Free myself from my beliefs
○ Come to accept that which I resist
○ Become a better writer
○ Speak in a laser like fashion
○ Become an effective public speaker
○ Find my voice and speak confidently
○ Distinguish truth from b.s. in every situation, instantly
○ Become a proactive person who never waits
○ Develop grace
○ Improve the relationship I have with my spouse or significant other
○ Improve the relationship I have with my children
○ Improve the relationship I have with my parents
○ Improve the relationship I have with my siblings
○ Improve the relationship I have with my in-laws
○ Improve the relationship I have with my neighbors
○ Improve the relationship I have with my boss
○ Improve the relationship I have with my colleagues
○ Improve the relationship I have with my clients

○ Improve the relationship I have with my coworkers
○ Improve the relationship I have with my minister
○ Become a better manager
○ Become a leader, not just a manager
○ Prepare my business for sale
○ Learn how to give advice without turning people off
○ Enjoy being human instead of trying to perfect myself
○ Identify what slows me down
○ Develop a marketing engine for my business
○ Increase the number of referrals I receive
○ Learn how to make requests that are accepted and fulfilled
○ Distinguish symptoms from sources when dealing with a situation
○ Become incredibly selfish
○ Sensitize myself so that I feel things when they occur instead of afterward
○ Lighten up
○ Deprogram myself from other people's expectations of me
○ Understand the relationship between memes and genes
○ Find my area of specialization or professional niche
○ Find a way to delegate my weaknesses so I can focus on my strengths
○ Transition smoothly into a new field
○ Shift the paradigm in which I exist
○ Perfect my environment so that it brings out my best
○ Create a vacuum that pulls me forward
○ Affect people profoundly
○ Position my services or products in the marketplace
○ Evolve from rational, logical, and linear thinking to operating well in a state of chaos
○ Be causal instead of reactive
○ Buff up my body
○ Buff up my life
○ Develop an edge in order to close a sale or make my point
○ Become part of a spiritual community
○ Develop compassion for people who I currently criticize
○ Learn to dance better with events instead of being so rigid
○ Be able to think abstractly instead of just logically
○ Come to enjoy change as opposed to resisting or disliking it
○ Reduce the emotional costs of my business or practice
○ Become a much more endorsing and encouraging person
○ Listen very, very well
○ Develop marketing materials for my business
○ Package my products and services better
○ Develop 10 profit centers instead of just one
○ Complete a project with less stress
○ Be sustainably motivated instead of operating in fits and starts
○ Become wise
○ Always have enough clean clothes, no matter what
○ Turn my bedroom into a place where I sleep perfectly
○ Have something to look forward to each evening
○ Not resist getting up in the morning
○ Get enough physical touching so that I don't shrivel up

- ○ Have a home that is always perfectly clean and organized
- ○ Improve the lighting everywhere in my home or office so that there is no strain
- ○ Have my teeth cosmetically perfected
- ○ Be able to recover quickly if I lose my wallet or purse
- ○ Keep my computer backed up, daily
- ○ Pay my bills early, always
- ○ Walk away from people who do not respect me
- ○ Never force myself to do anything that I don't want to
- ○ Rearrange my investments so that I don't lose sleep over them
- ○ Get the quality rest I need
- ○ Have more than enough confidence in virtually every situation
- ○ Always ask for more than I need, as a habit
- ○ Improve my judgment
- ○ Always arrive early and never feel rushed
- ○ Eliminate everything that distracts me during my day
- ○ Multitask, easily
- ○ Protect myself from the physical or environmental risks of life
- ○ Develop a rewarding life outside of work
- ○ Hire a coach to help me achieve what I want
- ○ Organize my files perfectly
- ○ Always be well groomed
- ○ Stay "present" throughout the day
- ○ Speak without a "charge" to my voice
- ○ Stop gossiping
- ○ Stop making promises, even if I feel I should
- ○ Stop doing errands and contract them out
- ○ Reduce volunteer activities that are getting in my way
- ○ Face a difficult legal, financial, or tax matter
- ○ Become aware of energy flows between others and myself
- ○ Deepen my relationship with God
- ○ Deepen my relationship with Jesus
- ○ Treat my body like the temple that it is
- ○ Toss out all of the clothes that don't make me look great
- ○ Learn to collaborate with people instead of debating or arguing
- ○ Break any past sabotaging patterns that I've had
- ○ Become more open and available to all that is already around me
- ○ Learn how to "get" someone instead of just listening to or hearing them
- ○ Learn coaching skills that I can use with my family and customers
- ○ Get a handle on what's coming, given how fast the world is changing
- ○ Have interdevelopmental relationships, not just interdependent ones
- ○ Raise my standards
- ○ Understand the basics of running a successful business
- ○ Identify the features and benefits that I offer my customers or clients
- ○ Evolve beyond being productive and become effective
- ○ Master my craft rather than just being an expert at it
- ○ Become fearless
- ○ Evolve from peace to a life of harmony
- ○ Arrange to have all my bills paid automatically
- ○ Design a system to complete projects two days before the deadline
- ○ Take up cooking

- Establish a family planning center in my home
- Increase productivity by 25 percent in six months
- Determine causes of procrastination and develop new skills
- Design each room of my home to complement its vision and purpose
- Implement a low-stress move or relocation
- Free up two extra hours of time each day
- Develop a motivational plan to lose 20 pounds in three months, safely
- Discover the root causes of stuckness and implement a plan for becoming unstuck
- Design a consistent discipline plan for my toddler
- Incorporate two acts of love per day toward my mate
- Establish a daily "dream work" time
- Cut television viewing to 45 minutes a day or less
- Design an annual physical maintenance program (doctors, dentists, etc.)
- Free my mind of clutter by establishing a recording and action system
- Free up $200–500 per month for my own self-improvement
- Be able to put my hands on most of the regularly used information in my office in two minutes or less
- Communicate love to my children in ways that are personally meaningful to them
- Establish and follow a seasonal shopping schedule to take advantage of seasonal sales
- Develop a phone call return system to ensure that calls are returned within four hours if they are important
- Attract a soul mate
- Define the top 10 qualities I am looking for in a soul mate
- Decrease stress level by 20 points in 90 days
- Become an "intrapreneur" in my organization by creating a small business idea and selling it to the decision makers
- Obtain a more senior position in my organization in less than six months
- Implement two new personal habits each month
- Maintain a daily quiet time
- Clarify my top 10 values and use them as a decision-making compass
- Cultivate a circle of five close friends
- Develop a plan to free up two evenings a week
- Double my income in two years
- Set up a one-year program toward taking a dream vacation
- Cut budget or spending by 25 percent
- Increase productivity in staff members by 30 percent
- Develop a system for recording and tracking my artistic or business ideas
- Implement a schedule for acting on ideas
- Incrementally increase salary over the next year
- Choose and take the self-assessment tools that would be of maximum benefit
- Define the legacy I wish to leave
- Discover a meaningful and rewarding career
- Reduce problem-solving time by 50 percent
- Refine the elements of my business plan
- Design a customer service satisfaction survey that identifies my customers' core needs
- Attract a client base that earns 25 percent more than my current client base
- Turn dreams into goals

○ Rearrange budget and food spending patterns in order to hire a personal chef within three months
○ Develop five personalized ways to say no to others in firmness and love
○ Get ahead of office equipment maintenance, reducing lost time by 30 percent
○ Eliminate major blocks to creativity
○ Eliminate 90 percent of office interruptions
○ Expand circle of influence by 50 people
○ Develop an annual goal-setting system
○ Increase customer retention by 25 percent
○ Learn to quickly identify people and situations that are not best for me
○ Navigate a successful transition for my staff
○ Identify, personalize, and memorize my vision
○ Enlarge Rolodex by 100 strong people
○ Reduce down time caused by adjustment to change by 50 percent
○ Reduce time commitments by 30 percent
○ Learn to make a point in 15 words or less
○ Design and implement an exercise program
○ Set standards for a clutter-free living environment
○ Set up a plan for the mastery of a new hobby
○ Add two pleasurable activities to my daily routine
○ Understand what drives and motivates me
○ Understand why I relate to people the way I do
○ Understand how I learn so that I can learn more easily
○ Understand my basic interests and how they affect my choices
○ Discover my fashion type and how it impacts other areas of my life
○ Design a customized reading plan
○ Discover my Enneagram type
○ Discover my Myers-Briggs type
○ Discover my DISC profile
○ Organize my closets
○ Design a personalized filing system
○ Set up a "90 Days to a Simpler Life" plan
○ Increase the speed of people's response to my needs
○ Add grace and beauty to my life through the arts
○ Learn to have an edge with people and events
○ Implement a personal prioritizing system to accomplish important rather than simply urgent things
○ Double my standards
○ Improve my skin tone
○ Develop a plan to deal with all undone details of my life
○ Develop a daily habit of journaling feelings
○ Learn how to effectively communicate feelings to my spouse
○ Eliminate 20 percent of my problems
○ Stop using caffeine within 30 days
○ Stop using sugar within 30 days
○ Implement a tailor-made nutritional plan
○ Develop a list of five boundaries that increase my quality of life
○ Increase my energy level
○ Set boundaries and standards around the relationship I have with my parents
○ Increase my job satisfaction so that I look forward to going to work

- ○ Develop a plan to implement the truest value into my life
- ○ Understand that I can be both a good person and a good boss
- ○ Get complete on relationships
- ○ Work through a career change
- ○ Get clear on priorities
- ○ Deal with and recover from burnout
- ○ Enjoy life more
- ○ Take on greater challenges at work
- ○ Become better at developing rapport with others
- ○ Deal with fears and concerns in a relationship
- ○ Manage time more effectively
- ○ Determine priorities
- ○ Explore or understand feelings and beliefs
- ○ Get my personal life in order
- ○ Strengthen my spiritual life
- ○ Overcome my fear of rejection
- ○ Deal better with interruptions
- ○ Develop the ability to say no and stick with it
- ○ Discover the inner peace that I know is possible
- ○ Surrender and accept what I am resisting
- ○ Catch myself within a minute whenever I step over something in a conversation
- ○ Become a participator in life, not just an observer
- ○ Identify a focus that expresses my values and uses my strengths
- ○ Stop trying to control everything and everyone
- ○ Identify a theme for my life in the coming year and orient my goals around that
- ○ Develop a morning routine that I totally enjoy
- ○ Let go of 10 shoulds that I've created for myself
- ○ Let go of people who are holding me back
- ○ Lessen the strain I put on people
- ○ Put people and relationships ahead of results
- ○ Develop more confidence in myself
- ○ Stop explaining myself
- ○ Stop justifying my actions
- ○ Stop selling or seducing others
- ○ Reduce how much I am drinking
- ○ Stop smoking
- ○ Resolve whatever childhood damage is causing me pain today
- ○ Start investing in the stock market
- ○ Create an outrageous business goal and enlist support to reach it
- ○ Start writing in a journal to express my thoughts and feelings
- ○ Subscribe to forward-thinking magazines
- ○ Learn to pace myself
- ○ Increase my ability to want and desire
- ○ Improve my self-esteem and self-worth
- ○ Learn to share the credit and glory of my accomplishments
- ○ Get completely free of what binds me
- ○ Always be 10 minutes early and never rushed
- ○ Start using a time management system
- ○ Stop tailgating
- ○ Hire someone to do my laundry

- ○ Maintain zero credit card debt
- ○ Be content with my life and myself; stop striving
- ○ Become wise in this lifetime
- ○ Expand what I see as possible
- ○ Reconcile my life with humanity
- ○ Be ready to die at any moment, without regrets
- ○ Become internally motivated
- ○ Learn to condition change instead of forcing it on others
- ○ Develop self-respect
- ○ Put jumper cables in my car's trunk
- ○ Have AAA (auto club) membership or equivalent
- ○ Have the right Internet service provider
- ○ Put all the serial numbers for my computer's software in a safe place
- ○ Have an attorney on retainer in case something really bad happens to me
- ○ Have my tax return completed by February 15th each year
- ○ Have a face lift if I want one
- ○ Hire a personal trainer
- ○ Start having fresh flowers in my home and office
- ○ Plan the next year by the end of the previous November
- ○ Know a professional gift service for last-minute solutions
- ○ Have a tailor or seamstress available to repair my clothes
- ○ Know a plumber I can call on a moment's notice
- ○ Install an alarm system in my house, so I can rest easily
- ○ Have my car washed each week
- ○ Have my closets professionally redone
- ○ Have a virtual assistant on call to handle stuff I don't want to do
- ○ Have healthy food delivered, so I don't have to cook when I don't want to
- ○ Have a weekly manicure
- ○ Get Rolfed

First-Year Checklist

You will want to compete all of the following during the first year. Check each box as you complete each step.

Client:	Start date:
Information/worksheets/assessments	
○ Clean Sweep	
○ NeedLess	
○ Tru Values	
○ Reserve Index	
○ Personal Foundation	
○ Irresistible Attraction	
○ Personal goals	
○ Business goals	
Conditions to have in place	
○ Client is saving money	
○ Truth is being told	
○ Client is working toward vision	
○ Client has solid personal foundation	
○ Client is well on road to being restored, recovered, healed	
○ Client is stress free	
○ Client is doing well in business or at work	
○ Client is not tolerating or suffering	
○ Client's needs are being met	
○ Client is oriented around values	

Coaching Evaluation

Our number one priority is you, my client. It is only through your honest and open feedback that I can continuously improve my services and learn and grow—to be the best coach I can be. I appreciate your taking the time to fill in this evaluation form and return it to me. Please use it as a guide and feel free to add anything you wish. Thank you.

What has been the greatest benefit coaching has brought you? What outcomes have you achieved?

_____

_____

Have any of your initial expectations of the coaching process not been met?

_____

_____

How effective was your coach?

☹		☺		☺	
○	○	○	○	○	My coach was a model for me on how to achieve.
○	○	○	○	○	I trusted my coach completely.
○	○	○	○	○	My coach always treated me with respect.
○	○	○	○	○	My coach was rigorous and committed to my success.
○	○	○	○	○	My coach was on time and present for all sessions.
○	○	○	○	○	My coach was available between sessions.
○	○	○	○	○	Within a month of starting, I felt confident in my coach.
○	○	○	○	○	My coach kept me focused, regardless of circumstances.

What was your coach's greatest strength, and how has that supported you? What areas do you feel your coach could focus his or her growth on?

_____

_____

Do you have any comments on the structure of our coaching sessions? (e.g., more or less time, frequency, reviews, paperwork, face-to-face versus telephone)

_____

_____

What do you want most from our future partnership, and what would keep this process rewarding?

_____

_____

Do you have any other ideas, insights, or suggestions on ways to improve?

_____

_____

Summary

☹		☺		☺	
○	○	○	○	○	My coach was able to bring out my very best.
○	○	○	○	○	I received full value for the fees I paid.
○	○	○	○	○	I will refer other people to my coach.

Evaluation of the Coach

Circle the numbers that most represent your response. How well are you being coached?

How valuable was/is your coaching?	NO				YES
I am achieving/have achieved the goals I intended to.	1	2	3	4	5
I am achieving/have achieved additional worthwhile goals.	1	2	3	4	5
I now produce results faster and easier because of coaching.	1	2	3	4	5
I now have skills that I will always benefit from.	1	2	3	4	5

How effective is the coach?	NO				YES
The coach is/was a model for me on how to achieve.	1	2	3	4	5
I trust/trusted my coach completely.	1	2	3	4	5
The coach always treats/treated me with respect.	1	2	3	4	5
The coach is/was rigorous and committed to my success.	1	2	3	4	5
The coach is/was on time and present for all sessions.	1	2	3	4	5
The coach is/was available between calls/sessions.	1	2	3	4	5
Within a month of starting, I felt confident in the coach.	1	2	3	4	5
I have the paperwork, forms, and worksheets I need.	1	2	3	4	5
The coach keeps/kept me focused.	1	2	3	4	5

Summary	NO				YES
I would refer/have referred coachees to the coach.	1	2	3	4	5
I receive/have received full value for the fees I pay/paid.	1	2	3	4	5
The coaching is/was a win for me.	1	2	3	4	5
The coach is/was a professional.	1	2	3	4	5
The coach knows his/her stuff.	1	2	3	4	5
The coach is/was able to bring out my very best.	1	2	3	4	5

Comments

Chapter 4

About Your Coaching Practice

Included in this chapter are tools and strategies for building and sustaining a successful coaching practice. They will support you in adding value and designing a practice that generates referrals. This chapter provides information on web sites, assistants, filling your practice, budgeting, cash flow and projection, and TeleClass leading.

The information, lists, forms, charts, tracking sheets, and programs will provide you tools and strategies for success. From practice design to client extras, you will have the foundation you need for a strong start to filling and maintaining a client base of ideal clients.

The following sections are included in this chapter:

1. 10 Steps to Developing a Successful Coaching Practice
2. Coaching Specialties
3. Choose Your Coaching Specialties
4. Practice Design
5. Client Extras
6. Ideal Coachee Characteristics
7. Client Retention Checklist
8. 25 Steps to Filling Your Practice
9. 100 Ways to Fill Your Coaching Practice
10. 101+ Ways to Fill Your Practice (and Keep It Full)
11. Team 100 Program
12. Start-up Budget for a Coaching Practice
13. Budget for the First 90 Days
14. Client Fee and Cash Flow Projection
15. Time and Billing Log
16. Checks Received This Month
17. Cash Receipts Log
18. Monthly Practice Checklist
19. Top Five Things Your Coaching Web Site Should Be Set Up to Do

20. Top Five Ways to Convert Your Web Site Visitors into Paying Customers
21. 90+ Ways to Use a Virtual Assistant
22. TeleClass Leading: 100 Skills and Steps of Designing and Leading TeleClasses

10 Steps to Developing a Successful Coaching Practice

This section is designed to educate individuals interested in finding out what it takes to be a coach with a successful practice. The key phrase is *successful practice,* because many folks coach naturally, as a hobby or for free. The steps provided here are written specifically for the committed and full-time professional coach. Feel free to copy this section to give to others you meet who you think would make a great coach.

Step #1

Discover why you really want to be a coach, and be turned on about it. People who coach well are people who love people and want the most for them. A coach usually has a knack for recognizing the strengths and assets of another human being. Given this ability, the coach can give good advice, listen between the words, and educate the coachee to take full advantage of opportunities. This turns the coach on, in a healthy, fulfilling way.

Step #2

Get in a good space, personally. Your coaching can only be as good as your life is. Coaching others is a responsibility; coachees entrust themselves, their visions, and their goals to you. You must be healthy, well, able, and balanced before you enter the coaching profession.

You should be in touch with yourself, clear of any past traumas or critical therapy issues, and in excellent health, free from addictions or attachments. In other words, no smoking, no alcohol, no drug or eating abuse, and no caffeine. You can't be addicted or attached and coach well.

Step #3

Hire a mentor coach; learn from an expert. People who attempt to develop a coaching practice by themselves rarely are successful. Why? Because coaching is both an art and a technology and requires a mentoring structure to insure the proper balance.

As a beginning or intermediate-level coach you will be faced with coaching situations that will shock, scare, and/or stump you. Your mentor coach has been there before and will assist you to handle the situation professionally and get you through the personal stuff that it brought up in you.

Plan to spend between $3,000 and $10,000 per year in coaching and training during your first three years in business. This investment pays off fully and quickly, so don't skimp. Coaching calls are an investment in you and your skills.

Step #4

Set a $100,000 per year earnings goal with an action plan. A professional, full-time coach should be earning $100,000 within three to five years of being mentored and trained. $100,000 would mean 40 hours a week of coaching at $50 per hour, or half-time at $100 per hour. To get to this level requires several things:

- Scheduled, bite-sized goals
- A willingness to work
- A financial reserve

Most coaches transition from a previous career, such as consulting or another profession. This transition is best achieved by designing an ultra-conservative plan, assuming a slow start to filling one's practice, and having a steady stream of income from a career or investment source.

A written plan makes the transition to full-time coaching easier and safer.

Step #5

Treat coaching as a business, not just a calling. The most successful coaches have business clients, not personal ones. Entrepreneurs, self-employeds, professionals, managers, and investors are the most likely group to benefit enough from coaching to pay you, and pay you well.

Those seeking just personal growth, spirituality, and help with crises can be viable clients but don't always have the budget to pay you $150 per hour or $10,000 per year.

Coaching is a business. You charge a fee for your time; the client should expect enough results to continue the relationship.

Send out bills monthly, and insist on timely payment. Be rigorous with clients to achieve their goals; don't back down. Know what you want for your clients, and hold that vision until they get it.

Make a substantial profit yourself; you'll attract more clients willing to pay more.

Step #6

Attract clients who are ready now for what you have to offer. A coach usually attracts clients who are either a step behind or a step ahead of you in life. Anything more and you're in over your head; anything less and you're bored.

Thus, you want to ask for and attract the clients who appreciate where you are in life and where you've come from. It inspires most clients to learn that you have courage, strength, and determination.

Some coaches coming into the field are concerned about their credentials. Must I have a degree? Should I wait to coach until I have more experience? Who would hire me?

Successful clients are your credentials. If prospective clients can't get that, they probably aren't ready for a coach. Know your current skills and natural abilities, and offer these to people you meet. You don't have to be an expert in every area of coaching.

Step #7

Deliver 120 percent and your practice will fill simply from referrals. The question most asked by prospective coaches is "How will I get my clients?"

A good question with an almost-too-easy answer: Deliver 120 percent of what the coachee expects, and your practice will fill itself.

And how does one deliver 120 percent? Another good question.

Here are a few ways:

- Keep expectations low.
- Be unconditionally constructive, always.
- Ask coachees to do more, a lot more.
- Don't accept excuses.
- Expect a lot from them.

Coachees want you to be straight, loving, and relentless.

Step #8

Know what you must know; then master it. After you have selected your niche, design a plan to learn and master everything about that area.

If your focus is entrepreneurs, read, study, practice, and interview. If turnaround situations turn you on, develop a model for that. If life transition work gets you up in the morning, learn the dynamics of people and change.

Whatever the specialty, don't just learn it; master it!

Step #9

Upgrade your practice; charge more than you think you are worth. Double your fees after a year of being in full-time practice, with the advice of your coach. There is a way to accomplish this and have your clients be empowered by it. And you'll attract people who would not pay you $75 per hour but will pay you $100 per hour.

Notice that the step is to charge more than you think you're worth. It does not say to charge more than you are worth. If you do, you will lose clients or it will come back to bite you. Charge what you're worth. And train to be worth much, much more.

Step #10

Mentor a novice coach; pass on the gift of coaching. Now it is your turn to teach others. Cherish the privilege. Mentoring another coach brings you to the next level.

Coaching Specialities: 100 Areas of Specialty

As the demand for coaching grows, so does the demand for coaching specialties. Here is a list of coaching specialties, many of which have already become popular. So, whether you are a coach in training wondering what the specialty options are, or a coachee seeking a specialist, the following list should be very useful. Note: Some specialties require special licensing or testing in certain states or countries. Others require advanced training qualifications and testing. Finally, some specialties are just beginning to become popular.

1. Corporate

○ Corporate coach

○ Executive/CEO coach

○ Organizational development coach

○ Management coach

○ Culture/paradigm shift coach

○ Leadership coach

○ Board of directors coach

○ Human resource coach

○ Quality coach

○ Staff/employee coach

2. Marketing/Sales

○ Sales coach

○ Public relations coach

○ Marketing coach

○ Brand management coach

○ Promotions coach

○ Pricing strategy coach

○ Buzz development coach

○ Advertising coach

○ Direct marketing coach

○ Personal marketing coach

3. Small Business

○ New business coach

○ Entrepreneur coach

○ Business turnaround coach

○ Multilevel marketing /network marketing coach

○ Networking coach

○ Budgeting/planning coach

○ Business financial coach

○ Mission development coach

○ Marketing coach

○ Partners' coach

4. Relationships

○ Marriage coach

○ Family coach

○ Romance coach

○ Team coach

○ Parent coach

○ Love coach

○ Divorce recovery coach

○ Couples' coach

○ Network development coach

○ Intimacy coach

5. Life Stage/Lifestyle

- Fresh start coach
- Generation X coach
- Baby boomer coach
- Retirement coach
- Lifestyle design coach
- Teen coach
- Students' coach
- Workaholics' coach
- Transition coach
- Personal turnaround coach

6. Quality of Life

- Nutrition/diet coach
- Exercise/fitness coach
- Vegan/vegetarian coach
- Recreation coach
- Travel/adventure coach
- Wellness coach
- Energy/Reiki coach
- Makeover coach
- Buff/style coach
- Stress reduction coach

7. Success Coach

- Motivation/edge coach
- Goals/results coach
- Idea/creativity coach
- Problem solving/solution coach
- Time management/leverage coach
- Strategic coach
- Attraction coach
- Financial/money coach
- Career coach
- Legacy/achievement coach

8. Special Markets

- Consultants/coaches' coach
- M.D./health professional/dentists coach
- Attorney/law firm coach
- Financial service professionals coach
- Trainers'/speakers' coach
- Gay/lesbian coach
- Single mom/parents' coach
- Realtors'/real estate coach
- Therapists'/counselors' coach
- Ministers'/caregivers' coach

9. Personal Development

○ Life perfection

○ Personal foundation coach

○ Integrity coach

○ Balance coach

○ Advanced development coach

○ Fear coach

○ Evolution coach

○ Resolution coach

○ Attainments coach

○ Spiritual coach

10. Special Skills and Situations

○ Communication coach

○ Cyber coach

○ Internet/web coach

○ Diagnostic coach

○ Futurist coach

○ Language/phrasing coach

○ Software/computer coach

○ Writing coach

○ Personal organization coach

○ General practitioner coach

Choose Your Coaching Specialties

What types of coaching do you most enjoy delivering? There are countless specialties in our field, and more are being added as professionals enter the field and develop new markets and as technology allows for specific applications. Which specialties appeal to you? Indicate your degree of preference by writing A+, A, B, or C in the spaces provided.

Business coach _____	Integrity coach _____
Vision coach _____	Professional networker _____
Turnaround coach _____	Spiritual coach _____
Career coach _____	Professional organizer _____
Personal manager _____	Balance coach _____
Energy coach _____	Executive coach _____
Relationship coach _____	Team coach _____
Life planner _____	Discovery coach _____
Reorientation coach _____	Fitness trainer _____
Project coach _____	Divorce recovery coach _____
Entrepreneurs' coach _____	Money coach _____
Recovery coach _____	New business coach _____
Attachment coach _____	Pleasure coach _____
Coaches' coach _____	Legacy coach _____
Professional trainer _____	Restoration coach _____

Top Three Specialties You Most Prefer, because You Like Them

1. _____

Why does this appeal to you so much? _____

_____

_____

_____

_____

2. _____

Why does this appeal to you so much? _____

_____

_____

_____

_____

3. _____

Why does this appeal to you so much? _____

_____

_____

_____

_____

Practice Design

Designing the ideal practice. Please respond to each question in the space provided.

I work with people who

Are: _____

Want: _____

Can: _____

I specialize in the following areas of coaching:

○ _____

○ _____

○ _____

Special features of my coaching:

○ _____

○ _____

○ _____

Specific benefits of my coaching to clients:

○ _____

○ _____

○ _____

Basic message I share with clients:

○ _____

What makes my coaching irresistible:

○ _____

○ _____

○ _____

Five service upgrades I offer that most consultants do not:

○ _____

○ _____

○ _____

○ _____

○ _____

Super six referral sources:

○ _____ has agreed to send me _____ clients

○ _____ has agreed to send me _____ clients

○ _____ has agreed to send me _____ clients

○ _____ has agreed to send me _____ clients

○ _____ has agreed to send me _____ clients

○ _____ has agreed to send me _____ clients

Financial Success

I charge $_____ per month and/or $_____ per hour.

My practice is full with _____ clients @ an average of $_____ per month = $_____ month.

My clients come via:

○ _____

○ _____

○ _____

I work an average of _____ hours per week.

I spend _____ hours per week marketing myself, which is _____% of my billing hours.

My entire business expenses are $_____ monthly, which is _____% of my income.

Ultimately, my practice looks like this:

Monthly revenue $_____

Number of clients   _____

Weekly billed hours   _____

Hourly rate $ _____

Client Extras

Have you noticed that just about every service firm, retailer, and manufacturing firm is adding value to what it offers its customers? Extras like more time, greater selection, and attractive pricing?

I am pleased to say that the services and the client extras I offer are fully aligned with this *give-more-to-the-customer* trend in business.

Why offer client extras? Because these, in addition to our weekly coaching sessions, give you everything you need to get more of what you want.

And, because I want your business and want to keep your business, the client extras are my way of inviting you to work with me. Here are the free extras to which each client is entitled.

Daily and Weekly TeleClasses

Many clients enjoy the convenience and effectiveness of the daily or weekly TeleClasses. Again, clients may enjoy these at no tuition cost. I can assist in the selection process also. Clients receive all printed materials that accompany the TeleClass. See current schedule for titles and times.

Free 800 Number, Internationally

It has always been my policy to pay the cost of your weekly long-distance coaching call regardless of where you live. You can still be in touch when you travel to or relocate anywhere in the United States, Canada, Mexico, or Western Europe because I'll pick up the cost of these calls also.

Special Seminars and Training

Many clients find that my coaching, communication, and business seminars help them to deepen their grasp of new principles, skills, and technologies. Clients have access to all of these trainings, whether offered in your city or elsewhere, regardless of any posted tuition.

One-Hour Orientation Session

New clients get off to a strong start with a special one-hour orientation session that focuses on what you want, what's in the way, and who you need to become.

Comprehensive Welcome Package

Every new client receives a 100-page welcome package, full of self-assessment tests, articles, goal-setting and tracking forms, tips, and suggestions to get the most out of the coaching.

Client Coaching Programs

Are you leading a workshop? Do you need source material? Checklists? Procedures? Clients may use my library of materials as the basis of their work.

Free Advice for Associates

I can help just about anyone better see where they are, what is really happening, and what the three key steps are to get to the next level. As a benefit to you, I will spend up to 30 minutes with anyone in your family or network who you think I can help.

Quality Referrals

I've been coaching for five years, have an extensive Rolodex, and do my best to match people up professionally. Need a tax person? Public relations (PR) person? Speaker? Need to get to know someone else in your field? I can probably help. It's all a part of my coaching service.

Ideal Coachee Characteristics

My ideal coachee would have these characteristics.

Gender	
Age	
Needs	
Wants	
Salary	
Education	
Lifestyle	
Qualities	
Dreams	
Problems	
Stresses	

Client Retention Checklist

Clients do leave, but use this list and they'll stick around twice as long.

- ○ Send birthday and holiday cards.

- ○ Never withhold anything from your client. Always share with them your concerns about them, a problem they are causing you, a fear you have about them. Don't censor or try to phrase it right. Get it out!

- ○ Tell your client what you want for them as often as you can.

- ○ Give flowers, a gift for their desktop, or something else that's special whenever they have a big win or need a lift.

- ○ Always make the client pay by the beginning of the month. Accept nothing else. Don't be nice.

- ○ Have a full practice and a waiting list.

- ○ Have a written agreement of at least three months.

- ○ Underpromise always. Never even hint that you can produce miracles.

- ○ Don't get into the client's (or your own) personality or issues—keep the focus on actions, distinctions, and coaching.

- ○ Be known for delivering the message, not for figuring out how to best run the client's business.

- ○ Speak with your client at least once per week between calls.

- ○ Invite your client to social events: dinner, special luncheons. Make it social, but only talk about them, not yourself.

- ○ Schedule special workshops for clients and their friends only.

- ○ Don't push your clients for referrals—let them know you appreciate the referrals, but don't bug them.

- ○ Send out a quarterly letter or newsletter to keep your clients abreast of all that you are doing.

- ○ Get the client focused on a very big and exciting goal or project. Challenge them; don't coddle.

- ○ Don't put up with anything—missed calls, tardy calls, complaining.

25 Steps to Filling Your Practice

... The easy way. Use this checklist to get a strong start. Do every item, and you should have a full practice within 6 to 12 months. Color in the left-hand circle if you are working on this step. Color in the right-hand circle when you have completed this step.

Full Practice Chart

		Step
○	○	Get your Clean Sweep score above 75.
○	○	Make a list of 25 people you know and write down three things that you want for each of them.
○	○	Schedule 10 lunches, 10 phone sessions, and five meetings to discuss this with these 25 people.
○	○	Schedule three workshops, one per month, on needs, business success, or other favorite areas.
○	○	Enroll at least five people into each at a nominal fee (just to make sure they show up).
○	○	Make a direct request of 10 people to work with them for 90 days.
○	○	Enroll in Coach U's free Q&A or similar training.
○	○	Hire a coach whose job is to help you fill your practice.
○	○	Spend 15 hours per week coaching—clients, friends, and/or associates—for pay or not; just coach.
○	○	Get promises from five people who will send you at least three referrals each.
○	○	Schedule yourself to speak about your favorite coaching topic to 10 groups or associations.
○	○	Spend twice as much time with the clients you have than they are paying you for.
○	○	Make huge requests of your current coachees so they produce breakthroughs in their lives.
○	○	Give unexpected gifts to your coachees.
○	○	Fire the client who is proving to be unwilling or not ready. Do not hang on.

		Step
○	○	Host a monthly evening seminar or luncheon for current clients and their associates.
○	○	Mentor another coach.
○	○	Have a strong opening line that attracts but does not hard sell.
○	○	Package your coaching services for what the market wants to buy, not just what you want.
○	○	Set the proper fee for where you are currently in your professional development.
○	○	Set up a phone line and office—be in business.
○	○	Have a 12-month practice plan and a budget that is extremely conservative.
○	○	Keep your day job.
○	○	Take all of the self-assessment tests so you know what it's like for the coachee.
○	○	Ask three friends or associates if you can coach them for 90 days for whatever fee they wish.

100 Ways to Fill Your Coaching Practice

This list contains steps and suggestions to help you fill your coaching practice. Some of the suggestions will help you to become a better marketer; others will help you network better and become better known; others are positioning and revenue-enhancing strategies. And some are quality-of-life improvement suggestions, which will help you become more attractive to yourself and thus to others.

1. Public Relations
Become known locally or nationally

- ○ Hire a PR firm
- ○ Write a column for a local newspaper
- ○ Appear on TV talk shows
- ○ Speak on radio talk shows

- ○ Get quoted as an expert
- ○ Send out press releases
- ○ Identify global need/link to coaching
- ○ Do something newsworthy
- ○ Offer free coaching to high-profile coachees
- ○ Develop a press kit

2. Electronic Marketing
Become Internet marketing–savvy

- ○ Develop a professional web site
- ○ Add useful content to your web site
- ○ Add meta tags for search engines
- ○ Link site to Yahoo or other search engines
- ○ Link site to or from other coaches' sites
- ○ Add yourself to findacoach.com
- ○ Create a weekly advice e-letter
- ○ Create or broadcast tips or nuggets
- ○ Ask for input from subscribers
- ○ Get links from other sites

3. Personal Marketing
Develop an extensive network

- Build a research and development (R&D) team
- Get to know top coaches
- Distribute self-intro/newsletter four times per year
- Join or form an alliance of coaches
- Develop a Team 100 network
- Improve your personality or style
- Become someone worth knowing
- Host soirees or groups in your home
- Offer to help people as a habit
- Read *Power Networking* by Sandy Vilas

4. Reputation/Credibility
Become respected as a coach

- Develop several specialties
- Become a certified coach
- Develop the "edge"
- Offer to teach for other coaches
- Take a poll or publish a report
- Correct or perfect your reputation
- Join the International Coach Federation
- Write a book
- Write magazine articles
- Teach for Coach U or Corporate Coach U

5. Professional Development
Become an expert at what you do

- Develop listening skills
- Develop diagnostic skills
- Speak simply, without jargon
- Know your coaching skills
- Know 100 key distinctions
- Read important magazines
- Complete Coach U or Corporate Coach U training
- Develop strong and savvy opinions
- Develop lasering skills
- Attend a coaching conference

6. Sales Skills
Know how to sell really, really well

- Create one sentence self-introduction
- Develop laser sales lines
- Know what you're selling
- Be fearless; ask for the order
- Develop conversion language
- Discern what's wanted or needed
- Ask open-ended questions
- Get to know the person or buyer
- Find a way to serve every buyer
- Tell buyers about themselves

7. Coachee Referrals
Become highly referable

- ○ Know your coaching strengths
- ○ Know where you need to improve
- ○ Let coachees know you have room for more clients
- ○ Ask coachees for referrals
- ○ Offer free introductory services
- ○ Help coachees to really succeed
- ○ Really challenge current coachees
- ○ Identify your ideal coachees
- ○ Let coachees go who aren't right
- ○ Specialize, specialize, specialize

8. Product/Services
Give everyone something to buy

- ○ Offer free audio tapes
- ○ Develop or sell an audiotape series
- ○ Lead local workshops
- ○ License your programs or work
- ○ Offer result-specific coaching
- ○ Offer industry-specific coaching
- ○ Offer coachee-type coaching
- ○ Offer group coaching
- ○ Teach four 12-week TeleClasses
- ○ Launch a virtual university

9. Personal Improvement
Perfect yourself and your life

- ○ Reach 90+ on Clean Sweep
- ○ Complete Personal Foundation
- ○ Master 28 attraction principles
- ○ Complete NeedLess program
- ○ Complete Tru Values program
- ○ Complete 100 Smiles program
- ○ Eliminate problems in your life
- ○ Develop reserve of space or money
- ○ Eliminate bad habits
- ○ Eliminate tolerations in your life

10. Marketing Tools
Give people a chance to experience you

- ○ Offer free TeleClasses
- ○ Offer free local workshops
- ○ Distribute a printed brochure
- ○ Give away 100-point checklists
- ○ Give away free audiotapes
- ○ Offer free coaching
- ○ Offer free call-in days
- ○ Develop or distribute a questionnaire
- ○ Host weekly telediscussions
- ○ Host a virtual community

101+ Ways to Fill Your Practice (and Keep It Full)

Do at least 25 of these.

1. Give your service away.
2. Give your services away to three clients who can fill your practice.
3. Lead a workshop for your current clients and don't charge them for it.
4. Lead a workshop for your friends, clients, prospects, and the public for a very affordable price.
5. Ask five key clients for five referrals each.
6. Host a weekly luncheon or monthly party.
7. Tell clients that their referrals are one of the ways you are paid.
8. Join three clubs or organizations where your ideal clients are likely to be members.
9. Deliver a measurable 20 percent more than what your average client expects.
10. Open an office that inspires you to do your best work.
11. Offer to help three people in trouble who cannot afford your fee.
12. Become a known resource by getting to know 50 highly qualified people who provide services that your ideal clients need.
13. Orient at least 25 percent of your practice around your special gift.
14. Host gatherings of your competitors.
15. Train your clients how to speak about you.
16. Become known as unconditionally constructive.
17. Write an article on something new in your profession.
18. Mentor an apprentice in your profession.
19. Hire an appointment setter.
20. Know and articulate your three basic messages.
21. Tell people the 10 things you want for them.
22. Set your practice standards high and honor them.
23. Clean out your closets.
24. Send out a monthly newsletter.
25. Send out a monthly personal practice letter.
26. Speak to groups at least once per week.
27. Move to the best part of town.
28. Send your clients birthday and holiday cards.
29. Write a book that breaks the rules.
30. Send "request letters" to colleagues.
31. Become known for three special things, but deliver all you can until your practice is full.
32. Invest 10 percent of your revenue in training, coaching, and development.

33. Dress better.
34. Be a professional.
35. Know what you are attached to and get released.
36. Know your vision and be able to share it.
37. Establish yourself as a center of influence.
38. Deepen your relationship with 10 centers of influence.
39. Make your clients and others right even when they aren't, because they are.
40. Raise your fees.
41. Get your personal needs met outside of your practice.
42. Give the right gift for each referral.
43. Master the skill of converting leads into clients.
44. Immediately acknowledge a referral.
45. Do not offer your business card; rather, ask for permission to call.
46. Have a full practice.
47. Ask, don't plead, for more business.
48. Be interested, not interesting.
49. Underpromise, but get the client anyway.
50. Fully handle everything.
51. Package your materials to stun people.
52. Have something worthwhile to say.
53. Have referrals call you; don't chase them.
54. Acknowledge others; don't compliment them.
55. Do more work for current clients.
56. Know what services you cannot or will not offer.
57. Expect a lot from your clients.
58. Package your services to create an annuity stream.
59. Upgrade your clientele.
60. Drastically cut business and personal expenses to be 25 percent profitable right now.
61. Get more permission than you'll ever need from everyone.
62. Be coached.
63. Handle the elephant in the living room.
64. Speak benefits, not features.
65. Speak from the "you," not the "I."
66. Take the initiative. Don't wait.
67. Don't gossip.
68. Put the relationship ahead of the result.
69. Establish a value on your time. No more errands.
70. Don't hide behind a brochure.
71. Advance your profession.
72. Take a vacation each quarter.
73. Have something to look forward to each evening.
74. Be straightforward, but don't spill your guts.
75. Offer to help when you can do so without such help costing you.
76. Know exactly what you can do for others, and let them know it.
77. Invite key people out.
78. Tell people what you want them to do.
79. Disqualify prospects.
80. Take rejection like an angel.

81. Be fully caught up.
82. Have time slots open, blank files prepared, and welcome packets printed.
83. Underinform instead of overinforming.
84. Anticipate and respond to client needs and concerns before the client even knows about them.
85. Use a written agreement in all cases.
86. Budget 5 percent for advertising, gifts, and referral source management.
87. Value each client as a key asset: a 10-year revenue stream.
88. Become attraction based versus promotion based.
89. Codesign work to be performed; let the client contribute to your success.
90. Think holistically; act specifically.
91. Align your goals with your values.
92. Reduce the hidden human costs of delivering your service.
93. Entice your clients to send you clients.
94. Find out why people have not been referring to you.
95. Make a list of your top 10 clients and who sent them to you: the referral tree.
96. Design a plan to fill your practice in half the normal time.
97. Introduce yourself in 10 words or less.
98. Know what would make you irresistible to your ideal clientele.
99. Serve, don't sell.
100. Cut out the distractions.
101. Have 50 percent more business than you need.
102. Identify the 20 percent who can get you the 80 percent.
103. Believe in the work you do.
104. Be responsible for how you are heard, not just what you say.
105. Dress well even when you don't have to.
106. Deliver the message; let people self-select.
107. Fully inform, don't hold back from your clients.
108. Have a self-introduction that engages people.
109. Meet with your advisory board weekly.
110. Write at least one acknowledgment note per day.
111. Say no (thank you) to most possibilities; say yes (thank you) to clients.
112. Value your time at $100–300 per hour.
113. Save at least 10 percent of your income, first.
114. Make one unscheduled call to a client each day.

Team 100 Program

Helping coachees get the results they need requires a team effort by the coach and other professionals.

The **Team 100** list works like a dance card: You select the 100 other professionals who you want on your team. With the right players here's what can happen:

- Your coachees have access to a strong network.
- You can tap into high expertise immediately.
- Most problems or needs can be solved, fast.
- Referrals start flowing among team members.

This program is dedicated to the model of networking: Sandy Vilas.

Instructions

1. Decide to get a full team within one year.
2. Fill in the team members you now know.
3. Start networking to fill in the other slots.
4. Pass around blank forms to associates.
5. Get yourself on others' Team 100 lists.

Progress Chart

Date	Points (+/−)	Score

Team 100 Program 100-Point Checklist

Sections					
#	A	B	C	D	E
20					
19					
18					
17					
16					
15					
14					
13					
12					
11					
10					
9					
8					
7					
6					
5					
4					
3					
2					
1					

Give yourself credit as you get points from the 100-point program. Fill in columns from the bottom up.

A. Business and Work

Running a business, managing a career, and finding work that you enjoy all come easier when you have experts and models to guide and inspire you.

Number of circles checked (20 max) _____

○ **New Business Specialist**
Name: _____
Contact info: _____

○ **Career Consultant/Planner**
Name: _____
Contact info: _____

○ **Graphic Artist**
Name: _____
Contact info: _____

○ **Printer/Copy Place**
Name: _____
Contact info: _____

○ **Turnaround Business Expert**
Name: _____
Contact info: _____

○ **Corporate Trainer**
Name: _____
Contact info: _____

○ **Professional Networker**
Name: _____
Contact info: _____

○ **Internet Marketing Expert**
Name: _____
Contact info: _____

○ **Web Presence Provider**
Name: _____
Contact info: _____

○ **Personal Marketer**
Name: _____
Contact info: _____

○ **Business Coach**
Name: _____
Contact info: _____

○ **Corporate Coach**
Name: _____
Contact info: _____

○ **Executive Coach**
Name: _____
Contact info: _____

○ **Business Diagnostic Coach**
Name: _____
Contact info: _____

○ **Marketing Coach**
Name: _____
Contact info: _____

○ **Professional Writer**
Name: _____
Contact info: _____

○ **Computer Consultant**
Name: _____
Contact info: _____

○ **Hard Disk Crash Recoverer**
Name: _____
Contact info: _____

○ **Software Consultant**
Name: _____
Contact info: _____

○ **Headhunter**
Name: _____
Contact info: _____

B. Money and Legal

The only thing in the way of your financial independence is great advice and the willingness to apply it.

Number of circles checked (20 max) _____

O **Small Business Attorney**
Name: _____
Contact info: _____

O **Real Estate Attorney**
Name: _____
Contact info: _____

O **Tax Attorney**
Name: _____
Contact info: _____

O **International Attorney**
Name: _____
Contact info: _____

O **Estate Attorney**
Name: _____
Contact info: _____

O **Copyright/Trademark Attorney**
Name: _____
Contact info: _____

O **Criminal Attorney**
Name: _____
Contact info: _____

O **Financial Planner**
Name: _____
Contact info: _____

O **Banker**
Name: _____
Contact info: _____

O **Realtor**
Name: _____
Contact info: _____

O **Venture Capitalist**
Name: _____
Contact info: _____

○ **Stockbroker**
Name: _____
Contact info: _____

○ **CPA**
Name: _____
Contact info: _____

○ **Insurance—Life/Health/Disability**
Name: _____
Contact info: _____

○ **Insurance—Liability**
Name: _____
Contact info: _____

○ **Insurance—Home/Auto**
Name: _____
Contact info: _____

○ **Bookkeeper/Bill Paying Service**
Name: _____
Contact info: _____

○ **Grant Writer**
Name: _____
Contact info: _____

○ **Property Manager**
Name: _____
Contact info: _____

○ **Money Manager**
Name: _____
Contact info: _____

C. Personal and Health

Our bodies, minds, and spirits can benefit from these experts.

Number of circles checked (20 max) _____

○ **M.D.—Internist**
Name: _____
Contact info: _____

○ **M.D.—Ophthalmologist**
Name: _____
Contact info: _____

○ **M.D.—Cosmetic Surgeon**
Name: _____
Contact info: _____

○ **M.D.—Dermatologist**
Name: _____
Contact info: _____

○ **M.D.—Sports**
Name: _____
Contact info: _____

○ **M.D.—Psychiatrist**
Name: _____
Contact info: _____

○ **Nutritionist**
Name: _____
Contact info: _____

○ **N.D. (Naturopath)**
Name: _____
Contact info: _____

○ **Massage Therapist**
Name: _____
Contact info: _____

○ **Chiropractor**
Name: _____
Contact info: _____

○ **Pharmacist**
Name: _____
Contact info: _____

○ **Movement Therapist**
Name: _____
Contact info: _____

○ **Acupuncturist**
Name: _____
Contact info: _____

○ **Diagnostician**
Name: _____
Contact info: _____

○ **Therapist—Depression**
Name: _____
Contact info: _____

○ **Therapist—Attention Deficit Disorder Expert**
Name: _____
Contact info: _____

○ **Therapist—Relationships**
Name: _____
Contact info: _____

○ **Fertility Expert**
Name: _____
Contact info: _____

○ **Dentist/Cosmetic Dentist**
Name: _____
Contact info: _____

○ **Speech Therapist**
Name: _____
Contact info: _____

D. Personal Services

These are services that make our lives easier.

Number of circles checked (20 max) _____

○ **Housekeeping/Cleaning**
Name: _____
Contact info: _____

○ **Travel Agent**
Name: _____
Contact info: _____

○ **Event Planner**
Name: _____
Contact info: _____

○ **Florist**
Name: _____
Contact info: _____

○ **Professional Gift Service**
Name: _____
Contact info: _____

○ **Portrait Photographer**
Name: _____
Contact info: _____

○ **Caterer**
Name: _____
Contact info: _____

○ **Seamstress/Tailor**
Name: _____
Contact info: _____

○ **Childcare/Babysitter**
Name: _____
Contact info: _____

○ **Minister/Clergy**
Name: _____
Contact info: _____

○ **Auto Mechanic/Car Care**
Name: _____
Contact info: _____

○ **Electrician**
Name: _____
Contact info: _____

○ **Air Conditioning/Heating Repair**
Name: _____
Contact info: _____

○ **Plumber**
Name: _____
Contact info: _____

○ **Professional Organizers**
Name: _____
Contact info: _____

○ **Personal Concierge/Errand Service**
Name: _____
Contact info: _____

○ **Dog Walker/Pet Sitter**
Name: _____
Contact info: _____

○ **Good Book Maven**
Name: _____
Contact info: _____

○ **Interior Designer/Decorator**
Name: _____
Contact info: _____

○ **Handyman/-woman**
Name: _____
Contact info: _____

E. Extreme Self-Care

Extreme self-care refers to the practice of taking exceptionally good care of your body, mind, and spirit. The professionals listed here can make a big difference in your emotional, physical, and energy levels.

Number of circles checked (20 max) _____

○ **Skin Care Specialist/Spa**
Name: _____
Contact info: _____

○ **Personal Assistant (Virtual)**
Name: _____
Contact info: _____

○ **Healthy Food Delivery**
Name: _____
Contact info: _____

○ **Spiritual Advisor/Clergy**
Name: _____
Contact info: _____

○ **Jeweler**
Name: _____
Contact info: _____

○ **Image/Color Consultant**
Name: _____
Contact info: _____

○ **Communication Coach**
Name: _____
Contact info: _____

○ **Reiki Master**
Name: _____
Contact info: _____

○ **Irresistible Attraction Coach**
Name: _____
Contact info: _____

○ **Lifestyle Design Coach**
Name: _____
Contact info: _____

○ **Personal Assistant (Real)**
Name: _____
Contact info: _____

○ **Personal Trainer**
Name: _____
Contact info: _____

○ **Personal Coach**
Name: _____
Contact info: _____

○ **Manicurist/Pedicurist**
Name: _____
Contact info: _____

○ **Certified Rolfer**
Name: _____
Contact info: _____

○ **Personal Makeover Coach**
Name: _____
Contact info: _____

○ **Feng Shui Consultant**
Name: _____
Contact info: _____

○ **Alexander Technique Expert**
Name: _____
Contact info: _____

○ **Visual Artist Consultant**
Name: _____
Contact info: _____

○ **Psychic**
Name: _____
Contact info: _____

Start-up Budget for a Coaching Practice

Figure a budget of between $1,000 to $5,000 to do it right. Create your budget by filling in the spaces provided.

Materials	Budget	Price Range
1,000 business cards	$	$10–500
500 sheets of letterhead and envelopes	$	$100–500
Office supplies	$	$100–500
500 brochures	$	$100–500
Other:	$	$ –
Other:	$	$ –
Other:	$	$ –
Equipment	Budget	Price Range
High-quality telephone	$	$50–200
Separate phone line	$	$50–200
Fax machine	$	$300–2,000
Computer	$	$500–4,000
Printer	$	$300–2,000
Large table or desk	$	$50–1,000
Ergonomic chair	$	$100–500
Telephone headset (a must)	$	$75–250

Large file cabinet	$	$50–350
High-quality lamp	$	$50–200
High-quality answering machine	$	$50–200
Software	$	$ –
Other:	$	$ –
Other:	$	$ –
Other:	$	$ –
Other:	$	$ –
Total	$	

Budget for the First 90 Days

Be conservative, not optimistic. It always takes longer than you think. Keep your day job. Create your 90-day plan by filling in the spaces provided.

	Month 1	Month 2	Month 3	
Income				
Coaching clients				+
Workshops/seminars given				+
Speaking engagements given				+
Other:				+
Other:				+
Total income				= A

	Month 1	Month 2	Month 3	
Expenses				
Telephone, voice mail expenses				+
Printing, materials, brochure				+
Promotion expenses				+
Coaching fee expenses				+
Training seminars/books				+
Office rent/payments				+
Other:				+

Other:				+
Other:				+
Total expenses				**= B**

Total start-up expenses				**= C**

Net profit from coaching				**= (A – B – C)**

Client Fee and Cash Flow Projection

Track how much is coming in, and from whom.

Client	Fee	Jan.	Feb.	Mar.	Apr.	May	Jun.	Jul.	Aug.	Sep.	Oct.	Nov.	Dec.	Year Total
	$													
	$													
	$													
	$													
	$													
	$													
	$													
	$													
	$													
	$													
	$													
	$													
	$													
	$													
	$													
	$													

Time and Billing Log

Time is money. Keep track of how much you are coaching and billing!

Date	Client	For	From	To		Time		Rate		Billed	Rec'd
Month: _____											
					=		X	$	=	$	○
					=		X	$	=	$	○
					=		X	$	=	$	○
					=		X	$	=	$	○
					=		X	$	=	$	○
					=		X	$	=	$	○
					=		X	$	=	$	○
					=		X	$	=	$	○
					=		X	$	=	$	○
					=		X	$	=	$	○
					=		X	$	=	$	○
					=		X	$	=	$	○
					=		X	$	=	$	○
					=		X	$	=	$	○
					=		X	$	=	$	○
					=		X	$	=	$	○
Total this page									=	$	

Checks Received This Month

Read and complete the following:

Date	From	For $	Comments

Total checks received this month _____ for $_____

Cash Receipts Log

Use this form to keep track of the money you receive. Write down every check or cash payment you receive on this form before depositing it. If you deposit several items together, use a separate line for each check and summarize the total so you can match up your deposits on the bank statement. Always fill in the Amount column and categorize the nature of the income, using one or more of the five columns on the right. Use categories like Coaching, Seminars, Public Presentations, Publications Sales, Bonuses, and Gifts. At the end of the month, quarter, or year, add up all of the columns to see how much money you received and how you earned it.

Date	From	For	Amount	Type of Income				
			$					
			$					
			$					
			$					
			$					
			$					
			$					
			$					
			$					
			$					
			$					
			$					
			$					
			$					
Total this page			$					

Monthly Practice Checklist

Stay ahead of your clients and on top of your practice with this list. Color in the square as you complete each step each month.

Action	J	F	M	A	M	J	J	A	S	O	N	D
1. Send birthday and holiday cards.												
2. Send progress reports.												
3. Identify three things you want for each client next month.												
4. Send/call with an acknowledgement for each client's growth.												
5. Collect all receivables.												
6. Prepare your monthly financial statement.												
7. Market until your practice is full.												
8. Schedule/enroll speaking engagements or workshops for clients.												
9. Buy more supplies or new equipment to do a great job.												
10. Send billing out.												
11. Pay your own bills—early.												
12. Make appropriate policy or pricing changes for the practice.												
13. Follow up with all leads and referrals.												
14. Ask for at least five referrals from current clients.												
15. Take plenty of time off.												
16. Update your Clean Sweep and other program scores.												
17.												
18.												
19.												
20.												

21.												
22.												
23.												
24.												

Top Five Things Your Coaching Web Site Should Be Set Up to Do

Gone—thank goodness—are the days of the "billboard website" (name, list of services, testimonials, "what is coaching?" section, etc.). Welcome to the website that actually serves the visitors instead of just informing them. Here are the five things your website should be set up to do when someone visits it.

Capture the Visitor's E-mail Address

Offer whatever you have to in order to get visitors to type in their e-mail address. Try a free report, e-book, subscription, coaching session, access to information on your website, TeleClass, or the like. You need an e-mail address in order to market to your visitors effectively—later—once they have gotten to know you a bit. Ease them in closer and closer to your inner circle.

Permit Visitors to Schedule Free or Fee Sessions or TeleClasses Online—Automatically and Immediately

It is good to give out your telephone number on your site and invite folks to call you, but it's even better if you set up a little calendar with the times and dates you are available today and in the next several days, so visitors book themselves into your schedule, right then, when they are at your site. Alternatively, install HumanClick (http://www.HumanClick.com) so visitors can click on the icon and ask you questions immediately. HumanClick has a free version available.

Demonstrate Your Expertise and Knowledge

The stuff that you know and take for granted is gold to someone who doesn't know it. Why not compile an e-book of your success tips or 10 Top 10 lists on your favorite subjects. Or tape yourself and post the recording as a RealAudio interview so the visitor can hear your voice, which is important given that most coaching is done over the telephone.

Help the Visitor to Buy Something You Are Offering, Online

Eventually, every coach will have a merchant account and a shopping cart that enables visitors to hire you on the spot and prepay for your coaching services, e-book, TeleClasses, etc. It's just a matter of time. And once you get started, you'll be hooked!

Directly Answer the Top 5 or 10 Questions Your Ideal Coachee Would Have

Everyone coming to your site (or any other coaching site) does have questions. If you can answer these questions, you will be building a relationship with your visitors. Relationships and credibility lead to coachees. Ask yourself, "If I were my ideal coachee, what are the 10 questions I would most want straight answers to?" Then post the answers to these questions prominently on your home page. Visitors love frequently asked questions (FAQs).

Top Five Ways to Convert Your Web Site Visitors into Paying Customers

Now that you have got 10 or 100 or 1,000 visitors coming to your web site each week, how do you convert them to clients instead of letting them slip by as lookie-lous? Here are five strategies that work very, very well.

Show visitors they have landed at the perfect web site for what they need right now.

Very few visitors to your web site need to learn about coaching. What they need is someone who can help them solve their problem or dilemma or to help them make the most of an opportunity.

Suggestion: Don't just list testimonials about how great a coach you are. Rather, describe the 10–25 specific situations in which your best clients have found themselves, in which you do your best work. This helps the visitor to see themselves and their situation versus just seeing you at your website.

Provide the option for visitors to sign up for your e-zine on your home page.

Most potential clients will only visit your site once, so it's key to get their e-mail address so that you can market to them later—and forever, if they let you. How many visitors are you losing as clients because you have no way to keep in touch with them?

Suggestion: Remember, most clients take time to warm up to you, and your weekly or monthly newsletter or e-zine is the most efficient way to let them do this. Start an e-zine today. It's free at Topica.com, or for more features try webvalence.com. Every e-mail is worth about $10–100 to you if you market your services well.

Offer an immediate take-away resource with your name on it.

Post some Top 10 lists, how-to guides, a free e-book, problem-solving steps, or life or business planning forms. These all act as brochures and remind the visitor who you are.

Suggestion: Remember, visitors to your coaching web site are probably surfing around a lot of web sites. Give them material to read and stuff to take with them on their journey.

Make a direct offer to help the visitor in any way that you can.

Most visitors to your web site are looking for something. They may know—or they may not know—exactly who or what they are looking for in terms of a coach. Make it quite clear that you can either help them directly or refer them to someone who can.

Suggestion: Position yourself as a well-connected resource, and make your e-mail address and telephone number prominent on every page. Educate the visitor in how you can help him or her decide whether to become a client, and/or offer a free session with no obligation.

Invest in a highly credible-looking web site.

Typically, web sites for coaches run between $1,000 and $10,000 to design, develop, and write. Also, generally, a client is worth between $3,000 and $25,000 over his or her customer life cycle.

Suggestion: Do the math. Then contract with a talented designer who understands how to convert visitors to clients and has the graphic flair to make your site credible, appealing, easy to use, and the best possible calling card for you. The #1 mistake coaches make around their web sites is in not having their site professionally designed. All the marketing in the world will not convince visitors to hire you if your site does not engender trust and credibility.

90+ Ways to Use a Virtual Assistant

The following list describes various ways clients are utilizing virtual assistants (VAs). This list is published to give new clients ideas on how they can personally benefit from the services of a VA. It may also give existing clients some new ideas or thoughts on how to expand the services of their VA. Remember, all documents created by or used by a VA can be quickly and easily transmitted via e-mail attachment, FTP, fax, or delivery of diskette or hard copy using overnight delivery, priority mail, or regular postal services.

Secretarial Services	
○	A client needs to confirm sales appointments made for the week. The list is faxed to a VA. The VA calls the appointments and notes who has confirmed and who must be rescheduled. The list is faxed back to the client.
○	A client needs directions to a prospect. The VA calls, obtains directions, and e-mails the directions to the client.
○	A client has routine paperwork that must be filled out on a daily basis (e.g., sales call recap). The client calls a VA with the information. The VA fills out the form and faxes or e-mails it to the home office.
○	A client makes a backup tape of computer files and sends it to the VA for safekeeping—a small task, but well worth it: In the event of a disaster, all the files are located off the premises.
○	A client travels frequently and needs a VA to coordinate air travel, car rental, and hotel reservations.

Research	
○	A client is selling business success tools and seminars. The client has the VA research a target industry. Once a list of companies has been prepared, the VA calls to identify a contact individual. The VA prepares and mails introductory material. After a specified time, the VA calls to verify that information has been received and to schedule a sale appointment.
○	A client needs a hotel conference room for a seminar and telephones a VA to do some research. The VA contacts several hotels in the area to determine availability of a room on the date in question that meets the size and other requirements of the seminar. The VA obtains written quotes from the hotels that can accommodate the request. The VA reviews each quote for completeness and reports the findings to the client.
○	A client needs CD-rom duplication and e-mails a VA with the assignment. The VA calls several vendors and obtains written quotes for the project. Upon approval, the VA coordinates sending the original CD-rom to the vendor, designs and prints labels, receives the completed order, attaches the labels, and sends the package to the client.

○	A client needs to buy some office equipment and e-mails a VA with the request. The VA calls several vendors, obtains pricing information, and e-mails the information back to the client.
○	A client needs software to do mail merge in e-mail. The VA researches on the Internet and inquires among business networking groups about such software. When the software is identified, the VA contacts the vendor to verify mail merge capability, the price, and availability. The VA then reports the findings to the client.
○	A client is interested in what competition exists online. The VA can do a keyword search and list the appropriate web sites and findings back to the client.
○	A client is preparing an advertising plan and e-mails what further information is needed. The VA contacts possible advertising places on the Internet and in magazines, periodicals, newspapers, and so on, and acquires information on pricing, publishing dates, publishing deadlines, payment policies, and so on. All information is compiled into a report for the client to review.

Word Processing and Presentations	
○	A client takes notes at meetings and needs them typed. The client faxes the notes to a VA, who types the notes.
○	A client is preparing a report and needs the draft copy to be formatted. The client sends the document via e-mail attachment to a VA. The VA edits and formats the document and returns the finished report via e-mail attachment.
○	A client writes a letter and faxes it to a VA. The VA types the letter, prints the letter on the client's stationery, and mails it.
○	A client needs a manual typed. The client mails the document to a VA. The VA types the manual, saves it to disk or CD-rom, and mails it to the client.
○	A client is preparing a seminar and needs a PowerPoint presentation prepared. He or she faxes sketches of diagrams and charts to a VA. The VA prepares the PowerPoint slides and sends the document to the client via e-mail attachment.
○	A client is preparing a seminar and needs a questionnaire fact sheet from each participant prior to the seminar. The client faxes the questionnaire along with a list of participants to a VA. The VA types the questionnaire; calls each participant, obtains their fax number, and faxes the questionnaire; tracks each completed questionnaire and calls the participants who did not respond on time; summarizes the questionnaire responses on a report; and delivers the report to the client via e-mail attachment.

Data Processing and Database Management	
○	A client collects business cards all month long. At the end of the month, he or she mails the collected business cards to a VA. The VA enters the data into the client's database, zips up the file, and returns the database to the client via e-mail attachment.
○	A client e-mails all new prospect leads to a VA. The VA enters the information into a contact database and, using mail merge, sends an introductory letter. The VA monitors the marketing follow-up program, sending a predetermined marketing piece every two weeks. Each week the database is sent to the client via e-mail attachment so the client has a record of the transactions. When a prospect responds, the client e-mails the VA to remove them from the active marketing follow-up program.

○	An insurance agent faxes new policy owner information to a VA. The VA enters the information into the client's database, zips the file, and sends the database to the client via e-mail attachment. The VA also prepares and mails a standard confirmation letter to the policy owner. The VA tracks the annual expiration date of the policy and, upon the due date, sends a reminder e-mail to the insurance agent.
○	A client is preparing a direct mailing and needs to verify his database. He or she sends the database to the VA via e-mail attachment. The VA telephones each name and verifies the name, spelling, title, and address. The VA makes all corrections, deletes old names, and adds new names. The corrected database is zipped and returned to the client via e-mail attachment.
○	A client is preparing a fax broadcast but has an incomplete database. The database is sent to a VA via e-mail attachment. The VA telephones those missing fax numbers and obtains the correct number. The updated database is returned to the client via e-mail attachment.
○	A client faxes copies of business cards he has gathered at a presentation to a VA. The VA enters the information into a contact database, uses mail merge to produce a follow-up letter, uses a signature font (and signature color ink) to sign the client's name, and mails all letters.
○	A client is changing database software and needs to convert his databases. A VA can handle the conversion.

	Desktop Publishing
○	A client needs a price list, product list, brochure, or schedule prepared. A VA can design, type, and prepare such items and use a variety of paper stock, clip art, or client-provided art.
○	A client needs a certificate for an employee of the month, an awards ceremony, a membership certificate, or participants completing a seminar. The VA designs and prints certificates and may use predesigned paper stock, seals, and/or ribbons. The completed certificates are delivered to the client to disperse as needed.
○	A client wants to publish a quarterly newsletter. The client provides the content and the mailing list to the VA. The VA types and prepares the newsletter, prepares labels, and mails the newsletter.
○	A client is distributing a CD-rom in a mailing and wants the company logo to be included on the labels. The VA can design and print labels using client-provided art, attach the labels, and coordinate the mailing or shipping.

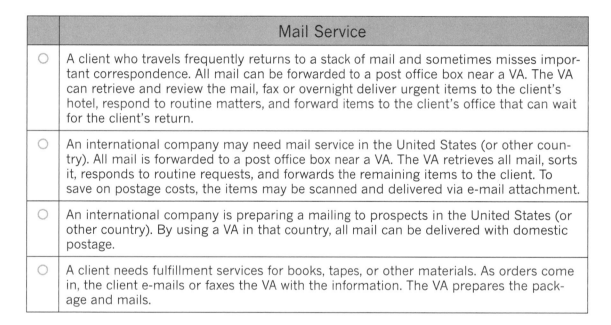

	Transcription Service
○	A lawyer sends microcassettes of a report via overnight delivery to a VA to transcribe. The VA types the report and sends it back to the lawyer via e-mail attachment.
○	A client needs a telephone conversation (e,g., conference call, teleclass, etc.) recorded. The VA records the call and transcribes the tape for the participants.
○	A client dictates letters and memos onto a cassette tape and mails it to the VA via overnight delivery. The VA transcribes the tape, prints the letters on the client's stationery, and mails them the following day.
○	A medical professional sends a report recorded on cassettes to a VA to transcribe. The VA types the report and returns it via overnight delivery.

	Mail Service
○	A client who travels frequently returns to a stack of mail and sometimes misses important correspondence. All mail can be forwarded to a post office box near a VA. The VA can retrieve and review the mail, fax or overnight deliver urgent items to the client's hotel, respond to routine matters, and forward items to the client's office that can wait for the client's return.
○	An international company may need mail service in the United States (or other country). All mail is forwarded to a post office box near a VA. The VA retrieves all mail, sorts it, responds to routine requests, and forwards the remaining items to the client. To save on postage costs, the items may be scanned and delivered via e-mail attachment.
○	An international company is preparing a mailing to prospects in the United States (or other country). By using a VA in that country, all mail can be delivered with domestic postage.
○	A client needs fulfillment services for books, tapes, or other materials. As orders come in, the client e-mails or faxes the VA with the information. The VA prepares the package and mails.

	E-Mail Service
○	A client cannot keep up with the volume of e-mail and is missing important messages. The client sets up a general e-mail account (info@mycompany.com). The VA retrieves all e-mail to this address, sorts it, responds to routine requests, and forwards items of importance to the client at his or her personal email account (myname@mycompany.com).
○	A client is going on vacation and doesn't want to miss important e-mail messages. The VA downloads all e-mail and notifies individuals that the client is out of the office. The VA contacts the client with urgent messages.
○	A client has or wants auto-responders on his or her website. The VA can write and setup the auto-responder. The VA can also monitor the number of requests and establish a database of who is requesting the information.
○	A client wants to fully utilize their e-mail software program (e.g., filters, auto-reply, signatures, etc.). The VA can walk them through the setup and teach the client how to do this over the telephone (while on the computer at the same time).

	Telephone/Fax Service
○	A client is going on vacation but needs to stay in touch with important business calls. The client records on his or her voice mail that urgent calls may contact his or her assistant and include the VA's telephone number. The VA can then contact the client with important messages.
○	A client is leaving on a business trip but doesn't want the phone to be left unattended. The client activates call forwarding to the VA's telephone and gives the VA the business itinerary. The VA answers all calls, responds to routine requests, and contacts the client with urgent messages.
○	A client is frequently out of the office or travels and cannot check voice mail on a regular basis. The VA calls and retrieves messages from voice mail, responds to routine requests, and contacts the client with urgent messages.
○	An international company needs a contact in the United States (or other country). Due to different time zones and costly international long-distance phone charges, it is difficult for prospects to contact the international client. Using a VA in the United States (or other country), prospects can easily call for information. If a question arises that a VA cannot answer, the VA e-mails the client for further instruction. In some cases, a separate phone line may be installed for the VA to answer.
○	A client is going out of town but needs to respond to any faxes received. The client places call forwarding on the fax machine to ring to the VA's fax machine. The VA handles the fax requests and contacts the client with urgent messages.
○	A client wants a human voice to answer the phone. A separate phone line is installed at the VA's location to be answered with the client's company name.
○	An international company sends many faxes to prospects in the United States (or other country). To save on international long-distance charges, the client uses a VA to send faxes from a domestic location.

	Internet Services
○	A client operates an automated e-mail mailing list or newsletter. Although it is automated, the client still receives incorrect subscription requests or failed mail messages. The client forwards all related e-mail messages to a VA to correctly process the requests to subscribe, unsubscribe, or delete bounced e-mail messages.
○	A client operates a manual e-mail mailing list or newsletter. The VA manages the e-mail database, adding subscriptions, deleting those wanting to unsubscribe, deleting failed mail addresses, and posting announcements or the newsletter to the list.
○	A client is trying to locate a hard-to-find item. Using the Internet, the VA can perform a search to try to locate the item.
○	A client needs changes on his or her web site. The VA can edit or upload new information to the client web site.
○	A client needs to promote his or her web site. The VA can submit the URL, keywords, and description to various search engines on a routine basis.
○	A client wants to increase the number of subscribers to his or her electronic newsletter. The VA can list the newsletter with a variety of online directories and follow up to make sure the listings are accurate.

○	A client wants to increase the number of subscribers to his or her electronic newsletter. The VA can contact other list owners of similar subjects to inquire about mutual cross-promotion.
○	A client wants to promote his or her company online. The VA can submit articles written by the client to electronic newsletters to increase the company's exposure.
○	A client doesn't have time to monitor web site traffic. The VA can monitor banner ad placements, click-throughs, and traffic reports, and make recommendations for adjustments.
○	A client wants to improve web site traffic with related links. The VA can contact similar web sites and request mutual link exchange.
○	A client doesn't have time to monitor his or her web site for errors or broken links. The VA can periodically review the web site and verify links.

Bookkeeping
---	---
○	A client needs bill-paying services. The client has all bills mailed to a post office box near a VA (or collects the bills and mails them to the VA twice a month). The VA sets up a checking account with payment authorization for both the client and the VA. As the bills are prepared for payment, the VA notifies the client how much money to deposit into the account. The bills are then paid. Another option, if available from the client's bank, is to use online bill payment services.
○	A client needs bill-paying services plus data entry into accounting software. The client's bills can be mailed to a post office box near a VA, or the client can collect all the bills and mail them to the VA periodically. The VA can do any of the following: (1) set up a checking account with payment authorization for both the client and the VA (as the bills are prepared for payment, the VA notifies the client how much money to deposit into the account); (2) prepare the checks for payment and mail back to the client for signature and mailing; (3) if available from the client's bank, use online bill payment services. As bills are paid, the VA then enters the transactions into accounting software. In addition, the VA can reconcile bank statements, enter credit card transactions, prepare invoices, make and/or enter deposits, and prepare end-of-month reports.
○	A consultant needs invoicing services only. A consultant sends an e-mail to the VA with the number of hours to be billed to a client. The VA prepares and mails the invoice.
○	An association mails annual dues invoices upon membership renewal. The VA prepares the invoices and mails according to schedule. The VA can also receive payments and deposit them into the association's account. All transactions are recorded in accounting software and sent to the association via FTP transfer or mailed on diskette or CD-rom.
○	A client has several account receivables that are past due. The VA can mail past-due notices or follow up via telephone to collect on past-due invoices.
○	A client continues to pay his or her own bills but needs monthly bank reconciliation. The client mails a copy of his or her check register along with the bank statement. The VA enters all data into accounting software and reconciles the account. The accounting software is sent back to the client via e-mail attachment.
○	A client continues to pay his or her own bills but needs reminders to pay in a timely manner. The VA can remind the client via e-mail or telephone when due dates arrive.

Purchasing Service	
○	On a prespecified basis, the VA faxes to the client a list of office supplies that are used on a regular basis. The client checks off what is needed and faxes the list back to the VA. The VA reorders the supplies and has them delivered directly to the client.
○	A client needs a new printer. After the VA researches the various makes, models, and so on, he or she sends written quotes to the client. Upon client authorization, the VA purchases the printer and arranges for delivery to the client. If the item to be purchased requires on-site setup, the VA makes those arrangements as well, confirming dates, times, and travel information.
○	When available, a VA can set up an online account on behalf of a client with stores that supply the client with supplies. When supplies are needed, the VA places the order with delivery to the client.
○	A VA working with the client's accountant can set up lines of credit with vendors and monitor them to keep the credit information current and accurate.
○	A client needs to order marketing materials (stationery, brochures, envelopes, etc.). The VA can obtain pricing quotes and coordinate ordering, delivery, and payment.
○	A client is preparing an awards ceremony for the annual company meeting and needs awards or employee recognition gifts. A VA can research for appropriate gifts and co-ordinate their purchase and delivery.

Writing/Editing Service	
○	A client is preparing a brochure, flyer, web site or manual and needs assistance with the copy. A VA can write, format, proofread, edit, spell check, and grammar check documents.

Marketing Service	
○	A client implements an advertising plan. The VA monitors the plan, submits ads by deadlines, tracks expiration dates, coordinates payment, handles correspondence with advertising vendors, and continually updates the advertising report and/or advertising budget report for the client's review.
○	A client maintains a variety of sales brochures. E-mail requests are forwarded to the VA. The VA's fax number is advertised. Postcards are mailed with the VA's address as the return address. The VA is stocked with a supply of each sales brochure and mails the appropriate brochure upon receipt of request. The VA also updates the client's database with name, address, date, and type of brochure requested.
○	A client wants to monitor customer satisfaction. The VA types a customer feedback questionnaire, mails it to customers, receives the completed questionnaire, summarizes the responses, and issues a report to the client.

	Personnel Services
○	A client receives employment applications and faxes them to a VA. The VA verifies past employment, calls the references, and reports the findings to the client.
○	A client needs to hire on-site office personnel. A VA can write a help wanted advertisement, place the ad, receive and review the resumes, conduct the initial phone interview, narrow the selection to three individuals, and schedule personal interviews with the client.
○	A client needs reminders for annual performance review dates. The VA can track the dates and send reminders to the client.
○	A client needs assistance with payroll requirements. A VA can monitor and verify that all payroll requirements have been met, appropriate taxes paid, and forms filed.
○	A client hires a new employee. The VA can prepare a welcome package and send it to the new employee.
○	An unemployed individual or individual desiring a career change needs a resume prepared. The VA can prepare or update a resume and include an introduction letter.
○	An individual seeking new employment can give a list of appropriate positions sought to a VA. The VA can research job openings online and submit resumes to online resources.
○	An unemployed individual or individual desiring a career change wants personalized resumes. Every time the individual finds a potential new employer, the individual telephones or faxes the VA with the information. The VA prepares a personalized cover letter and resume and faxes or mails them to the prospective employer.
○	An individual seeking new employment goes on an interview. He or she sends an e-mail or telephones the VA with the interviewer's name and address. The VA promptly mails out a thank-you follow-up letter to the potential employer.
○	An individual seeking employment can use a VA to conduct a practice interview. Virtual assistants specializing in personnel management services can offer many suggestions to ensure a positive, successful interview.
○	A client receives hundreds of resumes for an ad posted. Given some key specifications to look for, the VA reviews the resumes, types a short biography on each candidate, and sorts the resumes based upon the criteria given by the client.

	Personal Services
○	A client is planning a birthday party, anniversary party, or golf outing. The VA can send invitations, receive RSVPs, coordinate catering, and so on.
○	A client has a hard time remembering birthdays, anniversaries, and the like. The VA can e-mail or telephone the client with these important dates.
○	A client makes appointments and then forgets to keep them. The VA can keep a client's calendar and remind the client of dentist or doctor appointments, classes to teach, classes to take, or project deadlines.
○	A busy client needs an extra set of eyes. The VA can tape favorite TV shows or shows of importance and send the video to the client.

○	A busy client needs information on summer camps for his children. A VA is an extra set of hands to research the various options.
○	A VA can provide a clipping service. A VA can regularly monitor particular newspapers or magazines and clip articles of interest or take a trip to the library and copy specific articles. Either way, a VA can save a client a lot of time.
○	A client is planning a wedding. A VA can assist with the invitation list, mailing the invitations, tracking RSVPs, tracking gifts received, and even send thank-you cards.
○	A client was traveling and broke his tooth. The client called the VA and requested a dentist appointment in his destination city. The VA located a dentist, set up an appointment, and asked for directions.

TeleClass Leading: 100 Skills and Steps of Designing and Leading TeleClasses

1. Own the TeleClass

○ Teach only what you enjoy teaching

○ Don't be wimpy or too soft

○ Project your voice to reach people

○ Teach to one person at a time

○ Make individuals feel special

○ Come to the class eager to learn

○ Bond with the strongest three people

○ Challenge students to think big

○ Plant many seeds; don't reap yet

○ Tailor classes to students' needs

2. Design the TeleClass

○ Why are you leading this TeleClass?

○ How many sessions should it be?

○ How do you want students to change?

○ What do you want them to learn?

○ What three distinctions are important?

○ What three questions should you ask?

○ What is compelling about this class?

○ What long-term effect do you want for students?

○ What else do you want to offer them?

○ What should they do after the class?

3. Prepare for the TeleClass

- ○ Write up your class outline
- ○ Ask five smart people for suggestions
- ○ Set a date for your TeleClass
- ○ Arrange for a telebridge

- ○ Write up a class description or title
- ○ Announce, promote, and fill the Tele-Class
- ○ Invite five key, well-connected people
- ○ Spend 10 minutes with each registrant and find out what they most want out of the class
- ○ Run a beta or test class first
- ○ Write up class notes and share them

4. Basic Leading Skills

- ○ Weave in earlier student comments
- ○ Strongly endorse what students say
- ○ Ask for clarification regarding a share
- ○ Ask for more information regarding a share
- ○ Provide interesting facts
- ○ Focus on the strongest students
- ○ Include and call on quiet students
- ○ Ask big and provocative questions
- ○ Make people feel smart and special
- ○ Debrief at the end of the call

5. Intermediate Skills

- ○ Use coaching models or diagrams
- ○ Believe in the students' intelligence
- ○ Provoke reactions to foster discussion
- ○ Challenge students to be honest
- ○ Solve problems for students
- ○ Help students to network with each other outside of the class
- ○ Offer extras for students after class
- ○ Go with the flow and the needs of the students
- ○ Create wisdom from students' shares
- ○ Create credibility by asking for topic-based testimonials

6. Advanced Skills

- ○ Frame the call at the beginning
- ○ Identify and build up the class stars
- ○ Tell a humanizing story about yourself
- ○ Point to a developmental path
- ○ Label or articulate what is occurring
- ○ Identify a shift one might make
- ○ Get students laughing at themselves, life, you, their goals, their problems, and each other
- ○ Help students to share themselves
- ○ Tell them how they might mishear

7. Making Your Point

- Use metaphors, similes, and analogies
- Paint a picture or visual image
- Package points into messages
- Uplanguage what a student says
- Demonstrate (role-play) a point or skill
- Create context or relevance
- Point out benefits of your point
- Draw distinctions or progressions
- Plant seeds that will sprout later

8. Handling Difficult Students

- Interrupt the space hog
- Bring out the mouse
- Quiet down the boomer
- Notch down the impressor
- Uplanguage the digger
- Explain for the clarifier
- Cut off the resident coach
- Refocus the naysayer
- Challenge the Hallmark card
- Evolve the liner thinker to see 4 dimensions

9. Mistakes to Avoid

- Don't lecture continuously
- Don't assume you communicate well
- Don't assume the class will fill by itself
- Don't lose control of the class
- Don't worry about whether students like you
- Don't stop learning from students
- Don't become a walking cliché
- Don't teach what you don't believe in
- Don't teach alone
- Don't get your emotional needs met by leading TeleClasses

10. Communication Skills

- Tone is warm enough to charm across 3,000 miles
- Pace is fast enough to keep people's attention
- Volume is loud enough to reach people
- Pitch is deep enough to invite the listener to want more
- Vocabulary is extensive enough to recognize what students are saying
- Hearing is sharp enough to hear subtleties
- Students feel heard versus reached to
- Delivery is strong and confident without being loud
- Transition or segue from one point to another is smooth
- Leader is positive in everything he or she says

Chapter 5

About Working with Coachees

This chapter will provide you with a starting point for working with new coachees. You will understand what to say, where to start coaching, what to know about your new coachee, how to create value, what to listen for, and mistakes to avoid. By implementing this information you will create value while developing the relationship.

In addition to the information provided there are checklists, forms, powerful questions, strategies, and programs to use with coachees. Learning and utilizing the information will support you in working with your coachees and support your practice at the same time.

The following sections are included in this chapter:

1. New Client Checklist
2. Top 10 Places to Start Your Coaching
3. The Most Important Things to Know about Your Coachees
4. What to Say to Your Coachee
5. Coaching Session Agenda
6. First Coaching Session
7. Coachee's Life
8. About the Coachee
9. Client Laser Questions
10. Principles Discussed
11. Coaching Strategies
12. Listen For
13. Make Your Point
14. Success Formulas Program
15. Coaching Mistakes
16. The High Hidden Costs of Coaching
17. Master Coach Profile

New Client Checklist

Check each box as you complete each step.

	Client _____
	Before accepting a client
○	Do I really want to work with this person?
○	What are the three things I know I can do for them?
○	Will they stick around for at least six months?
○	Can I learn a lot from this relationship?
○	Will this person add to my practice and reputation?
○	Is this person going to be able to pay the coaching fee, on time?
○	Is this person ready for a coach, or do they need someone or something else?
	After acceptance, before first session
○	Schedule first call or appointment.
○	Find out what the person wants to work on most.
○	Get a minimum three-month agreement.
○	Get a check for the first month's coaching.
○	Send paperwork or assessments to complete prior to the first session.
○	Review the ground rules, agreements, and terms of relationship.
○	Double-check to make sure the client is ready and right for this.
	During the first session
○	Welcome the client.
○	Design up to three goals or projects to work on for 90 days.
○	Get all of the assessment scores.
○	Discern where the person is on path of development.
○	Discern the current block(s) to success.
○	Tell the client what to do during the session.
○	Give the client three pieces of homework.
○	Schedule next or subsequent sessions.

Top 10 Places to Start Your Coaching

Please note: This guide was written for the coach, but as the coachee, you will benefit from reading this.

What should you and your client focus on first when starting your coaching? Here's a list of 10 areas where the coach and coachee can start.

Welcome to coaching!

Tolerations

Ask the client what he or she is putting up with; he or she will give you a list of between 5 and 500 things. There will be many things in this list for you to help the client focus on handling. When the coachee starts getting rid of tolerations, he or she will feel like he or she is making progress in his or her life, and the momentum created (because energy is freed up) will keep the client motivated, which is very important when a client is new to coaching.

Shoulds

Find out what the client thinks he or she should be doing right now, personally and professionally. Most of us have lots of shoulds, and we do not feel that we can readily toss them out, given the potential consequences. Have the coachee make a list of at least 10 shoulds. This educates both you and your coachee about how much of his or her life he or she is living and how much of someone else's life he or she is living.

Frustrations

What is frustrating the client? Ask "What are the five things that are frustrating you right now about yourself, your life, your work, or others?" Feelings are a great place to start the coaching process because when the client gets in touch with (and shares) real feelings, the truth begins to come out, which will create relief and movement. Let truth, not you, drive your coachee.

Money

Money—or the lack of it—is at the heart of at least 50 percent of a client's current problems, whether the client recognizes it or not. Find out your client's earnings, debts, and savings, and see if the client is willing to make some financial changes, quickly. If he or she does so, he or she usually reduces stress right away, and this frees him or her up to better benefit from your coaching.

Client Programs

Coach U has numerous client programs, like Clean Sweep, Tru Values, Personal Foundation, Buff It Up, SuperReserve, Biz Whiz, and Attraction. Find out if your coachee likes working with this type of tool. If so, recommend one or two, or send the collection and let him or her pick out the one(s) that best fits his or her needs. You can still focus on other things, but many clients like the structure that these client programs provide. These programs can also help the client to discover something about himself or herself, so they meet the needs of the client who is into self-discovery and self-improvement.

Desires

What does your client *really* want in his or her personal or business life? What is the goal that he or she has given up on or put off for a while, due to circumstances? When a coachee feels that the coach cares enough to encourage him or her to reach for what will bring the greatest happiness, it may be all the coachee needs to succeed in that area. Remember, success is stressful, and getting what you want is sometimes a stretch; that's why the client has hired you—to help him or her get through whatever is in the way. When you help clients tap into what they most want, they get inspired and do not need constant motivation.

Integrity

It is very important to determine the strength of your client's integrity. In other words, are your clients doing the best for themselves and their bodies? Are they stressed out? Eating or drinking too much? Running on adrenaline? Stepping over problems? Avoiding the truth in a situation? Not taking time for themselves? Without enough integrity, whatever you help the client to achieve will eventually fade because the "container" for his or her life is cracked.

Outcomes

Many coachees know exactly what they want, and they want your support to achieve it, so by all means help them reach these outcomes. You can definitely have a tight focus with a client on outcomes, but also weave some of the other nine starting points into your coaching—but always get the client's permission. Some clients are very happy with focusing on outcomes, and they really do not want to work on the intangible or personal foundation strengthening type of stuff.

Strategies

Some clients want you to help them develop a strategy or a plan so they can achieve their result in the shortest period of time and with the least stress. If the client asks you how he or she can achieve X, then you know the client is asking for strategy. Sometimes the client will ask what action steps he or she should take, but you may want to begin by developing a strategy first because, with the right strategy, the steps become obvious.

A Change or Improvement

Most clients want to change or improve something. For example, they may want to change jobs or improve a relationship. The trick is to discover if their change goal is what they really want or if it is something they want to do because it will get them something else, as in "If I get a promotion, I'll be more fulfilled." As a coach, you might want to work with coachees on values first to find out what *would* fulfill them, because a promotion may not be the ticket.

The Most Important Things to Know about Your Coachees

The purpose of this article is to list, detail, and illustrate the seven primary aspects of a person. (Yes, including you.) Feel free to use yourself as a model as you read and "try on" this material. Enjoy.

Aspect #1: What They Are Not Clear Of

A mentor once said, "Our lives are spent doing what we are not clear of." In other words, until we completely and entirely clear out what is in our way of moving forward we do the same things over and over again in a futile attempt to get clear, so that we can move on and express our values.

Aspect #2: What Their Four Personal Needs Are

Each of us has a unique set of critical needs that, until completely satisfied, keep us away from our potential. Needs are those conditions in life that we *must* have to *fully* be ourselves. The needs satisfaction process assists the coachee to identify, articulate, and satisfy these critical needs. Please refer to the NeedLess program.

Most people are motivated (even compelled) by unknown or unsatisfied needs. Until these are taken care of, coaching requires effort by both parties.

Aspect #3: What Their Special Gifts Are

Everyone has a special, unique gift to share with others. However, few people move far enough along the path of personal and professional development to be able to orient their lives around their gift. Much of the work the coach does is to uncover the obstacles in the way of the coachee's seeing clearly and being that gift.

Aspect #4: What Their Core Values Are

Values are those activities that turn you on, such as creativity, learning, playing, loving, etc. Values are what we tend to do after our needs are met and after we are complete with the past. Values are not morals; values are our essence. Please refer to the Tru Values program.

Aspect #5: What They Really Want for Themselves

Most people do not know what they really want. Yes, they have a wish list and a "should want" list. But because most folks still don't have their needs met and their values clear, their wants are muddled or exaggerated. The coach can help a person discern what they really want—what will make him or her happy. These wants may be the same as the original list (or very different); it's just that the person will want, not crave or need, them. Wants are optional: They add to a life, but they don't *give* life, as a value or need does.

Aspect #6: How Well They Are Doing in Life's Six Areas

Coaches can measure the quality of a person's life in six areas: relationships, health, career, money, recreation, and personal development. It is important to know exactly how a coachee is doing in all six areas so that you can direct the coaching to bring all areas up to the desired level. (The tendency is to have one or two areas with low, low scores.) But the coach needs to have an overview in order to make the biggest difference.

In the area of personal development, the coach will know the following five things about the coachee:

- How willing he or she is to grow and be more
- How able he or she is to get what he or she wants
- How well the coachee relates with others
- How being-oriented the person is
- How attractive the person is to what is possible

Aspect #7: What They Want for Others

When we are well taken care of and in good shape, it is natural to want to give and to assist others. Some people have what is called a vision for others or for the world that motivates them. Others want the people around them to be happy and healthy. Any way you look at it, it is a sign of advanced personal development when your coachee wants to help others, can afford it (in time, love, and money), and is motivated by choice (versus need or compulsiveness).

That's it! When you know, and help the coachee to see, these seven aspects of themselves, the coachee is finally home and on the path to effortlessness.

What to Say to Your Coachee

100 helpful phrases and questions to share as you coach.

1. Encouragement

- ○ You're doing great! Keep going.
- ○ You've got what it takes.
- ○ Stick with it, especially now.
- ○ Don't even think about giving up.
- ○ I believe in you and your ability to reach this goal.
- ○ It will get better!
- ○ Whenever you try something new, surprises happen.
- ○ I am here for you.
- ○ Don't listen much to the naysayers.
- ○ Whose opinion matters to you most?

2. Empathy

- ○ I know exactly how you feel.
- ○ I am so sorry to hear that.
- ○ It must be frustrating.
- ○ That's terrible news!
- ○ How are you handling that?
- ○ How are you feeling right now?
- ○ What would you like to hear right now?
- ○ We'll get through this.
- ○ When's the last time you were this challenged?
- ○ How can I help?

3. Challenge

- ○ Your attitude sucks.
- ○ When will you reach the goal?
- ○ Try doing it this way.
- ○ You are not being responsible.
- ○ This situation is not okay with me, as your coach.
- ○ Stop doing that!
- ○ Why is that happening, do you think?
- ○ You need to face this head on.
- ○ Make this your first priority.
- ○ You can do better than that.

4. Clarification

- ○ Where did you learn that?
- ○ What is the truth in this situation?
- ○ Why is this happening to you?
- ○ How do you know that for sure?
- ○ You sound surprised by this.
- ○ How long has this been going on?
- ○ What's most important to you right now?
- ○ Is that a need or a want?
- ○ What's the worst part of the situation?
- ○ What's the source of the problem?

5. Refocus

○ Why won't you let go of this?

○ Let's focus on what is working.

○ You have special skills that can be developed.

○ Let's change the focus.

○ You're stuck on this goal; let's find a better one.

○ What do you want most?

○ Which of your resources isn't fully utilized?

○ Assume the worst. Now what?

○ Assuming life is perfect, what's the lesson?

○ What's an easier approach to take?

6. Strengthening

○ Is this solvable?

○ Fixing your cash flow is the first priority.

○ Your integrity is weak.

○ You sound tired.

○ Your boundaries are weak.

○ What's your number one character flaw?

○ Let's work on your selling skills.

○ Do you know how you come across?

○ Your standards are too low.

○ The Team 100 program will solve that.

7. Personal Development Programs

○ Let's work on the Clean Sweep program.

○ What are your values?

○ How strong is your personal foundation?

○ Let's buff up what you have.

○ Have your heard about the attraction principles?

○ Do you understand the Zen of attraction?

○ You need more space, not time.

○ What gives you pleasure?

○ Simplify your life.

○ The NeedLess program!

8. Expanding

○ Are you up to this?

○ What is your vision?

○ Describe your ideal life to me.

○ Is this solvable?

○ What motivates you in general?

○ You need to think a lot bigger.

○ How would an expert handle this problem?

○ You need a clear strategy.

○ What's the ultimate outcome?

○ What kind of person do you want to be?

9. Evoke

○ Tell me more about that.

○ What are the options here?

○ If there were a solution, what would it be?

○ Snap out of it.

○ Why are you so rigid and resistant?

○ How do I reach you?

○ Why are you tolerating that?

○ What part of you needs to be reached?

○ Tell me what to do.

○ There's a truth that needs to be said.

10. Action

○ What's the first step to take?

○ Are you ready to get to work?

○ Hang up, do that, and call me back in 20 minutes. What's next?

○ What's the single daily action to take?

○ What should you stop doing?

○ What do you need?

○ Who can you ask for help?

○ What's the most pivotal thing you can do?

○ What will you get done in the next hour?

○ How can I coach you even more effectively?

Coaching Session Agenda

Use this master checklist to make sure you are doing a masterful job. Fill in the first section prior to the call. Use this form during the session to document the coachee's activity and the content of the call.

Client _____

Date _____ Time _____

Before the Call

Get clear of the previous call.

Review this coachee's file, promise log, and goals list; outline what you want to accomplish or discuss now:

1. _____

2. _____

3. _____

4. _____

Starting the Call

_____, how are you? I am glad you called.

Tell me what's happened since our last call.

Shifts _____

Results/wins _____

Problems _____

Progress report _____

Content of the Call

Distinction shared _____

Requests made _____

Observations shared _____

Advice given _____

_____

_____

Toward the End of the Call

_____, we have about five minutes left.

Homework given _____

Confirm next call date, time, and procedure.

After the Call

Update the coachee's file and file this form.

First Coaching Session

These are essential questions to ask.

- ○ **What** do you expect from coaching?

- ○ **What** do you need most from me today?

- ○ **What** do you need most from me during our coaching?

- ○ **What** is the biggest change you are willing to make today?

- ○ **What** are the first three things you are going to do immediately after our session today?

- ○ **How** long will you be coaching with me?

- ○ **How** much of the work will you be willing to do during our sessions?

- ○ **What** is the one thing I should not say or do with you today?

- ○ **What** is the most exciting part of working with a coach?

- ○ **What** is the scariest part of working with a coach?

Coachee's Life

Help the coachee to see his or her life more clearly.

○ **Who** or what is holding you back the most right now, and how?

○ **How** much stress are you under right now, and what is causing the stress?

○ **What** are the 10 things that you are tolerating the most?

○ **What** about you makes your life work as well as it does?

○ **Who** are the key people in your life, and what do they provide for you?

○ **Is** your life one of your choosing? If not, which parts are not?

○ **Is** your life on an upward or downward trend?

○ **What** about your day do you like most?

○ **What** about your day do you like least?

○ **What** else, if anything, do you feel is important to accomplish for your life to be fulfilled and complete?

About the Coachee

Find out everything you can about the coachee, not just his or her goals or situation.

○ **What** are your three biggest concerns or fears about yourself?

○ **What** are your three biggest concerns or fears about life?

○ **What** are your three biggest concerns or fears about success?

○ **What** motivates you to want to improve or evolve?

○ **What** are the three most important things that you have learned about yourself?

○ **What** are you currently learning or accepting about yourself?

○ **What** is the best way for me to coach you?

○ **In what** areas are you foolish or irresponsible?

○ **What** is the best part of you? Why?

○ **What** habits do you have that make you feel bad about yourself?

Client Laser Questions: Creating Value in Coaching

Help the client to create value for himself or herself.

○ **How** will you know you're getting more than your money's worth in our coaching?

○ **What** changes will you need to make in order to make the most of what we talk about?

○ **How** much stress is the monthly coaching fee going to cause you?

○ **What's** the most empowering and helpful thing I can do for you during our sessions?

○ **Other than** support and advice, what are the five other ways I will be helping you most?

○ **What** should I do or not do if you get behind on your goals?

○ **Would** you like to be part of my TeleClasses or work on personal development programs such as Clean Sweep or Personal Foundation as a part of our coaching?

○ **What** should we do or talk about toward the end of each coaching session?

○ **What** should I do if you miss a coaching session?

○ **What** would have happened if we *hadn't* started coaching?

○ **What** is the one regret you don't want to have in this lifetime?

Principles Discussed

Keep track of the principles you share, and track the coachee's progress, with this tracking sheet.

#	Principle, Distinction, or Concept	STAGE				
		INT	INQ	GET	GOT	IS
1.		○	○	○	○	○
2.		○	○	○	○	○
3.		○	○	○	○	○
4.		○	○	○	○	○
5.		○	○	○	○	○
6.		○	○	○	○	○
7.		○	○	○	○	○
8.		○	○	○	○	○
9.		○	○	○	○	○
10.		○	○	○	○	○
11.		○	○	○	○	○
12.		○	○	○	○	○

SCORING KEY

INT   Concept has been introduced to the coachee
INQ   Coachee is thinking about it, inquiring
GET   Coachee is getting it
GOT   Coachee has clearly gotten it
IS   It now has the coachee

Coaching Strategies: 100 Ways to Help Your Coachees Get More of What They Want

There are many different ways that a coach can support a coachee to reach his or her goals and achieve both success and happiness. Some of the strategies are known as *front-door strategies,* such as goal setting, weekly coaching support, asking the right questions, making direct requests, and listening. Others are known as *back-door strategies,* meaning that they focus the coachee on something other than the goal itself.

Back-door coaching makes coaching powerful, easy, and sustainable. It's like the honeybee who gets up every morning and looks for pollen to bring back to the hive. It couldn't care less about man's desire for apples and other fruits, but as a by-product of the honeybee's flitting around, cross-pollination occurs, which permits the orchards to bear fruit. It's similar with coaching. Sometimes you focus the coachee on areas or activities that do not directly relate to the goal he or she wants to reach. But as a by-product of working in one of these back-door areas, the goal—or a better one—is reached, often in less time.

Whether you use front-door or back-door coaching strategies, this list should at least give you some ideas!

1. Modify Goals
Most goals need fine-tuning

○ Change the goal

○ Clarify the goal

○ Make the goal values-based

○ Abandon a goal

○ Abandon all goals/establish a goal-free zone

○ Simplify the goal

○ Make the goal clearly measurable

○ Eliminate pipe-dream goals

○ Change measures of success

○ Set intangible versus tangible goals

2. Strengthen Internally
Strength permits rapid growth

○ Resolve the past

○ Extend boundaries

○ Establish a super reserve

○ Build character

○ Improve self-esteem

○ Increase self-confidence

○ Restore integrity

○ Take daily exercise

○ Establish excellent eating habits

○ Create an absence of emotional stress or drain

3. Improve Environment
Environments support and shape

○ Establish support structure

○ Establish daily routine or habits

○ Expand professional network

○ Create loving home environment

○ Create productive work environment

○ Acquire the right tools or equipment

○ Live well but within means

○ Resolve toxic people or situations

○ Reduce clutter, clean up physical spaces

○ Focus on quality, not quantity

4. Create a Gap
Gaps pull a coachee forward

○ Help coachee to discover a truth

○ Help coachee find their vision

○ Point out a better paradigm

○ Plant a seed

○ Draw a distinction

○ Focus on financial independence

○ Focus on a perfect life

○ Fuel desire/find hot button

○ Set seemingly impossible goals

○ Point out unseen options

5. Use a Program Checklist
Coach 24 hours a day via programs

- ○ Clean Sweep program
- ○ NeedLess program

- ○ Tru Values program
- ○ Personal Values
- ○ 100 Smiles program
- ○ Attraction program
- ○ Extreme Self-Care program
- ○ Biz Whiz program
- ○ Team 100 Checklist
- ○ Super Reserve Checklist

6. Bond Fully
Trust accelerates growth

- ○ Listen to care, not to coach
- ○ Identify with coachee's feelings or situation
- ○ Validate coachee's concerns
- ○ Share inklings, sensings, and intuition
- ○ Be deeply respectful of coachee
- ○ Focus on coachee, not just the result
- ○ Empathize, no matter what
- ○ Find common ground
- ○ Tell the truth, always; be forthright
- ○ Remind the coachee who he or she is

7. Challenge and Push
We all need a push at times

- ○ Speak with "the edge"
- ○ Expect the coachee's best
- ○ Make a direct request
- ○ Correct assumptions

- ○ Demand a change
- ○ Be directive; instruct
- ○ Illuminate a path or steps to follow
- ○ Unhook from the future
- ○ Identify potential consequences
- ○ Refuse to coach coachee on "that"

8. Make Coachee Smarter
Educate them continuously

- ○ Share formulas or equations
- ○ Package thoughts into messages
- ○ Draw a Venn Diagram of dynamic
- ○ Devise overarching strategies or meta-strategies
- ○ Increase awareness
- ○ Introduce to right people
- ○ Share principles or maxims
- ○ Tell stories or parables
- ○ Recommend a book for coachee to read
- ○ Ask the coachee to teach others

9. Improve and Strengthen
Help the coachee to build skills and self

- ○ Communication skills
- ○ Selling or marketing skills
- ○ Internet or cyber skills
- ○ Relationships or network
- ○ Space or freedom
- ○ Talents or skill sets
- ○ Willingness or flexibility
- ○ Choices or options
- ○ Thinking process or openness
- ○ Bandwidth, RAM, or capacity

10. Reduce or Eliminate
Less creates space for more

- ○ Tolerations
- ○ Problems
- ○ Compromising
- ○ Resistance or blocks
- ○ Delay, waiting, and if ... then
- ○ Personality or emotional problems
- ○ Doubt or uncertainty
- ○ Fear
- ○ Stress
- ○ Bad habits

Listen For: 100 Things a Coach Listens For and Hears

There is so much to hear when working with a coachee, and the list provided identifies 100 of the most important things to listen for.

1. **Dissonance or Confusion**
   - Words don't match actions
   - Tone of voice doesn't match words
   - BS
   - Inability to identify or share feelings
   - No or slow progress
   - Easy steps not taken
   - Resistance to support
   - Reliance on clichés, jargon
   - Attracts continual problems
   - Playing dumb or dependent

2. **Desire or Readiness**
   - Excitement
   - Willingness
   - Eagerness to start
   - Flowing of ideas
   - Self-motivating
   - Exciting dreams
   - Fantasies
   - Performs faster than expected
   - Serendipity
   - Synchronicity

3. **Resources or Assets**
   - Inner strength
   - Unknown skills or talents
   - Size or power of network
   - Past experience or expertise
   - Resourcefulness
   - Specialized knowledge
   - Special way of thinking
   - Communication or selling skills
   - Strong reputation
   - Bandwidth or capacity

4. **Fears or Doubts**
   - Sharp intake of breath
   - Stopped breathing
   - Too many questions
   - Saying yes but meaning no
   - Talking slowly
   - Procrastination
   - Nervousness in voice
   - Pulling away from coach
   - Diversions away from goal
   - Changing of subject

5. Developmental Level

○ Strength of personal foundation

○ Knowledge of attraction principles

○ Personal maturity or self-responsibility

○ Flexibility

○ Response time to unexpected problems

○ High standards

○ Strong character

○ Adequate reserves

○ Ability to think conceptually

○ Type of emotional reactions

6. Coach's Reactions

○ Frustration or grrr factor

○ Resentment or anger

○ Funny feeling in stomach

○ Envy

○ Strong desire to help

○ Strong desire to protect

○ Confusion

○ Holding back

○ Pushing the coachee

○ Resignation

7. Personal Qualities

○ Honesty

○ Honor

○ Responsibility

○ Respectfulness

○ Accountability

○ Generosity

○ Maturity

○ Initiative

○ Caring

Strength

8. Quality of Relationships

○ Children

○ Spouse

○ Parents or family

○ Friends

○ Acquaintances or neighbors

○ Coworkers or colleagues

○ Vendors or service

○ Mentors or teachers

○ Clients or customers

Yourself

9. Quality of Life

○ Tolerations

○ Self-care

○ Commitments

○ Goals

○ Problems or struggles

○ Work environment

○ Home environment

○ Stress

○ Desires or needs

○ Pace

10. Mind and Intellect

○ Quickness

○ Intuitive ability

○ Type of learner

○ Opinions about things

○ General knowledge

○ Set of beliefs

○ Expectations about life

○ Reactions to life

○ Ability to process logically

○ Cultural restrictions or blocks

Make Your Point: 100 Creative and Powerful Ways to Make Your Point

There are many ways to make a point with a coachee, a reader, or an audience. We all have our favorite methods, but why not expand your repertoire by using this reference list? It will come in handy the next time you are crafting a speech, class, or program.

Select at least two items from each of the 10 sections and use them to help you craft a more powerful presentation.

1. Relevant
Make your point personal

○ Ask open-ended questions

○ Orient around listener's culture

○ Point to recent events

○ Offer a real-life example

○ Link to a current trend

○ Share personal experience

○ Emotionalize the point

○ Mention someone the audience knows

2. Compelling
Make your point irresistible

○ Point out consequences

○ Offer a conundrum

○ Show cause and effect

○ Tap into a source of fear

○ Make a bold, evocative statement

○ Provide a needed solution

○ Ask a premise-shaking question

○ Describe before and after states

○ Introduce a better paradigm

○ Offer a new thought or idea

3. Beneficial
Show how the listener or reader can do the following

○ Make more money

○ Have more time

○ Experience more happiness

○ Feel younger

○ Gain a competitive advantage

○ Reduce a financial cost

○ Have more love

○ Reduce emotional stress

○ Have more or better sex

○ Get more leverage

4. Comprehensible
Make your point easy to understand

○ Draw a distinction

○ Share an anecdote

○ Use a symbol

○ Use a quotation

○ Craft a metaphor

○ Use a simile

○ Create a vivid image

○ Use a formula

○ Foster a spirited discussion

○ Provide a demonstration

5. Credible
Prove the point; make it believable

○ Identify examples in nature

○ Quote a fact or statistic

○ Identify a universal truth

○ Describe a related historical event

○ Show how it's part of a bigger system

○ Relate to a well-known person

○ Outline point's source or provenance

○ Link to a physical or natural law

○ Mention related current research

○ Help people want to learn the point

6. Entertaining
Help people want to learn the point

○ Take the unconventional approach

○ Identify the meta-message

○ Use multimedia (video, music, etc.)

○ Share a dramatic yet true story

○ Give permission or foster acceptance

○ Share your vision in the area

○ Use humor; be funny, witty, quick

○ Point out an absurdity of life

○ Use a prop to make your point

○ Share a success story

7. Assimilative
Help people to integrate the point

- ○ Role-play with the audience
- ○ Custom fit your information
- ○ Give readers an exercise to do
- ○ Get people to share their views
- ○ Debrief or summarize what was said
- ○ Ask audience to further develop the point
- ○ Ask audience to apply or use the point
- ○ Describe the shift that is possible
- ○ Suggest what to stop doing
- ○ Share information about physical reactions

8. Useful and Practical
Show people how to use your point

- ○ Provide action steps
- ○ Identify unspoken objections
- ○ Point out easily missed fallacies
- ○ Explain implementation strategy
- ○ Identify or remove blocks to use
- ○ Correct false assumptions
- ○ Show how to use point with others
- ○ Inform possible reactions to using the point
- ○ Package points into Top 10 list
- ○ Give fieldwork or homework

9. Motivating
Get people excited about your point

- ○ Package point into a message
- ○ Ask a closed-ended (i.e., yes or no) question
- ○ Make a direct request
- ○ Plant seeds and water them
- ○ Point out what's possible
- ○ Suggest a life reorientation
- ○ Create urgency
- ○ Have a passion for your point
- ○ Identify a related toleration
- ○ Validate person's experience/views

10. Memorable
Make it easy to remember the point

- ○ Phrase point as a maxim
- ○ Create an acronym
- ○ Share your opinion
- ○ Package point as a life lesson
- ○ Repeat your point in different ways
- ○ Provide a model or example of use
- ○ Illustrate with a Venn Diagram
- ○ Describe smell, color, or texture
- ○ Create or relate to a slogan or jingle
- ○ Evolve the point while sharing it

Success Formulas Program

- Is life as simple as a success potion? No.
- Can you get a great life just by using a formula? No.
- Does every formula work every time? No.

With that said, welcome to the **Success Formulas** program. We've come up with 100 formulas that are mini-recipes for success that professional coaches sometimes use from time to time with their coachees.

Take a look at what we've put together here and try a couple of them out to see if they'll work for you.

Our goal is to simplify the success process.

We'd really enjoy hearing from you and including your suggestions and formulas in a future edition, so please write. Our address is on the last page.

Instructions

There are four steps to completing the Success Formulas program.

Step 1: Answer each question.

If the statement is true, check the square. If not, leave it blank until you've done what it takes for it to be checked. Be rigorous; be a hard grader.

Step 2: Summarize each section.

Add up the number of squares for each of the 10 sections and write those amounts where indicated. Then add up all 10 sections and write the current total in the box on the front of this form.

Step 3: Color in the progress chart on the front page.

If you have five checks in the Accounting section, color in the bottom five boxes, and so on. Always start from the bottom and work up. The goal is to have the entire chart filled in. This will indicate that you are managing your company well. In the meantime, you have a current picture of how you are doing in each of the 10 areas.

Step 4: Keep playing until all boxes are filled in.

This process may take 30 or 360 days, but you can do it! Use your coach or advisor to assist you. And check back quarterly for maintenance.

Progress Chart

Date	Points (+/−)	Score

Success Formulas Program 100-Point Checklist

Sections										
#	A	B	C	D	E	F	G	H	I	J
10										
9										
8										
7										
6										
5										
4										
3										
2										
1										

Give yourself credit as you get points from the 100-point program. Fill in columns from the bottom up.

A. Communication

Number of circles checked (10 max) _____

○ Nonaddiction	+ Needs met	= Be present
○ Whole	+ Restored	= Forgiveness
○ Gratitude	+ Grace	= Compassion
○ Restored	+ Reserve	= Charge neutral
○ Subtle difference	+ Words	= Articulation
○ New truth	+ Motivating	= Message
○ Awareness	+ Shift	= Clarity
○ Experience	+ Awareness	= Understanding
○ Holding vision	+ Possibility	= Focus
○ Gentleness	+ Self-Trust	= Touch

B. Success

Number of circles checked (10 max) _____

○ For	+ Community	= Performance
○ Efficiency	+ Effectiveness	= Productivity
○ Desire	+ Evidence	= Dedication
○ Discipline	+ Structure	= Sustainability
○ Incentive	+ Possibility	= Willingness
○ Network	+ Information	= Resources
○ Result	+ Growth	= Accomplishment
○ Cash in bank	+ Family/love	= Success
○ Belief In	+ Endorsement	= Management
○ Consistent action	+ Results	= Momentum

C. Money

Number of circles checked (10 max) _____

○ Revenue	+ Low expenses	= Profit
○ Added value	+ Service	= Referrals
○ Capital	+ Opportunities	= Wealth
○ High-touch	+ Meet needs	= Sale
○ Service	+ Mastery	= Full practice
○ Insurance	+ Alarms	= Security
○ Controls	+ Reporting	= Budget
○ Investment	+ Wisdom	= High return
○ Certified public accountant	+ Tax planning	= Tax savings
○ Consistent savings	+ Time	= Retirement fund

D. Quality of Life

Number of circles checked (10 max) _____

○ Desire	+ Acceptance	= Present perfect
○ Good food	+ Exercise	= Physical fitness
○ Peaceful	+ Selfish	= Being
○ Extreme self-care	+ Freedom	= Poise
○ Integration	+ Prioritize	= Balance
○ Boundaries	+ Steps over nothing	= Problem-free
○ Whole	+ Boredom	= Peace
○ Flossing	+ Brushing	= Good teeth
○ Boundaries	+ Protection	= Safety
○ Abstinence	+ Self-care	= Sobriety

E. High-End Living

Number of circles checked (10 max) _____

○	Gratification	+ Love	= Happiness
○	Tru Values	+ Accomplishments	= Fulfillment
○	Inspiration	+ Experimentation	= Creativity
○	Underpromise	+ Excellence	= Freedom
○	Synthesis	+ Pleasure	= Creation
○	Options	+ Patience	= Choice
○	Touch	+ Grounding	= Joy
○	Reserve	+ Possibility	= Abundance
○	Present perfect	+ Anticipation	= Future
○	High standards	+ Self-worth	= Self-esteem

F. Spirituality

Number of circles checked (10 max) _____

○	Honesty	+ Awareness	= Truth
○	Selfishness	+ Community	= Oneness
○	Now	+ Wholeness	= Eternity
○	Perspective	+ Awareness	= Consciousness
○	Fullness	+ Connection	= Bliss
○	Judgment	+ Connectedness	= Wisdom
○	At Cause	+ Timing	= Miracle
○	Trust God	+ Surrender	= Acceptance
○	Style	+ Love	= Grace
○	Understate	+ Overdeliver	= Self-esteem

G. Development

Number of circles checked (10 max) _____

○	Innovation	+ Practice	= Mastery
○	Possibility	+ Shift, performance	= Evolution
○	Tru Values	+ Gifts	= Who
○	Today	+ Present	= Eternity
○	Contribution	+ Selfishness	= Legacy
○	Recovery	+ Perfection	= Restoration
○	Self	+ Expert	= Source
○	Idea	+ System	= Invention
○	Development	+ Honesty	= Readiness
○	Internally driven	+ Maintaining	= Self-managing

H. Relating

Number of circles checked (10 max) _____

○	Relationships	+ Creativity	= Culture
○	Gratitude	+ Bond	= Granting
○	Inclusion	+ Love	= Connectedness
○	Is right	+ Doesn't care about it	= Ease
○	Endorsement	+ Challenge	= Empowerment
○	Action	+ Vision	= Support
○	Faith	+ Insurance	= Trust
○	Champion	+ Challenge	= Loyalty
○	Prepare	+ Challenge	= Change
○	Partnership	+ Needs met	= Interdevelopmental

I. Potpourri

Number of circles checked (10 max) _____

○   Intuition   + Experience   = Good judgment

○   Accomplishment + Leadership = Model

○   Experience   + Simplicity   = Success formula

○   Love   + Support   = Community

○   Self-respect   + Self-care   = Self-esteem

○   Wanting for   + Caring for   = Coaching

○

○

○

○

J. Types of Coaching

Number of circles checked (10 max) _____

○   Restorative coaching:
Awareness   + Honesty   = Truth

○   Linear coaching:
Focus   + Action   = Result

○   Adult coaching:
Responsibility   + Foundation   = Ease

○   Self-esteem coaching:
Integrity   + Gratitude   = Pride

○   Progressive coaching:
Integrity   + Needs met   = Wants

○   Attraction coaching:
Investment   + Reserve   = Attraction

○   Perfection coaching:
Reserve   + Desires   = Perfection

○	Vision coaching: Tru Values	+ Life purpose	= Contribution
○	Training coaching: Observation	+ Demonstration	= Training
○	4th dimension coaching: Attraction	+ Buff	= Effortlessness

Coaching Mistakes:100 Mistakes You Can Avoid

Most coaches were *born* coaches. We naturally attract people who want our support and advice. But, as is true with any profession, there is a learning curve in the process of mastering the coaching skill set. This list is compiled from the experience of hundreds of coaches. All of these coaching mistakes are fixable, once you become aware of them. As you find yourself making fewer and fewer mistakes, your confidence will grow, thus adding to the power and effectiveness of your coaching. Fortunately, we get to stand on the shoulders of hundreds of veteran coaches, a number of whom helped compile this list.

Coaches generally make mistakes for two reasons. The first reason is that there has not been enough formal or comprehensive training for coaches. A high level of competence can be reached via the coach training available from one of the CoachInc.com training programs, accompanied by 2,000– 5,000 hours of coaching coachees. The second primary reason coaches make mistakes is because we do not hear or see all that is occurring with the coachee, in the coachee's life, or in a specific situation. Situational training via CoachInc.com is very effective in helping the coach to easily and immediately discern and assess the situation or needs. But we also need to evolve as human beings in order to be aware of the many important nuances present in every coaching situation and in life. This process takes time, individual coaching, and willingness. Having a mentor coach helps a lot as well.

1. Wrong Focus

○ Focusing on the coachee's goal or achievement to the exclusion of the person

○ Working on wants and needs when, in fact, the coachee's integrity is way off the scale

○ Trying to help by sharing tips or techniques when, in fact, the coachee just needs to be heard

○ Getting led down diversionary tunnels by your coachee because you can't see the real problem, opportunity, or situation

○ Letting coachees select goals that they have not had much luck with in the past

○ Getting sidetracked by a coachee's personal stuff

○ Trying to push coachees through blocks instead of helping them fully understand the block's dynamic

○ Paying more attention to what the coachee is saying than to his or her behavior

○ Letting coachees set their coaching goals without fully buying into them

○ Forcing a topic the coachee does not want to focus on, even if you feel it really needs to be discussed

2. Weak Coaching

○ Passively coaching and responding during the coaching sessions instead of asking for more (much more) from the coachee

○ Focusing on tactical matters or details when strategic coaching is needed, and vice versa

○ Being too nice or patient to the point that you are not saying what needs to be said

○ Slipping into the role of motivator or cattle prod instead of being the collaborative partner

○ Working too hard to make your coachees successful instead of inspiring or challenging your coachees to do that for themselves

○ Not setting specific enough goals or focusing enough on performance (unless coachee wants a discovery-type focus)

○ Not directly and immediately addressing the coachee's personality problems, communication flaws, bad attitude, or resistance

○ Not knowing or asking the right question(s)

○ Accepting what the coachee says at face value, without clarifying or asking for evidence

○ Coaching all coachees the same way

3. Communication Flaws

○ Using jargon instead of simple words

○ Interrupting the coachee in a desire to help or to save time

○ Not interrupting a coachee who is rambling on because you do not want to be rude

○ Being blunt because you feel you are correct, and not being mindful of its possible impact on your coachee's feelings

○ Using e-mail with coachees without going out of your way to make sure you add extra warmth, encouragement, and respect

○ Not taking responsibility for how you are being heard

○ Not sharing the inklings you are having—positive or negative

○ Using a patronizing tone with coachees, relating to them as people who need what you have to say

○ Not hearing the often subtle clues that coachees always give the coach about what is most important to them and the changes that they really want to make

○ Trying to teach a concept to the coachee instead of just taking a piece of the concept and showing the coachee how to use it in a specific situation

4. Egocentricity

○ Laying your tip, views, or agenda on the coachee in your eagerness to help

○ Not asking enough of your coachee because you are afraid of pushing him or her too hard

○ Not asking your coachee to do more than you would be willing to do in the same situation (holding a coachee to *your* limits)

○ Forcing your coachee to adopt your life approach, principles, or beliefs

○ Getting your emotional needs met via your coachees

○ Taking or needing credit for your coachees' successes, even if you were instrumental in the process

○ Thinking that your coachees should do what you coach them to do because you are the coach

○ Underestimating coachees' strengths, willingness, resources, and resourcefulness

○ Expecting more of coachees—because you see their potential—than they are truly capable of doing right now

○ Encouraging coachees to step out and follow their hearts or pursue a dream before they are emotionally ready or financially responsible

5. Coachee Management

○ Letting the coachee consistently pay late

○ Trying to coach in a restaurant or other public venue

○ Not charging enough or charging too much

○ Assuming your coachees are not evolving and thus falling behind their changing or emerging needs

○ Not tightly managing every logistical aspect of your practice (billing, prompt callbacks, etc.)

○ Getting into business with your coachees without first ending the coaching relationship or having a very clear partnership agreement

○ Assuming your practice will build quickly and quitting your day job with that expectation

○ Telling the coachee about your personal life, successes, failures, or problems, except in the direct interest of the coachee

○ Letting coaching sessions run late or making the coachee call back in a "couple of minutes"

○ Having call waiting or background noise that the coachee can hear during the session

6. Unprofessional Coaching Practices

○ Firing coachees because they are not performing or succeeding

○ Collecting a percentage or bonus based on the coachee's results

○ Thinking your job is mostly to share useful information and advice (as opposed to being a full, collaborative partner)

○ Telling coachees not to worry so much or otherwise disrespecting them

○ Taking sides with your coachee against the coachee's employer, spouse, friend, or other person

○ Getting emotionally invested in the outcome of your coaching of a coachee

○ Talking about a coachee to a third party without having been cleared to do so by the coachee

○ Hanging on to an unsuitable or unproductive coachee for the money

○ Fining coachees who do not take their promised actions

○ Pigeonholing the coachee as a type

○ Coaching on a problem or subject that you do not know enough about, unless you first tell the coachee of your ignorance or lack of experience, and this ignorance cannot hurt the coachee

7. Marketing and New Coachee Selection

○ Overpromising results in any way instead of underpromising or not promising anything

○ Talking people into hiring a coach instead of helping them to see or create the value of coaching for themselves

○ Selling people on the value of coaching instead of first selling people on themselves

○ Working with a noncoachable coachee or someone who is not emotionally ready for coaching

○ Coaching friends or family members

○ Coaching coachees who need you or coaching too much, thus creating dependency or pressure.

○ Asking or pressuring current coachees for referrals instead of finding more professional ways to let them know you have time for more business

○ Not spending enough time learning about your coachee's learning styles and ways of doing things

○ Not knowing what to say or do with a potential coachee who calls you as a result of a referral or web link

○ Assuming someone knows in advance how to be a great or successful coachee

8. Coachee Retention and Coaching Flow

○ Having even one bad coachee who is causing you stress

○ Not continually planting seeds to help the coachee see the next objective or focus

○ Not helping coachees to see the connection between a recent success and the changes or evolution they have been making

○ Assuming that your coachees know or remember how much they have benefited from your coaching

○ Not periodically asking your coachees to specifically tell you what to do differently or better so that they will better benefit from your coaching because you have become a better coach

○ Not knowing exactly what the coachee feels you are contributing to the relationship and coaching process

○ Taking on more coachees than you have the intellectual or emotional space for (not just time for)

○ Failing to inquire why a coachee terminates the coaching relationship and to make improvements as a result

○ Assuming that, because you have made a commitment to the coachee, the coachee has made a commitment to you

○ Not initiating or bringing up the themes, issues, or foci that your coachees will likely benefit from

9. Erroneous Assumptions

○ Assuming that X (situation, issue, stress) is a problem for the coachee because it is or would be a problem in your life

○ Assuming you can and should coach anyone if they are ready, willing, and able

○ Assuming that your coachees want or are ready to be successful just because they say they are

○ Assuming that your coachees want to or can hear your advice at any given point if what you have to say is really good

○ Assuming your coachees are just like you and need the same advice or type of support that you would

○ Assuming the coachee can get it quickly instead of giving the coachee enough time to process or accept your suggestions

○ Assuming shared standards and boundaries

○ Assuming that you are a terrific coach and thus stopping your own learning process

○ Assuming that you have to know everything about coaching before you can be a really effective coach

10. Bad Advice

○ Telling the coachee what to do rather than helping to create the plan/strategy

○ Giving only one suggestion or option for what could be done

○ Giving the right advice at the wrong time

○ Giving legal, psychological, or medical advice without a license

○ Getting too personal with your coachee, even if you are close

○ Referring coachees to other professionals when you are not adequately familiar with their competency or services

○ Using a one-solution-fits-all approach for all coachees

○ Making recommendations without having all the relevant information and knowing the needs of the coachee

○ Telling the coachee what will probably happen as a result of following your recommendation

○ Giving the same advice to all coachees without customizing it

The High Hidden Costs of Coaching

There are about 30 costs—many subtle or hidden—of coaching. All these costs must be eliminated in order for you to have a successful and sustainable practice, and to qualify to be a master coach.

Y	N	Foundation: How solid is your relationship with the client?
○	○	Have you overpromised results?
○	○	Have you misrepresented your experience or expertise in your rush to get the client?
○	○	Has the client taken the Coachability Index test and not passed?
○	○	Is this the wrong type of client for *you* to be coaching at this point in your development?
○	○	Does your client follow your advice blindly? (Dangerous!)
○	○	Does this client bring out your worst? (Don't use clients to settle your own issues.)
○	○	Are you undercharging?
○	○	Did you accept too many, too few, too big, too small, or too vague goals?
○	○	Did you violate your boundaries by accepting call times outside your desired schedule?
○	○	Do you *not* have a coach yourself? (The *hard* way.)
○	○	Does the client see you as a technician (consultant) or as an artist (coach)?
Y	N	Flow: How easy is it to coach and work with the client?
○	○	Is the client a complainer? (Stop this, now.)
○	○	Does the client pay more than seven days late? (Enforce your rules.)
○	○	Does the client come to the call more than three minutes late? (Retrain them.)

Y	N	Flow: How easy is it to coach and work with the client?
○	○	Does the client question everything you say? (Some trust is essential.)
○	○	Does the client fight your suggestions, only to accept them later? (This client needs to grow up.)
○	○	Does the client not give you credit when credit is due you? (Greatness takes two.)
○	○	Does the client blame you for advice that didn't work out? (Share the responsibility.)
○	○	Does the client keep breaking his or her word? (Request they only commit to what they are going to do.)
○	○	Does the client not take action, or enough action? (You should be impressed each week.)
○	○	Is the client full of excuses? (Have them stop.)
○	○	Does the client just use you to talk to? (The client should ask for your opinion.)
○	○	Do you gossip about your clients? (Stop now.)
N	Y	Future: Is a fantastic future being built between you? (Questions in this section are phrased in the positive mode versus the negative tone of previous sections. Notice new position of N and Y.)
○	○	Is this client on a solid, fast track?
○	○	Is this client going to be able to pay increasing fees?
○	○	Does this client keep you on your toes?
○	○	Does this client send you business?
○	○	Does this client make you an extraordinary coach?
○	○	Is this client full of projects and ideas for the future?
○	○	Does this client have his or her vision, purpose and mission clearly defined?
		Total second-column circles checked

SCORING KEY

25–30 You are virtually cost free and should have an effortless practice.
20–24 Pretty good; your practice should be moving along. Go for 30!
15–19 Not bad, but you are being dragged down by your clients.
0–14 Not good; you have an expensive practice—eliminate five costs, fast!

Master Coach Profile

We've identified the 100 key skills, behaviors, and conditions to become a Master Coach. A Master Coach is at an advanced level of the coaching profession. He or she has demonstrated a proven ability to coach a client in virtually any coachable situation.

A Master Coach is a magical person, whose personal and professional life reflects the quality of work delivered to clientele.

This profile covers the 100 skills and conditions that qualify a coach to be a Master Coach.

This checklist may be used by a newly trained or intermediate-level coach to further his or her development. It is designed to be used as you are being coached.

Instructions

There are four steps to completing the **Master Coach** profile.

Step 1: Answer Each Question

If true, check the box marked True. Be rigorous; be a hard grader. If the statement is sometimes or usually true, please *do not* check the box until the statement is virtually always true for you. (No credit until it is really true!) If the statement does not apply to you, check the True box. If the statement will never be true for you, check the box. (You get credit for it because it does not apply or will never happen.) And you may change any statement to fit your situation better.

Step 2: Summarize Each Section

Add up the number of True boxes for each of the four sections and write those amounts where indicated. Then add up all four sections and write the current total in the box on the front of this form.

Step 3: Color In the Progress Chart on the Front Page

If you have nine points in the Coaching Skills section, color in the bottom nine boxes, and so on. Always start at the bottom and work up. The goal is to have the entire chart filled in. In the meantime, you have a current picture of how you are doing in each of the four areas.

Step 4: Keep Playing Until All Boxes Are Filled In

You can do it! This process will take between one and five years, but you can reach 100 points and be a Master Coach! Use your coach or a friend to assist you, and check back once a year for maintenance.

Benefits

In the spaces provided, jot down specific benefits, results, and shifts that happened in your life because you accomplished an item in the Master Coach profile.

Date	Benefit

Progress Chart

Date	Points (+/−)	Score

Master Coach Profile 100-Point Checklist

#	Sections			
	A	B	C	D
25				
24				
23				
22				
21				
20				
19				
18				
17				
16				
15				
14				
13				
12				
11				
10				
9				
8				
7				
6				
5				
4				
3				
2				
1				

Give yourself credit as you get points from the 100-point program. Fill in columns from the bottom up.

A. Practice and Success

Number of circles checked (25 max) _____

○ My receivables are all current (and I know who owes me what).

○ All clients pay within 10 days of date due.

○ I consistently send birthday, occasion, and anniversary cards.

○ My practice is full of clients who nourish and inspire me.

○ I have a waiting list of clients.

○ I prepare monthly profit and loss statements by the 15th of the next month.

○ I am not tolerating any clients.

○ I have the right equipment—telephone head set, computer, laser printer, fax machine, answering machine, separate phone line.

○ I put 20 percent of my gross income into savings.

○ I have a reputation as a powerful coach.

○ Every client is moving forward well.

○ I spend only 5 percent of my time marketing.

○ I am not practicing therapy with my clients.

○ I spend less than eight hours a day working.

○ My clients stay for more than one year.

○ I receive 90 percent of clients via referral.

○ I know and honor my "Coach-Free Zones."

○ I have the highest quality letterhead and cards.

○ All clients honor my *very* high standards.

○ I maintain no unattended paperwork.

○ I have signed agreements for all clients.

○ I am on time for 98 percent of my client calls.

○ Clients come to or call me; I rarely travel.

○ I have a simple, interesting statement that describes who I am, what I do, and who I work with.

○ My clients win, win, and win and they thank me for it.

B. Coaching Skills and Communication

Number of circles checked (25 max) _____

○ I share powerful messages that move the client.

○ I give the needed phrasing to the client to articulate what is occurring.

○ I get my clients back on track within two sessions.

○ I step over nothing; I do not wait to point out what I see happening.

○ I listen fully, adding nothing; I can bear 120 seconds of client silence.

○ Clients get my acknowledgement of them.

○ I've mastered the AIM model (advocate, instruct, and manage).

○ I am coaching at least one coach.

○ I zero in on the source of the problem.

○ I fully discern a client in the first session.

○ I recognize distinctions.

○ I recognize and label coachee's 10 common blocks.

○ I make huge requests of my clients.

○ Clients get exactly what I mean.

○ I deliver 20 percent more than is expected.

○ I say very few words, but they have extraordinary impact.

○ I am known for getting people instantly.

○ I always see the clients' best and speak to their strengths—my clients' weaknesses don't distract or bother me.

○ I let clients go who aren't up to coaching with me.

○ I will go to any length to assist the discouraged client.

○ I dance (two-way) in my client conversations—I adjust immediately to where they are and to what they've just gotten.

○ I proactively manage my clients' promises and keep their vision alive.

○ I share observations without hogging the space.

○ I almost always say the right thing at the right time in the right way.

C. Essence and Effortlessness

Number of circles checked (25 max) _____

○ I know and share the 10 things I want for my clients.

○ I separate coaching from loving and caring.

○ I am free of feeling that I have to produce a result.

○ I accept acknowledgment gracefully.

○ I am the most grateful person I know.

○ I've helped a coach fill his or her practice.

○ I let clients teach me what I do not know.

○ I speak slowly, simply, and clearly and use virtually no jargon or clichés.

○ I stand up for, but do not caretake, my clients.

○ Just by being with me, clients produce miracles.

○ I coach effortlessly: no suffering, no trying, no struggling.

○ I have a coach whom I honor and respect.

○ I speak with no charge in my voice.

○ I am happy, fulfilled, and able.

○ I score above 90 on the Clean Sweep.

○ I score above 70 on the Reserve Index.

○ I can be with a client who is disturbed.

○ I am known for my compassion.

○ I think on my feet and am able to share all that I feel in the moment.

○ I do not need to coach to be whole.

○ I really enjoy my clients, no matter how well or how poorly they are doing at the moment.

○ I am building a future with my clients.

○ I put the truth ahead of immediate client or practice gains. I will not excuse, rationalize, or accept anything less.

○ I have a limitless amount of compassion for clients, my life, and myself.

○ I can easily be with myself.

D. Expertise and Confidence

Number of circles checked (25 max) _____

○ I have coached at least five clients to the 100 score on the Clean Sweep program.

○ I have led at least three 27-day programs.

○ I have led workshops with a cumulative total of at least 100 people.

○ I have coached at least 10 clients to the 100 score on the NeedLess program.

○ I am recognized locally as a specialist.

○ I put people first and results second.

○ I have assisted 10 clients to completely turn around their financial problems.

○ I have assisted 10 clients to reorient their lives around their three Tru Values.

○ My clients tell me they want to be more like me.

○ I have fully integrated the personal and professional lives of 10 entrepreneurs to the point of sustainable balance.

○ I have helped 10 clients make the authentic choice to be fully alive for the rest of their lives.

○ I have been fired at least five times for attempting to hold clients to my high standards.

○ I have assisted 20 clients get out of a tough spot and go on to find their true life's work.

○ People have a simple, vibrant, and powerful vision because of me.

○ I have developed my own seminar, workshop, program, or assessment tool that has been shared with over 100 people.

○ People credit me with being the most empowering influence in their lives.

○ I have had 10 clients reach 100 in the 100 Smiles program.

○ I have coached five coaches to have a full practice.

○ I am at 90+ on Irresistible Attraction.

○ I am "over" myself. I have a healthy ego state.

○ I have passed CoachInc.com's certification exam.

○ I have 25 client recommendation letters.

○ I have left a legacy for at least 1,000 folks.

www.coachinc.com

Part 2
Personal Coaching

Chapter 6

Life Coaching

This chapter deals with the life side of personal coaching. It is designed for self-exploration and to bring awareness to who and where you are in your personal life.

In this chapter you will find information to learn from, assessments, self-examining questionnaires, a personal inventory, self-tests, and programs to work through. You may use them for your own personal growth or with your coachees to further their development. Working through these materials takes time and commitment.

The following sections are included in this chapter:

1. Skills to Work on with a Coach
2. 15 Human Conditions
3. Problems, Concerns, and Blocks
4. Uncovering the Fundamental Lie
5. Emotional Reactions
6. Reaction Free
7. The Attachment Index
8. Letting Go
9. Stress Index
10. The Adrenaline Lifestyle
11. Adrenaline Self-Test
12. Who Are You?
13. What Fuels You
14. Strengths Inventory
15. Personal Wins
16. Resources and Assets
17. Spending and Debt Questionnaire
18. Daily Report
19. 10 Goals to Reach in the Next 90 Days
20. Clean Sweep Program
21. 25 Secrets to Having the Life You Want
22. The Success Process

Skills to Work on with a Coach

Please mark the goals you *most* want to work on during the first year of coaching. A list of popular skills to master, using the services of a coach.

Success Skills		
Build a team	Remove obstacles	Take bigger risks
Prioritize opportunities	Use leverage	Ask for what you need
Stay focused	Delegate	
Demonstrate leadership	Manage others	
Self-Management Skills		
Be on time	Keep one's word	Get needs met
Underpromise/overdeliver	Protect oneself	Develop routine
Ask for what you need	Stop tolerating	
Stop suffering	Love oneself	
Fulfillment Skills		
Integrate all of one's life	Discover purpose	Surround oneself with love
Build a reserve	Find spiritual path	Design personal mission
Discover source/higher power	Include, hold it all	
Know oneself	Create a legacy	
Listening Skills		
Listen, adding nothing	Hear behind the words	Care
Read body language	Discern who the person is	Discern what's true
Get the person	Empower silence	
Get to the source of the problem	Immediate sensing	

Speaking Skills		
Discern what's happening	Hear versus talking	Dance in conversation
Language feelings	Speak straight	Use captivating voice
Fully communicate	Be fully constructive	Evoke others
Ask for all you want	Speak with the edge	Say what is so
Directly request	Acknowledge	
Say no, no, no	Educate environment	
Being Skills		
Sticking by requirements	Know what you want	Effortlessness
Gratitude	Grace	Surrender to self
Be with anyone	Feel self, others	
Ability to inquire	Courage	
Integrate	Include it all	
Contributing Skills		
Empathy	Compassion	
Give freely without guilt	Able to receive	
Invest in a person	Able to give love	

15 Human Conditions

What is really causing your problems? Circle the number that comes closest to representing how true the statement is for you right now. Then, score yourself using the key at the bottom of the page.

Less True			More True		Statement
1	2	3	4	5	I have not really made the authentic choice to be fully alive for the rest of my life.
1	2	3	4	5	I need to be right.
1	2	3	4	5	I have unresolved matters and issues.
1	2	3	4	5	My personal values are not clear or are not fully expressed.
1	2	3	4	5	I am addicted or attached to substances, people, or behaviors.
1	2	3	4	5	I am currently living a lie.
1	2	3	4	5	I really do not have anything better to do than what I am doing now.
1	2	3	4	5	I am not really engaged in the game of life.
1	2	3	4	5	I have financial problems or major concerns.
1	2	3	4	5	I am missing key, empowering relationships in my life.
1	2	3	4	5	My needs are not being met.
1	2	3	4	5	My life is primarily about me.
1	2	3	4	5	I do not really understand how life works so well for certain other people.
1	2	3	4	5	I have not experienced very much in life yet.
1	2	3	4	5	I am under a lot of stress.
					Total score (add up all numbers)

SCORING KEY

61–75   Now you know why life is such a struggle!

41–60   You've started to live, but you have a lot to learn about yourself and how life works effortlessly.

26–40   You're on your way—keep going! You'll get there.

15–25   Congratulations: You have what it takes to be extraordinary, now.

Problems, Concerns, and Blocks

Please respond to each question in the space provided. What is in your way?

Primary Attachments
Please take the Attachment Index. List your three primary attachments here. Score from test: ___

_____

_____

_____

Lightning-Rod Attraction
What kind of problems and crises do you keep attracting?

_____

_____

_____

Recurring Behavior Patterns, Bad Habits, and Blocks To Success
What do you keep doing that limits your success?

_____

_____

_____

Accountability Deferment Tactics
What games are you playing with yourself and others? (Where do you fool or kid yourself? Where do you cause problems or sabotage yourself?)

_____

_____

_____

Uncovering the Fundamental Lie

The Fundamental Lie is that false assumption, life misunderstanding, or stale formula that dictates many of our thoughts, actions, and results. It is the kind of thing that takes the shock of an auto accident, a spiritual experience, or a knock on the side of the head to see and tell the truth about. Use the space provided to tell the truth about your Fundamental Lie.

What is true about your parents that you've never been able to see or articulate until now?	
What is true about the failures you've had in life? Whose fault were they?	
What do you say you are ready for but have not had significant results in or progress toward in the last two years?	
What childish fantasies are you hanging on to?	
What are you still hoping for?	
What's the secret you are most concerned about people discovering?	
List three possible Fundamental Lies.	
What is the next step?	

Emotional Reactions: How Are You Feeling?

Consider the following:

Fear

- ○ Dread
- ○ Panic
- ○ Alarm
- ○ Horror
- ○ Terror
- ○ Worry
- ○ Distrust
- ○ Misgiving
- ○ Timidity
- ○ Anxiety

Hesitancy

- ○ Pause
- ○ Break
- ○ Stop
- ○ Postponement
- ○ Deferral
- ○ Procrastination
- ○ Unwillingness
- ○ Wavering
- ○ Diffidence
- ○ Slowing down

Dissatisfaction

- ○ Frustration
- ○ Exasperation
- ○ Impatience
- ○ Irritation
- ○ Annoyance
- ○ Discontent
- ○ Thwarted
- ○ Displeasure
- ○ Nonfulfillment
- ○ Restlessness

Disappointed

- ○ Dismayed
- ○ Discouraged
- ○ Disillusioned
- ○ Disenchanted
- ○ Thwarted
- ○ Foiled
- ○ Miscarriage
- ○ Baffled
- ○ Chagrined
- ○ Fizzled

253

Anxiety (symptoms of)

- Palpitation
- Trembling/quivering
- Shaking/shuddering
- Butterflies
- Cold feet
- Second thoughts
- The creeps
- Hollow feeling in pit of stomach
- Hard to breathe
- Speaking quickly
- Stop speaking

Pain

- Anguish
- Ache
- Discomfort
- Twinge
- Throbbing
- Torture
- Torment
- Distress
- Trial
- Burden

Sadness

- Sorrow
- Joylessness
- Discouragement
- Disheartened
- Gloominess
- Bleakness
- Dejected
- Depressed
- Despondent
- Melancholy

Hesitation

- Trepidation
- Apprehension
- Uncertainty
- Suspicion
- Qualm
- Disquiet
- Concern
- Reluctance
- Indecision
- Balking

Anger

○ Angst

○ Ire

○ Bitterness

○ Wrath

○ Temper

○ Rage

○ Fury

○ Resentment

○ Acrimony

○ Enmity

Resigned

○ In a funk

○ Tolerating

○ Depressed

○ Down

○ Given up

○ Abdicated

○ Submitted to

○ Ceded

○ Surrendered

○ Endured

Reaction Free

For you to be perfect, what are the 25 things that you would simply stop reacting to?

In a perfect life, what are the specific situations, people, roles, problems, events, experiences, stresses, surprises, and life dynamics that you would simply no longer react to? How would you work through these in order not to react, without resorting to self-control or self management?

	How?
1.	
2.	
3.	
4.	
5.	
6.	
7.	
8.	
9.	
10.	
11.	
12.	
13.	
14.	
15.	
16.	
17.	
18.	
19.	
20.	
21.	
22.	
23.	
24.	
25.	

Would support be helpful?

Crafting and creating a perfect person is a lot more fun when you can focus with a friend, partner, colleague, or professional coach. Especially important is how you identify and articulate each of your 25 elements. Properly phrased, each element would excite and naturally motivate you. Poorly phrased, you may feel pressure to perform or the items become just more shoulds or coulds in your life.

The Attachment Index

Circle the number that comes closest to representing how true the statement is for you right now. Then score yourself, using the key provided.

Less True			More True		Statement
1	2	3	4	5	I watch more than 10 hours of TV or videos per week.
1	2	3	4	5	I smoke more than five cigarettes per week.
1	2	3	4	5	I drink more than five alcoholic beverages per week.
1	2	3	4	5	I have more than one caffeinated beverage per day.
1	2	3	4	5	My thoughts often revolve around sex and having sex.
1	2	3	4	5	I critique my appearance in the mirror more than four times per day.
1	2	3	4	5	I gamble more than once per month or lose more than 10 percent of my take-home pay per month.
1	2	3	4	5	I use cocaine, dope, other drugs more than once per month.
1	2	3	4	5	I virtually always get my way.
1	2	3	4	5	I must be in a relationship to feel great.
1	2	3	4	5	I usually put myself and my needs last.
1	2	3	4	5	I suffer or tolerate far too much.
1	2	3	4	5	I barely pay my bills and often pay them late.
1	2	3	4	5	I go shopping more than four hours per week.
1	2	3	4	5	I attend more than one workshop or personal growth seminar per month.
1	2	3	4	5	I sleep more than nine hours per night.
1	2	3	4	5	I am often late and/or rushed.
1	2	3	4	5	I try to manage the impressions people have of me.
1	2	3	4	5	I eat sugar (cake, candy bars, drinks) more than four times per week.
1	2	3	4	5	I often think about food and my next meal.
1	2	3	4	5	I work more than 45 hours per week.
1	2	3	4	5	I have to be the best at everything I do.
1	2	3	4	5	I use adrenaline to get the job done or to meet deadlines.
1	2	3	4	5	I overpromise or don't keep my word.
1	2	3	4	5	I am always busy.
Total score (add up all numbers)					

SCORING KEY

25–50	You are very free.
51–75	You are human, but you would benefit from some detachment work.
76–90	You are human, but you are being held back by your attachments.
91–100	You are human, but not really yourself.
101–125	You are an attachment machine!

Letting Go

In the left column, write down the 10 elements, behaviors, or things that are not best for the rest of your life. You may include elements that you have already let go of or have done, as well as elements that you want to let go of and that are not done. In the right column, write down the 10 elements, behaviors, or things that you want to have or do, or want to continue to have and do, for the rest of your life.

–	0	+	To Let Go of, Not Do		–	0	+	To Do or Have
			1.					1.
			2.					2.
			3.					3.
			4.					4.
			5.					5.
			6.					6.
			7.					7.
			8.					8.
			9.					9.
			10.					10.

Scoring

Check the box below the minus sign if you have not made much progress with that item.
Check the box below the zero if you are definitely making progress with that item.
Check the box below the plus sign if that item has been true for at least 90 days.

Stress Index

How stressed out are you, right now? Circle the number which comes closest to representing how true the statement is for you right now. Then, score yourself, using the key at the bottom of the page.

Less True			More True		Statement
1	2	3	4	5	A close family member died in the past 12 months.
1	2	3	4	5	I moved to a new town in the past 12 months.
1	2	3	4	5	I changed jobs in the past 12 months.
1	2	3	4	5	My son or daughter left home in the past 12 months.
1	2	3	4	5	A close friend or family member who is ill depends on you for care.
1	2	3	4	5	I have had a major health problem in the past 12 months.
1	2	3	4	5	A close relationship ended in the past 12 months.
1	2	3	4	5	I lost my job or retired in the past 12 months.
1	2	3	4	5	I got married in the past 12 months.
1	2	3	4	5	I took on a lot of debt in the past 12 months.
1	2	3	4	5	I got divorced or separated in the past 12 months.
1	2	3	4	5	I lost a lot of money in the past 12 months.
1	2	3	4	5	I have ongoing marital problems.
1	2	3	4	5	I have ongoing sexual problems.
1	2	3	4	5	I have ongoing financial problems.
1	2	3	4	5	I have ongoing trouble with friends or relatives.
1	2	3	4	5	I have ongoing problems meeting family demands.
1	2	3	4	5	I have ongoing pressure at work or school.
1	2	3	4	5	I have ongoing pressure with emotional problems.
1	2	3	4	5	I am constantly facing do-or-die deadlines.
Total score (add up all numbers)					

SCORING KEY

20–35	Virtually stress free
36–50	Somewhat stressed
51–75	Stressed—watch out
76–100	Super stressed—reduce all pressures in your life or someone will be calling 911

The Adrenaline Lifestyle

Do you fully understand what an adrenaline lifestyle is?

Adrenaline Is

A Source of Energy

Humans will go to any length to get the quickest, easiest source of energy. Adrenaline produces energy; this is not the most healthful source, but is continually available.

A Racket

Humans succumb to this drug instead of finding healthy energy sources.

A Medicant

Adrenaline rushes help a person to blast thorough difficult times. The problem is that the adrenaline junkie creates crises just for the rush. When a person is on adrenaline, he or she has a respite from pain, and feelings are covered up.

A Nasty Habit, Which Creates a Lifestyle

To get the rush, humans do soul-damaging things: overworking, acting greedily, insisting on getting ahead or winning, keeping self in survival mode in order to have something to win at, and so on.

A Toxin, Which Keeps Healthy People Away

Those who are over adrenaline or are not adrenaline dependent usually won't develop close relationships with adrenaline addicts; it is too upsetting and painful. So the addict is surrounded by those with broken wings—codependents or other addicts.

Adrenaline addiction is a recoverable condition.

- Adrenaline addicts (ADAs) can recover from adrenaline addiction, usually by simply changing select behaviors.
- ADAs identify their personal 20 triggers that start the rush and eliminate these triggers.
- ADAs recover faster with the help of a therapist or adrenaline-recovered coach.
- ADAs will go through a withdrawal period (see the section on the recovery process) of between 6 and 12 months.

What Others Will Say or Think about the ADA

- Boy, is he on all the time. How can his spouse take it?
- I know he listened to what I said, but I don't think he heard me.
- You can count on Karen to be late; that's just her.
- Jerry is always so busy. What is he always doing?
- Susan works too hard. What's with her?
- Why does Michael put himself through all that stress? I think he likes it or something.
- He always says he works best under pressure, but he's including us, too.

The Recovery Process

- Stop the triggering behavior.
- Be willing to be very bored until your new energy source kicks in (three to six months).
- Speak truthfully and completely to everyone and yourself in order to let go of the residue of adrenaline, and heal.
- Hire a coach, therapist, or experienced consultant.
- Install a strong personal foundation to keep you well and adrenaline free.

Adrenaline Trigger	Solution
Overpromising results, even a little bit	Deliberately underpromise, regardless of the person's reaction or consequence
Arriving exactly on time or late	Leave 15 minutes early for every appointment
Involvement in nonessential projects or activities	Cut out 50 percent of all personal and professional projects and goals
Shoulds and have-tos; someone else's agenda	Get rid of all shoulds, regardless of the consequences
Being optimistic during a rough time	Surrender to the tough time; don't try to see it better than it is
Doing one thing in order to get another thing	Just do the latter and see if it works
Having current unresolved matters in your life	We have at least 100; get them done
Holding back from another; being nice, being mad, not owning up to something you did	Have a heart-to-heart conversation and become intimate
Not asking for what you need	Be specific and ask before you need it
Tolerations; things you're putting up with	Put up with nothing; reeducate people
Letting people walk all over you	Expand your boundaries
Trying to prove something by your results	Shift from results to people and pleasure

Adrenaline Self-Test

Adrenaline is the drug of choice of a stressed society. Furthermore, most people are connected in some way with a stressed environment, which is why so many of us overuse our adrenaline. Originally, adrenaline gave us a jolt of superhuman energy when we were faced with a threat. But now, we use adrenaline in order to get an exciting rush or high. The authors have nothing against adrenaline highs—in fact, they can be quite fun. However, there are both physical and emotional or spiritual costs: physical costs being the overuse of the adrenal gland and the stress that circulating adrenaline puts on the body, and emotional or spiritual costs that arise because when we are high, we are not present. Also, there is the stress involved in creating situations in which our body is triggered to circulate the adrenaline.

Wondering if you are an adrenaline addict? Your score on the following questionnaire will tell the story. Again, no one is saying that you must stop adrenalizing, but if you recognize the cost and wish to make some changes in your life or way of living, then we suggest you work with a coach who understands the adrenaline addiction process and knows how to help you redesign the areas of your life that trigger your need for the rush.

Y	N	#	Statement
○	○	1.	I drink coffee, colas, or other caffeinated beverages in order to get going and keep going.
○	○	2.	I eat sugar to calm myself down.
○	○	3.	I tend to overpromise and then rush to get the project done at the last minute.
○	○	4.	I arrive at work rushed and already "on."
○	○	5.	I feel an inner rush or lack of stillness or peace much of the time, and I can't get rid of it.
○	○	6.	I tend to be impatient with the pace or performance of others.
○	○	7.	I often drive 10 mph or more over the speed limit or tend to tailgate.
○	○	8.	I tend to run late or arrive just in time. After all, why waste time by being early?
○	○	9.	It often seems that there is a problem, hassle, or difficult situation I'm having to deal with.
○	○	10.	I don't give myself plenty of time during the day for the things I do know will come up.
○	○	11.	I love a challenge and pushing through it to reach a solution.
○	○	12.	I get grabbed by surprises or upsetting events and can't calm down for a day or two.
○	○	13.	I find it boring or difficult to simply hang out with people sometimes.

Y	N	#	Statement
○	○	14.	I am at my best when under pressure, especially deadline pressure.
○	○	15.	Sometimes I wonder if I deliberately set myself up to wait until the last minute.
○	○	16.	I do not arrive at the airport an hour before my flight.
○	○	17.	I carry my cell phone even when I do not really need it.
○	○	18.	Sometimes I think I unconsciously try to find the hardest way of getting something done.
○	○	19.	People sometimes complain that I am not there with them, even though I am.
○	○	20.	I tend to be a driven type of person.
		Score (# of Ys)	

SCORING KEY

15–20   You are a certified adrenaline junkie.

11–14   An unhealthy level of adrenaline is probably coursing through your body.

6–10   You have a possible adrenaline problem.

0–5   Congratulations! You appear to not have an adrenaline problem.

Who Are You? 100 Elements of a Person

Who are we? What are we made of? What makes us tick? What makes us unique? What makes a human—human?

In the list that follows, you will find at least 100 answers to these questions. This list is helpful to both coach and client because it provides 100 focus areas for coaching, as well as acting as an interesting emotional and lifestyle blueprint of a human being. Clients often use this list as a way to select and prioritize what they want to work on with a coach.

Possessions: tangible and intangible	**Reserves:** how much extra you have	**Relationships:** who you know, who knows you, who you spend time with
1. Home/property 2. Car/vehicles 3. Computer/tools 4. Clothing 5. Accessories/jewelry 6. Money/investments 7. Knowledge/wisdom 8. Books/music/art 9. Memories 10. Reputation	11. Time 12. Money 13. Love 14. Opportunities 15. Marketability 16. Space 17. Ideas 18. Network/relationships 19. Bandwidth/capacity 20. Energy	21. Children 22. Spouse 23. Parents/family 24. Friends 25. Acquaintances/ neighbors 26. Co-workers/colleagues 27. Vendors/service 28. Mentors/teachers 29. Clients/customers 30. Yourself
Character: what you're made of	**Experiences:** how you have been affected	**Life:** what's going on around you

31. Honesty
32. Honor
33. Responsibility
34. Respectfulness
35. Accountability
36. Generosity
37. Maturity
38. Initiative
39. Caring
40. Strength
	41. Childhood experiences
	42. Love experiences
	43. Romance experiences
	44. Work experiences
	45. Vacation experiences
	46. Cultural experiences
	47. Success/failure experi-
	    ences
	48. Images (TV/movies)
	49. Schooling experiences
	50. Threatening experiences
		51. Tolerations/
		    requirements
		52. Commitments
		53. Goals
		54. Problems/struggles
		55. Work environment
		56. Home environment
		57. Stress
		58. Desires/needs
		59. Pace
		60. Stimulation

Personal Foundation: what you have developed to support you in life	Life Skills: what you're good at	Thoughts: what's upstairs
61. Values	71. Creativity	81. Inklings
62. Assumptions	72. Communication	82. Intuition
63. Boundaries	73. Thinking/analysis	83. Facts
64. Wants	74. Multitasking	84. Opinions
65. Self-esteem	75. Understanding	85. Knowledge
66. Spirit	76. Prioritizing	86. Evidence
67. Safety	77. Self-management	87. Beliefs
68. Roles	78. Evolving	88. Expectations
69. Balance	79. Relating	89. Reactions
70. Self-care	80. Loving	90. Ideas
Feelings: what you are feeling		
91. Fear/dread		
92. Acceptance/ understanding		
93. Expectation/obligation		
94. Excitement/thrill		
95. Happiness/contentment		
96. Sadness/depression		
97. Anger/rage		
98. Freedom/relief		
99. Joy/bliss		
100. Powerful/able		

What Fuels You

Choose your sources of motivation and energy carefully. Color in the chart from left to right as you shift your source of fuel. Nothing is wrong with the items on the left; they do motivate a person—however, at considerable cost. It takes practice, discussion with your coach, learning new distinctions, and seeing the early stages of the shift to continue in this game—and make sure you treat it that way. This is not a should—it's an opportunity!

Fools You	Start >>>> Achieve					Fuels You
Emotional reactions						True, simple feelings
Anger, revenge, judging						Pure compassion for others
Take, win, prove						Being perfect as you are
Keeping things the same						Surrendering to the flow
Chasing unmet needs						Responsibly fill one's cup
Drama, crises, intrigue						Peace, boredom, and freedom
Compulsions and addictions						Choice
Self-criticism and self-blaming						Granting full forgiveness
Unhealed past traumas or events						Awareness and healing
Tripping over unresolved matters						Restoring 100 percent integrity
Shoulds, coulds, have-tos						Wants and desires
Managing others' impressions						Honoring own standards
Avoiding consequences						Building trust with others
Catching up, adrenaline						Building reserve: time and money
Resignation, reacting						Dedication, have a vision
Searching, looking						Enjoy beauty
Pleasing others						Servings one self

Strengths Inventory

To get a view of your strengths, score yourself in each of these areas, with A being the greatest and C being the lowest.

Personal

Health

A	B	C	My life is full of only healthy stress.
A	B	C	I have lots of energy, vim, and vigor.
A	B	C	I look great physically.
A	B	C	My body is healthy and well taken care of.
A	B	C	I recover well from illness.
A	B	C	

Financial

A	B	C	I am financially independent or clearly on track to becoming so.
A	B	C	I am free of credit cards and installment debt.
A	B	C	I can count on my income each month.
A	B	C	I have extra money in a safe and available space.
A	B	C	Money (or lack of it) doesn't hold me back.
A	B	C	

Career

A	B	C	I like—and get what I need from—the work that I do.
A	B	C	I have the training and education I need to advance.
A	B	C	I am respected at work.
A	B	C	I get paid well for the work I perform.
A	B	C	

Relationships

A B C My friends love me even more than I need.

A B C My family loves me even more than I need.

A B C I feel a special connection with certain people.

A B C I have a best friend.

A B C People are there when I need them.

A B C

Outlook

A B C I am optimistic about myself and my future.

A B C I trust in a higher power.

A B C I recover well from challenges and difficulties.

A B C I am actively engaged in creating my future.

A B C

Self-Care

A B C I readily put myself first when I need to.

A B C I am free from addiction to substances and food.

A B C I get help quickly and appropriately when I need it.

A B C

Situational

Communication

A B C I get my point across powerfully and consistently.

A B C People listen and respond to me and what I say.

A B C I often willingly share my thoughts and ideas.

A B C I hear beyond what others are saying.

A B C I can articulate what is really happening.

A B C

Social

A	B	C	I attract great people to me.
A	B	C	I am graceful in social situations.
A	B	C	I make people feel great about themselves.
A	B	C	I deliver parties or events that others love.
A	B	C	My social calendar is full or nearly full.
A	B	C	

Professional

A	B	C	I lead a group or staff well.
A	B	C	I am a great people manager.
A	B	C	I handle myself well in business situations.
A	B	C	I know my stuff (technology, info, procedures).
A	B	C	I meet and exceed my targets and goals at work.
A	B	C	

Challenges

A	B	C	I recover well from disappointments and problems.
A	B	C	I anticipate problems and handle them early.
A	B	C	I don't mind risk. I use it to get what I want.
A	B	C	I adapt to and make the most of changes around me.
A	B	C	I can count on myself to always survive the worst.
A	B	C	

Style

A	B	C	People can count on me to be on time and keep my word.
A	B	C	I am very organized and neat.
A	B	C	I ask for, and get, what I need.
A	B	C	I don't gossip; I keep confidences and am trustworthy.
A	B	C	

Proaction

A	B	C	I have and honor my personal standards.
A	B	C	I make and follow through on my commitments.
A	B	C	

Personal Wins

Write down your wins, successes, blockbuster results, shifts, and miracles.

Date	Specifically, what is it?	Financial Benefit
		$
		$
		$
		$
		$
		$
		$
		$
		$
		$
		$
		$
		$
		$
		$
		$
		$

Resources and Assets

Please respond to each question in the space provided. What do you have going for you?

Personal and Professional Strengths

Evaluate your strengths on the Strengths Inventory and list the top five below.

_____

_____

_____

_____

_____

Most Significant Personal and Professional Accomplishments

What are you most pleased and proud of having accomplished?

_____

_____

_____

_____

_____

Personal and Professional Assets

Who do you know? What do you know? What gifts do you have? What makes you unique and powerful?

_____

_____

_____

_____

_____

Spending and Debt Questionnaire

How bad are you with money? Circle the number that comes closest to representing how true the statement is for you right now. Then score yourself, using the key provided.

Less True			More True		Statement
1	2	3	4	5	This month's bills come in before I have paid last month's bills.
1	2	3	4	5	I receive at least one cutoff or past due notice per month.
1	2	3	4	5	I have a stack of unopened bills or notices.
1	2	3	4	5	I keep a negative running balance in my checkbook.
1	2	3	4	5	I search for products I can buy with minimal down payments.
1	2	3	4	5	I get excited about how much credit line I have left.
1	2	3	4	5	I get at least one cash advance per month from my credit card.
1	2	3	4	5	I am frequently short a few dollars and borrow from friends or others.
1	2	3	4	5	I get high from telling the clerk to "charge it."
1	2	3	4	5	I am always interested in getting new charge cards.
1	2	3	4	5	I feel inordinately good when I pay routine bills like the phone or the rent.
1	2	3	4	5	I am reticent to discuss the subject of money and walk away from social conversations about it.
1	2	3	4	5	I have had an account closed in the last six months and am angry about it or have blamed others.
1	2	3	4	5	When my paycheck or loan money comes in, I experience a great sense of relief.
1	2	3	4	5	I rarely keep a running balance in my checkbook.
1	2	3	4	5	My credit card balances run near the maximum credit line.
1	2	3	4	5	I have little or no savings, investments, or assets; nothing is available for contingencies.
1	2	3	4	5	I bounce more than three checks per year.
1	2	3	4	5	I have only a vague idea of my various financial obligations.
1	2	3	4	5	Money is tight, but there is always someone I keep turning to who won't let me starve.
					Total score (add up all numbers)

SCORING KEY

20–35	Doesn't look like a problem.
36–50	Get on a budget!
51–75	Borderline situation.
76–100	Clearly a problem.

Daily Report

Read and complete the following report daily.

Theme for today:

Schedule	
6:00	
6:30	
7:00	
7:30	
8:00	
8:30	
9:00	
9:30	
10:00	
10:30	
11:00	
11:30	
12:00	
12:30	
1:00	
1:30	
2:00	
2:30	
3:00	
3:30	
4:00	
4:30	

5:00	
5:30	
6:00	
6:30	
7:00	
7:30	
8:00	
8:30	
9:00	
9:30	
10:00	
10:30	
11:00	

10 Daily Habits	
1.	
2.	
3.	
4.	
5.	
6.	
7.	
8.	
9.	
10.	

Goals for Today	
1.	
2.	
3.	
4.	
5.	
6.	
7.	
8.	
9.	
10.	

Completions
1.
2.
3.
4.
5.

I Am Grateful For:
1.
2.
3.
4.
5.

Accomplishments
1.
2.
3.
4.
5.

Daily Biz Points

Goal	Act	%	Action
			Total

Requests Made
1.
2.
3.
4.
5.
6.
7.
8.
9.
10.

10 Goals to Reach in the Next 90 Days

What are the goals you most want to set for yourself for the next 90 days?

Please select only those goals that you really want, not the ones you should, could, oughta, or might want. Look deep inside, write down your 10 personal and professional goals, and discuss these with your coach. When you set the right goals for yourself, you should feel excited, a little nervous, and ready and willing to go for them!

Don't select the goals you historically have chosen but never reached, unless you're in a much better position to reach them now.

Start Date	Finish Date	The Specific Measurable Goal	Completed
		1.	
		2.	
		3.	
		4.	
		5.	
		6.	
		7.	
		8.	
		9.	
		10.	

Please develop a three-step action plan or strategy for each goal and fine-tune this with your coach.

What are the personal or professional benefits to you of accomplishing these goals?

Clean Sweep Program

Summary

You have more natural energy when your environment, health and emotional balance, money, and relationships are all operating at a high level.

The **Clean Sweep** program consists of 100 items that, when completed, give you the vitality and strength you want.

The program can be completed in less than one year.

Instructions

There are four steps to completing the Clean Sweep program.

Step 1: Answer each question.

If true, check the box. Be rigorous; be a hard grader. If the statement is sometimes or usually true, please *do not* check the box until the statement is virtually always true for you. (No credit until it is really true!) If the statement does not apply to you or will never be true for you, check the box. (You get credit for it because it does not apply or will never happen.) You may change any statement to fit your situation better.

Step 2: Summarize each section.

Add up the number of True boxes for each of the four sections and write those amounts where indicated. Then add up all four sections and write the current total in the box on the front of this form.

Step 3: Color in the checklist.

Always work from the bottom up. The goal is to have the entire chart filled in. In the meantime, you will have a current picture of how you are doing in each of the four areas.

Step 4: Keep playing until all boxes are filled in.

You can do it! This process may take 30 or 360 days, but you can achieve a Clean Sweep! Use your coach or a friend to assist you. And check back once a year for maintenance.

Clean Sweep Program 100-Point Checklist

			Sections		
#	A	B	C	D
25				
24				
23				
22				
21				
20				
19				
18				
17				
16				
15				
14				
13				
12				
11				
10				
9				
8				
7				
6				
5				
4				
3				
2				
1				

Give yourself credit as you get points from the 100-point program. Fill in columns from the bottom up.

A. Physical Environment

Number of circles checked (25 max) _____

○ My personal files, papers, and receipts are neatly filed away.

○ My car is in excellent condition (doesn't need mechanical work, repairs, cleaning or replacing).

○ My home is neat and clean (vacuumed, closets clean, desks and tables clear, furniture in good repair, windows clean).

○ My appliances, machinery, and equipment work well (refrigerator, toaster, snowblower, water heater, toys).

○ My clothes are all clean and pressed, make me look great (no wrinkles, baskets of laundry, or torn, out-of-date, or ill-fitting clothes).

○ My plants and animals are healthy (fed, watered, getting light and love).

○ My bed and bedroom let me have the best sleep possible (firm bed, light, air).

○ I live in a home or apartment that I love.

○ I surround myself with beautiful things.

○ I live in the geographic area I choose.

○ There is ample and healthy light around me.

○ I consistently have adequate time, space, and freedom in my life.

○ I am not damaged by my environment.

○ I am not tolerating anything about my home or work environment.

○ My work environment is productive and inspiring (synergistic, with ample tools and resources, and with no undue pressure).

○ I recycle.

○ I use non-ozone-depleting products.

○ My hair is the way I want it.

○ I surround myself with music that makes my life more enjoyable.

○ My bed is made daily.

○ I don't injure myself or bump into things.

○ People feel comfortable in my home.

○ I drink purified water.

○ I have nothing around the house or in storage that I do not need.

○ I am consistently early or easily on time.

B. Health and Emotional Balance

Number of circles checked (25 max) _____

○ I use caffeine (chocolate, coffee, colas, tea) less than three times per week, total.

○ I rarely eat sugar (less than three times per week.).

○ I rarely watch television (less than five hours per week).

○ I rarely drink alcohol (less than two drinks per week).

○ My teeth and gums are healthy (have seen a dentist in the last six months).

○ My cholesterol count is healthful.

○ My blood pressure is healthful.

○ I have had a complete physical exam in the past three years.

○ I do not smoke tobacco or other substances.

○ I do not use illegal drugs or misuse prescribed medications.

○ I have had a complete eye exam within the past two years (glaucoma check, vision test).

○ My weight is within my ideal range.

○ My nails are healthy and attractive.

○ I don't rush or use adrenaline to get the job done.

○ I have a rewarding life beyond my work or profession.

○ I have something to look forward to virtually every day.

○ I have no habits that I find to be unacceptable.

○ I am aware of the physical or emotional problems or conditions I have, and I am now fully taking care of all of them.

○ I consistently take evenings, weekends, and holidays off and take at least two weeks of vacation each year.

○ I have been tested for the AIDS antibody.

○ I use well-made sunglasses.

○ I do not suffer.

○ I floss daily.

○ I walk or exercise at least three times per week.

○ I hear well.

C. Money

Number of circles checked (25 max) _____

○ I currently save at least 10 percent of my income.

○ I pay my bills on time, virtually always.

○ My income source or revenue base is stable and predictable.

○ I know how much I must have to be minimally financially independent, and I have a plan to get there.

○ I have returned or made good on any money I borrowed.

○ I have written agreements and am current with payments to individuals or companies to whom I owe money.

○ I have six months' living expenses in a money market–type account.

○ I live on a weekly budget that allows me to save and not suffer.

○ All my tax returns have been filed, and all my taxes have been paid.

○ I currently live well, within my means.

○ I have excellent medical insurance.

○ My assets (car, home, possessions, treasures) are well insured.

○ I have a financial plan for the next year.

○ I have no legal clouds hanging over me.

○ My will is up to date and accurate.

○ Any parking tickets, alimony, or child support I owe is paid and current.

○ My investments do not keep me awake at night.

○ I know how much I am worth.

○ I am on a career or professional or business track that is or will soon be financially and personally rewarding.

○ My earnings are commensurate with the effort I put into my job.

○ I have no loose ends at work.

○ I am in relationships with people who can assist in my career or professional development.

○ I rarely miss work due to illness.

○ I am putting aside enough money each month to reach financial independence.

○ My earnings outpace inflation, consistently.

D. Relationships

Number of circles checked (25 max) _____

○ I have told my parents in the last three months that I love them.

○ I get along well with my sibling(s).

○ I get along well with my coworkers and/or clients.

○ I get along well with my manager and/or staff.

○ There is no one who I would dread or feel uncomfortable running across (in the street, at an airport, or at a party).

○ I put people first and results second.

○ I have let go of the relationships that drag me down or damage me. ("Let go" means to end, walk away from, state a problem with, handle, or no longer be attached to.)

○ I have communicated or attempted to communicate with everyone who I have damaged, injured, or seriously disturbed, even if it wasn't fully my fault.

○ I do not gossip or talk about others.

○ I have a circle of friends and/or family who love and appreciate me for who I am, more than just what I do for them.

○ I tell people how they can satisfy me.

○ I am fully caught up with letters and calls.

○ I always tell the truth, no matter what.

○ I receive enough love from people around me to feel good.

○ I have fully forgiven those people who have hurt or damaged me, whether it was deliberate or not.

○ I am a person of my word; people can count on me.

○ I quickly clear miscommunications and misunderstandings when they do occur.

○ I live life on my terms, not by the rules or preferences of others.

○ There is nothing unresolved with my past loves or spouses.

○ I am in tune with my wants and needs and get them taken care of.

○ I do not judge or criticize others.

○ I do not take personally the things that people say to me.

○ I have a best friend or soul mate.

○ I state requirements rather than complaining.

○ I spend time with people who don't try to change me.

Benefits

On the lines below, jot down specific benefits, results and shifts that happen in your life because you handled an item in the Clean Sweep program.

Date and Benefit

○ _____

○ _____

○ _____

○ _____

○ _____

○ _____

○ _____

Intellectual Property Notice

25 Secrets to Having the Life You Want

These are simple to learn, though not necessarily easy to achieve.

- ○ You will accomplish much more, much more easily if you take the time to first strengthen your personal foundation.

- ○ Come to see how perfect your life is today, even if it doesn't look or feel that way.

- ○ Proactively choose the type of energy that you want to use during your life.

- ○ Decide that you want to learn, continuously and forever. Then choose to learn how to learn.

- ○ Reorient your life around the gifts you have, no matter what they are.

- ○ Put your integrity first, your needs second, and your wants third.

- ○ Let yourself have it all, even if it feels like too much.

- ○ Before you create a future, resolve the past and perfect the present.

- ○ For an effortless life, get more than you need and far more than you deserve.

- ○ Invest 10 percent of your time in maximizing the other 90 percent.

- ○ Set your goals based on your values, not on coulds, woulds, wills, or shoulds.

- ○ Start on your path to financial independence even if it doesn't seem realistic.

- ○ Stop trying to change your behavior; instead, start shifting and evolving.

- ○ Triple your personal boundaries until your heart and spirit have the room they need.

- ○ Stop hanging around people who have less to lose than you do.

- ○ Stop waiting for anything. Instead, initiate 100 percent of the time.

- ○ Solve your problems, even if you didn't cause them.

- ○ Build a community of people who bring out your best without trying to.

○ Develop your spirituality in a way that feels right to you.

○ Educate your environment until it responds to you the way you like.

○ Have more than enough love in your life.

○ Let your vision set your goals and guide your life.

○ Expand your vocabulary so you can be and share yourself.

○ Get comfortable with change and chaos.

○ Get a coach.

The Success Process:
Ten Steps to Sustainable,
Fulfilling Success

○ Stop tolerating.
When you stop putting up with stuff, you will have more energy.

○ Get complete.
When you complete unfinished business and fully communicate, you will experience peace.

○ Simplify everything.
When you simplify your life, you will have much more space, and you will experience balance.

○ Strengthen your foundation.
When your needs are met and your personal foundation is solid, confidence replaces fear.

○ Orient around what matters.
When your life is oriented around what is most important to you, you will have clarity about what's next.

○ Experiment and improve continuously.
When you try new things or ways of thinking, you will become a more creative person.

○ Strengthen your strengths.
When you build on what you have, you will become more successful.

○ Stockpile.
When you build a reserve in every area, you can leverage more opportunities more quickly.

○ Integrate your life.
When you make sure your life's components fit together well, you will experience effortlessness.

○ Polish everything.
When you buff up every aspect of your life, you will feel even more proud to be a human being.

Chapter 7

Personal Foundation

Your personal foundation is the same as the foundation on a building. The deeper and stronger the foundation, the taller the structure can be built. You want your coachees to build a strong foundation for their life in order to live a life of authenticity that is aligned with their values and gets their needs met once and for all. With a strong personal foundation they will be able to deal with life on life's terms.

This chapter includes lists of information, tracking forms, and in-depth programs that will strengthen their foundation. It is designed to walk them through the core structure that forms the base from which they live their life.

The following sections are included in this chapter:

1. 25 Steps to a Strong Personal Foundation
2. Personal Foundation Program
3. 10 Daily Habits
4. 200+ Tolerations
5. What Am I Tolerating?
6. NeedLess Program
7. Tru Values Program
8. Reserve Index Program
9. Super Reserve Program

25 Steps to a Strong Personal Foundation

These steps are based on the Personal Foundation program.

- ○ Decide that you want a strong personal foundation.
- ○ A strong foundation is a choice. Want it.
- ○ Zap the tolerations.
- ○ Whatever you are putting up with eats away at your personal foundation.
- ○ Simplify your life dramatically.
- ○ Resolve unfinished business.
- ○ Identify and focus on your 10 daily habits.
- ○ Restore your integrity wherever it's broken.
- ○ Get your needs met. You can.
- ○ Handle the money. Period.
- ○ Treat your body like the temple it is.
- ○ Extend your boundaries until you are fully respected.
- ○ Raise your standards until you feel terrific.
- ○ Create reserves in all areas of your life.
- ○ Perfect the present, especially if it's not.
- ○ Strengthen your family. Heal if necessary.
- ○ Extend your community.
- ○ Start attracting instead of striving.
- ○ Select and reach your preferred living states.
- ○ Be well protected.
- ○ Choose your work so that you can be all of yourself.
- ○ Reorient your life around your values.
- ○ Become a problem-free zone.
- ○ Improve your attitude.
- ○ Invest in your life.
- ○ Thank the people who've made your life as rich as it is.
- ○ Choose your postfoundation steps.

Personal Foundation Program

Personal Foundation is a self-paced personal development program for the individual who wants more—much more—in life and understands the value of investing in oneself by strengthening what we call one's personal foundation.

A personal foundation has 10 parts—each distinct, yet interrelated—forming a solid base on which to develop a most wonderful, satisfying, and fulfilling life. Also, this program requires work on several other programs, notably Clean Sweep, Tru Values, and NeedLess.

The 10 areas that you will be working on are:
- Clearing unresolved matters
- Restoring your integrity
- Getting all of your needs met
- Extending your boundaries
- Raising your personal standards
- Eliminating what you are tolerating
- Coming from positives
- Resolving key family relationships
- Developing a supportive community
- Reorienting around your Tru Values

This is a fairly rigorous program. Take it one piece at a time. Your first score may be less than 10 or 20. Do not worry. You'll get to 70, 80, or 90+ sooner than you may think. Once started, the personal foundation process carries on its own momentum.

Instructions

There are four steps to completing the **Personal Foundation** program.

Step 1: Answer each question.

If the statement is true, fill in the circle. If not, leave it blank until you've done what it takes. Be rigorous; be a hard grader. If the item does not apply or will never be true for you, give yourself credit. (You may do this with up to five items.) Feel free to rewrite or reword up to five of the items in this program to better suit you, your needs, and your life.

Step 2: Summarize each section.

Add up the number of checked circles for each of the 10 sections and write those amounts where indicated. Then add up all 10 sections and write the current total in the progress chart provided.

Step 3: Color in the checklist.

If you have five circles filled in the Clearing Unresolved Matters section, color in the bottom five boxes of column A, and so on. Always work from the bottom up. The goal is to have the entire chart filled in. This will indicate how strong your personal foundation is. In the meantime, you have a current picture of how you are doing in each of the 10 areas.

Step 4: Keep playing until all the boxes are filled in.

This process takes between six months and five years, but you can do it! Use your coach to assist you. Check back quarterly for maintenance.

Progress Chart

Date	Points (+/−)	Score

Personal Foundation Program 100-Point Checklist

					Sections					
#	A	B	C	D	E	F	G	H	I	J
10										
9										
8										
7										
6										
5										
4										
3										
2										
1										

Give yourself credit as you get points on the 100-point program. Fill in columns from the bottom up.

A. Clearing Unresolved Matters

Past experiences—what we did, didn't do, should have done, did poorly or wrongly—are always with us in some way. In this section, you get clear of the past, doing what you can and letting go of the rest. You are not your past, yet you may still be living as if you are.

When clearing unresolved matters with the past, a person:
- Feels free of what he or she has done, yet responsible for it all
- Can be with themselves, as they are today, with no compensating
- Is able to set goals and reach them more easily

What happens when one isn't clear:
- One continues to repeat the past in some new way.
- One is reacting to life's unresolved matters instead of flowing with it.

The 10 Steps to Clearing Unresolved Matters

Number of circles checked (10 max) _____

- ○ Develop strong compassion for yourself: understand that we always do our best, even when we know we aren't.
- ○ Come to see how staying unresolved with someone or something in your past gives you unhealthy energy.
- ○ Come to recognize the six signs of being unresolved: regret, remorse, shame, anger, denial, continuing sadness.
- ○ Make a list of at least 50 things you have left unresolved and start working that list down until it is at zero!
- ○ Take the Clean Sweep program and work it until your score is above 95.
- ○ Make a list of the 10 actions you took against others or lies you told; then communicate them fully.
- ○ In your "clearing" conversations, expect nothing of the other person; it's about you clearing, not their response.
- ○ Start doing the maximum in work, in your tasks, conversations, and actions, so that nothing comes back to bite you for five years.
- ○ With someone you really trust, share the five things about you that you feel worst about and/or that are your biggest secrets.
- ○ Make five changes to prevent unresolved matters from occurring.

B. Restore Integrity

To be our best, we must be whole: that is, be responsible for our actions and inactions, respond fully to the lessons being offered to us, honor our bodies and our selves, and respect the realities of the physical universe.

When a person is "in integrity":
- He or she experiences fewer problems.
- Consistent feelings of peace, health, and emotional balance are present.
- He or she reacts to others very little.

What happens when one is "out of integrity":
- Disturbances occur regularly.
- Others are blamed, criticized; one reacts a lot to others.

The 10 Steps to Restoring Integrity Wholeness

Number of circles checked (10 max) _____

- ○ Make a list of the 10 ways you are currently not in integrity.
- ○ Get to the source of each and every item; resolve all fully.
- ○ Dedicate yourself to start living in integrity, as you see it.

○ Let go of at least 10 shoulds, coulds, woulds, oughts, and wills.
○ Involve a coach or other strong, able person to help you.
○ Start getting 50 percent more reserve than you feel you need.
○ Get your score up to 95+ on the Reserves Index program.
○ Stop hanging out with people who are not the best models.
○ Eliminate adrenaline and other unhealthy rushes in your life.
○ Let go of everything that you know is not good for you.

C. Get Your Needs Met

We know we all need air, water, shelter, and food—these are our physical needs. But what about our personal needs? These are things we must have to be ourselves but somehow have not been able to get enough of. Now, it is possible to get enough.

When a person is getting their needs fully met:
- He or she has room and love for other people; there is no competing.
- He or she has a dramatic sense of self-confidence without arrogance.
- Wants naturally decrease: There are no compulsions or musts.

What happens when one's needs are not met:
- Much time is wasted trying to get needs partially met.
- One attracts needy people.

The 10 Steps to Getting Your Needs Met

Number of circles checked (10 max) _____

○ Identify your top four personal needs using the NeedLess program.
○ Ask four special people to each meet one need fully.
○ Train, manage, and coach them to do so until it is done right.
○ Understand that personal needs are fully satisfiable.
○ Set up a SASS (see NeedLess) for each of your four needs.
○ Understand that people who love you will meet your needs.
○ See the difference between neediness and needs satisfaction.
○ When it is true, assert that your personal needs are met.
○ Extend a boundary that will help you satisfy two needs.
○ Ask three friends to tell you what they see your needs to be.

D. Extend Boundaries

Boundaries are imaginary lines we establish around ourselves to protect our souls, hearts, and minds from the unhealthy or damaging behavior of others. It is recommended that you extend your boundaries at least two or three times beyond where they are currently.

When a person has healthy boundaries:
- Fear diminishes significantly; trust is rarely an issue.
- Willing, healthy family members and true friends respect the person.
- The person starts growing more emotionally and developmentally.

What happens when a person's boundaries are weak:
- The person attracts needy, disrespectful people into his or her life.
- The person wastes energy keeping life going.

The 10 Steps to Having Extensive Boundaries

Number of circles checked (10 max) _____

- ○ Understand that you need to dramatically extend your boundaries.
- ○ Be willing to educate others how to respect your new boundaries.
- ○ Be relentless, yet not punitive, as you extend boundaries.
- ○ Make a list of the 10 things that people may no longer do around you, do to you, or say to you.
- ○ Sit down with each person involved and share with them your process; get an agreement to honor you.
- ○ Require that every single person in your life is always unconditionally constructive in every single comment to you: no more digs, make-funs, deprecating remarks, criticisms—no matter who or what or the situation!
- ○ Have and use a four-step plan of action whenever someone violates your boundaries: Inform them what they are doing, implore that they stop immediately, require that they stop, walk away without any snappy or get-even comments.
- ○ Make a list of 10 ways you are violating others' boundaries.
- ○ Stop violating the boundaries on that list.
- ○ Reward and congratulate those who are respecting boundaries.

E. Raise Standards

Personal standards refer to the behavior and actions you are willing to hold yourself to. You'll find as you work on the first four areas of the personal foundation program that you'll much more easily expect (and enjoy) more of yourself and of your behavior.

When people have and honor high standards:
- They feel very, very good about themselves, and others, too.
- They become irresistibly attractive to high-quality people.
- They don't get near people or situations that cause problems.

What happens when one's standards are too low:
- One continues to operate "below the line" emotionally.
- Self-esteem drops; self-worth is questioned.

The 10 Steps to Raising Personal Standards

Number of circles checked (10 max) _____

- ○ Make a list of 10 people you admire. Identify their admirable qualities, natural behavior, and how they handle tough situations and people. What standards could you raise that would make you more like them, yet still be you, today?
- ○ Start being unconditionally constructive every single time you open your mouth, yet still say all you need to say.
- ○ Stop spreading gossip, good or bad, about anyone.
- ○ Let go of the standards you believe you should have; make a list of the 10 standards you most want and are ready for today.
- ○ Understand that standards are a choice, not a requirement.
- ○ Fully respond to everything that occurs in your space; assume you had something to do with it, but don't take the blame. Just handle it and raise your standards so it doesn't happen again.
- ○ Always put people and relationships ahead of results.
- ○ Always put your integrity first, needs second, and wants third.
- ○ Understand that others are right, and so are you.
- ○ Always maintain a reserve of time, money, love, and wellness.

F. Stop Tolerating

Humans tolerate a lot. Often, we're taught not to complain, to accept that life is difficult, not to rock the boat, to go along with others, to be grateful for what we have, to be understanding. Not bad advice, but we can still stop tolerating what is bugging us!

When people have stopped tolerating:
- They are happier, more fun to be around.
- They have extra energy to express their values versus their egos.
- They have the edge: they step over nothing.

What happens when they tolerate?
- They and their work become mediocre; they are tired.
- Natural creativity is squashed.

The 10 Steps to a Toleration-Free Life

Number of circles checked (10 max) _____

- ○ Understand that putting up with things is good for no one.
- ○ Make a list of 10 things you are tolerating at home.
- ○ Make the requests or take the actions to eliminate these items.
- ○ Make a list of 10 things you are tolerating at work.
- ○ Take the actions to eliminate these items.
- ○ Understand that you're getting juiced (negatively energized) by tolerating things.
- ○ Be focused on being toleration free.
- ○ Stop complaining; instead, make a strong request.
- ○ Invest $1,000 to handle the tasks or chores that pain you.
- ○ Do steps 1–9 again after you've done them once!

G. Come from Positives

There is a wonderful feeling that comes from making the shift from focusing on the problems in life to realizing that life is pretty good. This shift may take time, development, and a high score on the Personal Foundation program, but you'll get there! We promise!

When people come from a positive place in life:
- They still live in reality but choose to live a better way.
- They create more positive things happening.

What happens until one makes this shift:
- Nothing is good enough, especially oneself.
- Problems are attracted, like bees to honey.

The 10 Shifts to Make to Come from This Place

Number of circles checked (10 max) _____

- ○ From feeling that one doesn't have enough to being enormously grateful, always
- ○ From having problems to being a problem-free zone
- ○ From just getting by to having a healthy reserve of time, love, money, and space
- ○ From fighting, resisting, and denying the circumstances, problems, and disturbances in life to realizing that you had a lot to do with whatever is happening
- ○ From doubting yourself to trusting your inklings and intuition
- ○ From being complacent to making the choice to be fully alive

○ From being passive and waiting to always initiating, being at cause, and creating your life
○ From putting others first to becoming healthfully selfish
○ From talking or being "about" life to being actively "for" life
○ From thinking you're alone to developing a relationship with God, self, spirit, soul (or whatever term you wish)

H. Strengthen Family

Family, whether biological or chosen, is an important part of our personal foundation. Why? Because we need to know we belong, that we are loved, that we can afford to take risks in life because we know there are key people behind and with us.

When a person has a strong family:
- More needs are met, automatically.
- Values are expressed more often.

What happens if one doesn't have a strong family:
- One doubts oneself more often.

The 10 Steps to Strengthening Your Family

Number of circles checked (10 max) _____

○ I understand that families are people, not perfect, probably learning how to be better, not there to give me everything I deserve or need; they need love and support from me.
○ I've done everything possible to restore any family relationships that hurt me. It is okay with me not to spend time with family members who pain me.
○ I have owned up to my role in problems between me and other family members.
○ I operate from choice versus obligation or duty when doing things for my family.
○ I have nothing negative or unresolved with any of my children.
○ I have nothing negative or unresolved with my spouse or mate.
○ I have nothing negative or unresolved with an ex.
○ I have nothing negative or unresolved with a parent.
○ I have nothing negative or unresolved with a relative.
○ I have nothing negative or unresolved with a sibling.

I. Strong Community

Nothing worth doing is worth doing alone. Given that, it helps to have a strong personal and professional community: people you can share your love, life, dreams, and concerns with at a level of intimacy once reserved for family.

When people have a strong community:
- They are well-rounded and well-connected; they have a reserve in case of trouble.
- It expands their personal and professional horizons.
- They move in new, more rewarding directions.

What happens if one doesn't have a community:
- One relies excessively on family members to meet needs.
- One misses out on opportunities for personal or professional growth.

The 10 Steps to Developing a Community

Number of circles checked (10 max) _____

- ○ I have a best friend.
- ○ I have a soul mate.
- ○ I have at least 10 social friends who I enjoy.
- ○ I have a successful professional network of at least 25 folks.
- ○ I contribute daily (in some way) to people in my community.
- ○ I am loved by people in my community.
- ○ My friends are happy and healthy; they don't "need" me.
- ○ I feel good enough about myself to be part of a community.
- ○ I actively seek out people whose company I enjoy.
- ○ I can and do say no to people who want to be a part of my community but with whom I do not feel comfortable.

J. Reorient on Values

As you strengthen your personal foundation, you'll find yourself having a lot more time, energy, and space in your life. What should you do with this? Start fully expressing yourself by setting goals based on your Tru Values.

When people orient around their values:
- Goal setting is easier and goals are reached more quickly.
- Their life purpose or vision comes to them clearly.
- Fewer distractions occur; life is simple but rich.

What happens until one does this:

- They are frustrated in the area of goals and lack a strong reference point in life.
- Their goals, wants, and ideas keep changing.

The 10 Steps to Fully Expressing Your Values

Number of circles checked (10 max) _____

- ○ Read through and complete the Tru Values program worksheet.
- ○ Understand that you are your Tru Values and that expressing these values is what will make you feel fulfilled in life.
- ○ Understand that goals are more fun when linked to your values.
- ○ Identify 10 key Tru Values: set one goal to match each value.
- ○ Let go of goals that can't be linked to one of the 10 Tru Values (unless they strengthen your personal foundation).
- ○ Begin working on each of these 10 goals immediately.
- ○ Reach each of these 10 goals.
- ○ Identify your number one value: your key value.
- ○ Raise a personal standard through the roof in order to help you more fully orient around your key value.
- ○ Discover your life purpose as expressed by your number one value.

Intellectual Property Notice

This material and these concepts are the intellectual property of Coach U, Inc. You may not repackage or resell this program without express written authorization and royalty payment. The exception is that you may deliver this program to single individuals without authorization or fee. If you lead a workshop or develop or deliver a program to a group or company based on or including this material or these concepts, authorization and fees are required. You may make as many copies of this program as you wish, as long as you make no changes or deletions of any kind.

10 Daily Habits

Write down your 10 daily habits in the space provided and fill in the box underneath each day of the month that corresponds with the habit(s) you completed that day.

Habits	Mon.	Tues.	Wed.	Thurs.	Fri.	Sat.	Sun.
1.							
2.							
3.							
4.							
5.							
6.							
7.							
8.							
9.							
10.							

Wins for the Month

1.	11.	21.
2.	12.	22.
3.	13.	23.
4.	14.	24.
5.	15.	25.
6.	16.	26.
7.	17.	27.
8.	18.	28.
9.	19.	29.
10.	20.	30.

200+ Tolerations

Here's an idea list of things to stop tolerating.

- Not enough storage space for all my office files
- A desk full of stacks of papers
- Peeling wallpaper
- A partner who is not unconditionally constructive with my child or children
- Being overweight
- A web page that needs updating
- Hair that doesn't look good
- A guest bedroom that needs cleaning up (it looks like a storage room)
- A partner's messy office
- A kitchen that needs a dishwasher (and it shouldn't be me)
- Not enough time scheduled for dreaming
- Not enough time spent in the garden
- Not setting time aside to meditate
- Not saving money every month
- Not getting paid on time by all of my clients
- Clients who cancel appointments at the last moment
- Excessive clutter
- Storage shed that is so full you can't get into it
- Investments that should be reevaluated but haven't been
- Needing a water purifyer
- Solar panels on the roof that need fixing
- House walls that need painting
- Kitchen floor that needs new tile
- Not having a spare key for the car
- Not having a well pump for the well
- The fact that I must park four blocks from work
- The no-leadership style of my boss
- A half-finished kitchen
- Tripping over my dog's toys throughout the house
- Having to get up each morning before the sun rises
- Evening telephone solicitations
- Limited trunk space in my car
- Mortgage and car payments
- Negative attitudes of people with whom I work
- Needy relatives
- Poor customer service and inadequate responses from vendors
- Eating too much sugar and salt
- Low levels of reserves
- Too many possessions that need to be cleaned
- A backyard that is an eyesore
- A constant need for home maintenance and repairs
- The invasiveness of e-mail and the Internet

- People or institutions that don't return my calls
- My lack of creative outlet
- Being part of a profession whose goals and standards I can no longer relate to
- Knowing all my debt will not be paid off for another 10 years
- Inadequate retirement fund
- Demands on my time by my children
- A former spouse who does not contribute time or money to raising our children
- The insanity of television newscasts
- Not having replacement belts for my vacuum cleaner
- Mildew in the grout of the tiles in my shower
- Mildew on the plastic shower curtain
- A crack in the sealer around the base of the shower
- The outdated or broken tile in the bathroom
- Missing lights on the medicine cabinet
- Spiderwebs in the corners
- Stuff on top of my fridge that has not been put away since I had that Christmas party 10 years ago
- The dog hair that shows up somewhere else the minute I clean it up
- Keeping the end table by my chair cluttered in order to put my coffee cup on it because if it's cleaned off the cat will lie on it, leaving no room for my coffee cup
- Cat food on the kitchen table because it's the only surface the dog won't get to
- New slipcovers that aren't quite the right shade
- An area rug that doesn't match the living room
- Thirty-year-old wall-to-wall carpeting that resists cleaning attempts
- A dining room table currently covered with stuff not related to dining
- Whites that have yellowed because of hard water
- A humidifier that needs a new filter to work properly
- An inherited chest of drawers that has a broken piece of veneer
- Fixing one toleration by putting up a window shade only to have it become a new toleration because it doesn't fit properly
- A cat that lies on my wrists when I'm working on the computer
- A living room window that is cracked and so dirty I can't see out of it when the sun is shining
- Having a nice attic but not being able to get into it because the steps are falling apart
- Cleaning supplies that won't fit under the sink
- Spending eight hours a day in a room with no window
- A coworker who has more tolerations than I do and spends all day talking about them
- Being the office dumping ground because I'm such a good listener
- Having a sugar and caffeine addiction
- Taking antidepressants and experiencing more severe PMS symptoms than before
- Taking antidepressants and gaining weight because I can't seem to care about changing my eating habits any more
- Wearing only what's comfortable even if I don't like the way I look
- Squirrels getting in the bird feeder
- Having gotten very good at acting patient and hating every minute of it

- ○ Not making time for art or music or crafts
- ○ Water stains on the walls
- ○ A roof that is only half reshingled
- ○ Rusty iron porch railings
- ○ Trim on the house that needs to be painted
- ○ House that needs to be repainted
- ○ Being deep in debt with no end in sight
- ○ Not having a coach because I can't afford one
- ○ Not being able to do much about most of my tolerations because they need money to be resolved
- ○ Not having a nice stereo
- ○ Having a saddle and riding boots and no horse
- ○ Loving to travel and not knowing when I'll next be able to take a trip somewhere
- ○ Not being able to come up with a concrete way to describe what I'm doing as a coach
- ○ Having so many talents and interests that I'm constantly being pulled in lots of directions
- ○ Being very good at maintaining acquaintances but having few close friends
- ○ Not knowing how to build a network or not being able to figure it out in a way that isn't too overwhelming
- ○ Being easily overwhelmed and trying to act like I'm not
- ○ Being surrounded by people that think following your dreams is a needless, self-indulgent activity
- ○ Throwing away money on things I don't really need or use
- ○ Being from and living in a community where it's ingrained in the collective consciousness that the more you're tolerating, the more righteous you are
- ○ Hating the way animals are processed for food and yet not being able to give up eating beef because it's comfort food
- ○ Fearing that if I move to someplace I love to visit, it will be ruined forever
- ○ Knowing that I'm the only reliable sibling and that when the time comes that my parents need to be cared for, it's all going to fall on me
- ○ Knowing I can't afford to move anywhere even if I wanted to
- ○ Knowing that techniques like affirmations, self-hypnosis, and guided imagery work for me but still not practicing them
- ○ Not having 20 clients that are like my one wonderful client who will pay me $200 a month (or more)
- ○ Not having a garage for my car
- ○ Large parts of my lawn being covered in weeds
- ○ Writing a volunteer weekly column for the local newspaper for months, wanting to be paid for it now, and not knowing what to do about it
- ○ The fact that my laptop computer has needed a new battery for months
- ○ Having boxes of things that need to be donated but that I haven't taken to the donation center
- ○ Being so intent on being true to myself that it gets in my way
- ○ Not having enough time to read and understand all that I want to
- ○ Believing things that people say when I know they are not true for me
- ○ Spending 95 percent of my waking hours struggling with frustration of some sort or another

○ Being hungry but not wanting to stop what I am doing to get something to eat
○ Having more books than bookshelves
○ Working at a job I don't enjoy
○ Having friends who are almost all 10 to 20 years older than I am
○ Not knowing how to ask for space from people without getting snippy because I've waited too long to ask
○ Having health insurance that doesn't pay for massage therapy or other alternative therapies
○ Having lower back problems from sitting in a nonergonomic chair all day
○ Having one of those combination copier/scanner/answering/fax machines when all I really need is a flatbed scanner
○ Having someone in my life who always tries to tell me what to do
○ Not knowing how to tell someone in my life to stop hurting my feelings without hurting his or her feelings
○ Feeling that if my parents died tomorrow, it would be catastrophic for me, even though I think I've been trying to plan ahead
○ Living in an uninsulated house in a place where it gets really hot or really cold
○ Being designated the keeper of the peace in the family
○ Being really sentimental
○ Having a poorly designed kitchen
○ Having a neat-looking 1950s stove or oven, only part of which works
○ Being crabby a lot
○ Not having a friend in the same town that I can just call up on the spur of the moment to go out with to do something
○ Feeling like I don't really have time to do things that are just for fun
○ Living too far away from places I enjoy visiting: museums, specialty shops, like-minded organizations, but not wanting to move
○ Living with a constant inner sense of deep frustration
○ The lack of sunlight in winter
○ Fear of ice on the sidewalks
○ Living in a dangerous area
○ Beating myself up because I can't seem to apply all the things I know to myself
○ Not getting enough deep belly laughing every day
○ Having brains and talent but not knowing of any means of making a living from them
○ Feeling victimized and helpless and hating myself when I see others being victims too
○ Experiencing lots of synchronicity with tiny things every day, but not with the big important things
○ Not having a life plan that seems doable
○ Forty-year-old carpet in my bedroom and a mismatched bedroom set
○ The pile of stuff on top of the dresser that I can't seem to throw away
○ Not having organized Christmas decorations
○ A brown splotch on the wall from where I killed an insect
○ Having insects show up every now and then high on my bedroom walls where I can't reach them
○ Having insect invasions every summer
○ Visible dust collected on the top of the ceiling fan in the bedroom
○ Not being able to see my clock or radio without my glasses

○ A partner who chews food noisily
○ A partner who hates where we live
○ No table light in my bedroom
○ No reserve of income
○ Not taking a holiday every year
○ Not visiting friends or family as often as I'd like to
○ Having old, worn-out shoes
○ A car that needs washing
○ A back bumper that needs replacing
○ Clothing of dissatisfying quality
○ Living on a noisy main road
○ Not having a strong community
○ No recreation in my life
○ Not going dancing regularly
○ Underselling myself
○ Shelves waiting to go up
○ New light fittings waiting to go up
○ Cupboard door hanging off
○ Sock drawer broken
○ Upstairs room still waiting to be upgraded
○ A kitchen that has room only for one person at a time
○ Carpet that needs cleaning
○ Insufficient income
○ Few visitors to the house
○ Weak networks
○ No fun opportunities
○ Credit card debt
○ Lack of discipline in myself
○ An echo in my phone line
○ My spouse's tone of voice with me
○ A client who changes appointments frequently
○ Too much e-mail
○ Clothing that doesn't complement my body shape
○ My frying pan–everything sticks
○ A phone headset that doesn't fit my head or ear properly
○ A lack of consistent income
○ Telemarketing calls at inconvenient times
○ Cell phone battery that needs replacing
○ A stock of magazines and not enough time to read them
○ A lack of support in my local professional group
○ My tenant's late rent payments
○ A lack of closet space in my home
○ Too much television
○ A lack of communication with my spouse
○ Too much paperwork
○ A lack of an up-to-date business plan
○ Fleas on my pets
○ A lack of clients
○ Software that doesn't work

- ○ A messy studio/home/bedroom/other room
- ○ A web site that doesn't reflect me
- ○ Dandruff
- ○ Cooking dinner every night when I don't want to
- ○ People who go beyond the bounds of decency
- ○ A dent in the front door of my car
- ○ An overcrowded filing cabinet
- ○ Not having a car I enjoy driving
- ○ Feeling depressed and not taking enough action
- ○ Dissatisfaction with my sexual relationship with my partner
- ○ Unsorted boxes of stuff in my closet
- ○ Holding on to clothes I don't really like
- ○ Gophers tunneling under my new front lawn
- ○ Termite damage to my house
- ○ A floor that needs refinishing
- ○ A broken sun visor in my car
- ○ Holding on to some stocks that have lost me a lot of money
- ○ My fear of analyzing my investments and taking the steps I need to get on the right track
- ○ Doing without an office assistant even though I need one
- ○ Not getting enough sleep to feel rested
- ○ My attitude that I should be able to handle everything on my own, even though I can't
- ○ People who criticize me
- ○ Not making enough money to afford what I want
- ○ A garage so full of stuff I can hardly move around in it
- ○ Windows that need cleaning
- ○ A garden shed that is rusting and needs replacing
- ○ Mildew on my roses
- ○ Lack of flowers in front of the house
- ○ Bedroom furniture that is no longer up to my standards
- ○ A backyard that needs landscaping
- ○ Not working out at least three times a week
- ○ A neighbor's pet that poops in my yard

What Am I Tolerating?

Humans sure have learned how to tolerate a lot! We put up with, accept, take on, and are dragged down by people's behavior, situations, unmet needs, crossed boundaries, unfinished business, frustrations, problems, and even our own behavior.

You are tolerating more than you think. So what are you tolerating? Please take a couple of minutes to write down stuff you sense that you are tolerating. As you think of more items, add them to your list. Do you have to do anything about them? No, not really. Just becoming aware of and articulating them will bring them to the forefront of your soul and you'll naturally start handling, eliminating, fixing, growing through, and resolving these tolerations.

What Am I Tolerating?	
1.	16.
2.	17.
3.	18.
4.	19.
5.	20.
6.	21.
7.	22.
8.	23.
9.	24.
10.	25.
11.	26.
12.	27.
13.	28.
14.	29.
15.	30.

NeedLess Program

It is possible to have all of your needs met permanently. Now, that might make your life just a bit too effortless, but we hear that people find some rewarding way to fill up the time that is freed up when they are not chasing needs.

This three-step program is designed to be used in conjunction with a professional coach, but you can start the process by completing the steps outlined here.

It takes most people about a year to reach the 25-point level for all four needs. Make it a great time in your life. You needn't suffer as you get your needs fully satisfied.

Purpose of the Program

The purpose of the **NeedLess** program process is to help you to:

- Identify what your personal needs are
- Understand how to get your personal needs met
- Design an effective system to have them vanish

What are personal needs?

Personal needs (versus bodily needs such as water, food, and shelter) are those things we must have in order to be our best. One can get through life fairly well not having these needs met, but for an effortless, rewarding, and successful life, personal needs must be identified, addressed, and handled.

Many of us spend our lives trying (consciously or not) to get these needs met. At best, we treat the symptoms or get temporary relief from them. This is for two reasons: Most of us assume these needs will always be with us and that's just the way things are. This is not true.

It does take a special technique to handle personal needs once and for all. We call that the NeedLess process. Your professional coach can assist you to more fully understand the dynamic of needs and the steps to make them vanish.

Progress Chart

Date	Points (+/–)	Score

NeedLess Program 100-Point Checklist

Top Four Needs			
# 1. _____	2. _____	3. _____	4. _____
25			
24			
23			
22			
21			
20			
19			
18			
17			
16			
15			
14			
13			
12			
11			
10			
9			
8			
7			
6			
5			
4			
3			
2			
1			

Give yourself credit as you get points from the 100-point program. Fill in columns from the bottom up.

Instructions

Please read these instructions twice, and read them carefully to let the subtleties show themselves.

Step 1: Select 10 needs.

Read the list of needs and circle approximately 10 that resonate as a need for you. You are looking for a need—not a want, a should, a fantasy, or a wish. A need is something that must be met for you to be your best. Part of the first step is to tell the truth about what you actually need. This may be the first time you have ever admitted this to yourself. Some of these you will know innately. Others require some straight looking. Please be willing to "try on" words you might normally skip over. These may be hidden needs. If so, you may have one or more of the following reactions:

- "No, no, no; I don't want that to be a need."
- You can't get to the next word quickly enough.
- "If that were true, I'd have to change my life a lot!"
- You flush, blush, or shake when reading the word.

Now circle the 10 words you believe to be personal needs. Ask yourself: "If I had this, would I be able to reach my goals and vision without effort?" (Work yes, struggle no.)

Be Accepted	Approved	Be included	Respected	Permitted
	Be popular	Sanctioned	Cool	Allowed
	Tolerated			
To Accomplish	Achieve	Fulfill	Realize	Reach
	Profit	Attain	Yield	Consummate
	Victory			
Be Acknowledged	Be worthy	Be praised	Honored	Flattered
	Complimented	Be prized	Appreciated	Valued
	Thanked			
Be Loved	Liked	Cherished	Esteemed	Held fondly
	Be desired	Be prefered	Be relished	Be adored
	Be touched			
Be Right	Correct	Not mistaken	Honest	Morally right
	Be deferred to	Be confirmed	Be advocated	Be encouraged
	Understood			
Be Cared For	Get attention	Be helped	Cared about	Be saved
	Be attended to	Be treasured	Tenderness	Get gifts
	Embraced			
Certainty	Clarity	Accuracy	Assurance	Obviousness
	Guarantees	Promises	Commitments	Exactness
	Precision			

Be Comfortable	Luxury	Opulence	Excess	Prosperity
	Indulgence	Abundance	Not work	Taken care of
	Served			
To Communicate	Be heard	Gossip	Tell stories	Make a point
	Share	Talk	Be listened to	Comment
	Informed			
To Control	Dictate to	Command	Restrain	Manage
	Correct others	Be obeyed	Not ignored	Keep status quo
	Restrict			
Be Needed	Improve others	Be useful	Be craved	Please others
	Affect others	Need to give	Be important	Be material
	Be a critical link			
Duty	Obligated	Follow	Obey	Have a task
	Satisfy others	Prove self	Be devoted	Have a cause
	Do the right thing			
Be Free	Unrestricted	Privileged	Immune	Independent
	Autonomous	Sovereign	Not obligated	Self-reliant
	Liberated			
Honesty	Forthrightness	Uprightness	No lying	Sincerity
	Loyalty	Frankness	No censoring	No secrets
	Tell all			
Order	Perfection	Symmetry	Consistent	Sequential
	Checklists	Unvarying	Proper	Literalness
	Regulated			
Peace	Quietness	Calmness	Unity	Reconciliation
	Stillness	Balance	Agreements	Respite
	Steadiness			
Power	Authority	Capacity	Results	Omnipotence
	Strength	Might	Stamina	Prerogative
	Influence			
Recognition	Be noticed	Be remembered	Be known for	Regarded well
	Get credit	Acclaim	Heeded	Seen
	Celebrated			
Safety	Security	Protected	Stable	Fully informed
	Deliberate	Vigilant	Cautious	Alert, Guarded
Work	Career	Performance	Vocation	Press, push
	Make it happen	At task	Responsibility	Industriousness
	Be busy			

Step 2: Narrow your needs to four.

We all need a little of everything on this list. But we want you to pick the four personal needs from the ones you circled. You may wish to compare each of your 10 needs with each of the others and ask yourself, "Now, do I need X or Y? Which ones could I live well without? Which ones, when met, make the other ones not as important?" Choose your four personal needs and write them down on the top of the checklist provided.

Step 3: Create a system to get your needs met.

Now that you have your personal needs identified, you will want to design a way to have them all met, permanently. This satisfaction system has three parts, as described in the following sections.

Establishing Boundaries

A boundary is a line you draw all around you that permits only the behaviors of others that are acceptable and nourishing to you. You may set a boundary of not allowing anyone to hit you, yell at you, be critical of you, take advantage of you, not show affection, call you only when they need something, interrupt you when you are working, and the like. You may be permitting these behaviors now for some pretty good reasons. But there are no excuses or reasons to let anyone do anything to you that hurts you, distracts you, uses you, or commands your attention. You will want to establish a boundary that is much more than you actually need. Be rigorous with yourself on this one. You cannot get your needs met if you are unwilling to set significant boundaries, so no excuses. Be selfish on this one!

When you set a boundary, you are protecting your heart, your soul, and what we call self. So you cannot be your self without the protection provided by strong, healthy boundaries. The people who really care about you will honor these boundaries and will care for you more, but give everyone time to get used to them.

Getting a Selfish Automatic Sprinkler System

Once boundaries are identified and installed, the next step is to design what we call a Selfish Automatic Sprinkler System, or SASS. A SASS is just what the term implies. You want your need to be satisfied (watered) whether you're thinking about it or not (automatically). This takes a little creative work to put together—your professional coach has experience with this one and is a good person with whom to brainstorm.

SASS examples include getting friends to satisfy your need by saying or doing specific things you have designed for them to do, like calling you, including you, doing things for you (that you asked for), telling you how they appreciate you, and so on. You will want to be shameless in this process of designing and implementing a SASS. It is good to tell the people around you how they can satisfy your needs. Remember, it is only temporary, because when the SASS is operating properly, these needs vanish.

Raising Your Personal Standards

After you have started on boundaries and your SASS, begin to substantially raise your personal standards (PSs). These are the behaviors you hold yourself to in order to become a bigger person. Examples of PSs range from the obvious to the advanced: Don't steal, always tell the truth, speak straight, be unconditionally constructive, be responsible for how you are heard rather than what you say, don't smoke or abuse your body, always be early, avoid all adrenaline rushes.

Set PSs that are a stretch, but not ones that will cause you to fail. You will have plenty of time to upgrade them with the extra energy you receive as your needs become met.

NeedLess Program Checklist

Use this checklist to guide yourself through the program. Fill in the circle when you have *started* on the step. Fill in the square when you have *completed* the step. Fill in the appropriate box on the checklist provided when you have completed the step. Work these 25 steps in order.

Do this process for each of the four needs you've chosen as personal needs.

○ ❑   1. Select the personal needs, using the procedure described in step 1. Write in the needs at the top of the checklist provided.

○ ❑   2. Ask yourself, "Why is this need important enough to me to be a personal need?" Write down five specific reasons on a sheet of paper.

○ ❑   3. Ask, "Who am I when I get this need met? How do I act? What do I think about? What motivates me?" Write down five specific examples on a piece of paper.

○ ❑   4. Ask, "Who am I not when I don't get this need met? How do I behave? How do I feel about myself? About others? About life?" Write down five specific responses on a piece of paper.

○ ❑   5. Ask, "How well am I getting this need met? What am I doing in my life that permits this need to be satisfied to the point of its vanishing?" Write down five specific ways that you are currently satisfying this need.

○ ❑   6. Ask, "Where am I not getting this need met? What I am doing that restricts, dishonors, or does not give this need the room and nourishment it requires and deserves?" Write down five specific things you are doing that don't serve your needs.

○ ❑   7. Ask, "What three changes would I make in my life in order to fully meet and satisfy this need?" Write down the three specific (and probably large) changes to make in the next 90 days. Examples of changes: change jobs, face and handle something tough, stop smoking, start fully communicating, let go of duties, get special training, let go of the future, let go of draining people.

○ ❑   8. Make change #1—permanently.

○ ❑   9. Make change #2—permanently.

○ ❑ 10. Make change #3—permanently.

○ ❑ 11. Ask, "What are the three boundaries I can install to protect myself so that this need has a chance of getting met? What do I no longer permit others (or situations) to do to or with me?" List these on paper.

○ ❑ 12. Install each of these three boundaries to a degree greater than you need.

○ ❑ 13. Ask, "What are the three things that people must do for me to satisfy this need?" (This is your SASS.) Write these down on a piece of paper.

○ ❑ 14. Arrange for part one of your SASS.

○ ❑ 15. Arrange for part two of your SASS.

○ ❑ 16. Arrange for part three of your SASS.

○ ❑ 17. Ask, "What are the three high personal standards that I must honor in order for this need to vanish?" List these on paper.

○ ❑ 18. Honor high personal standard #1.

19. Honor high personal standard #2.
20. Honor high personal standard #3.
21. Ask, "What must I now upgrade in my life to have this need fully satisfied forever?" Come up with three substantial changes.
22. Make these changes.
23. Eliminate any residue or clean up anything left from this process.
24. Share this process with a friend and help them get started with it.
25. Throw a party to celebrate your new life.

Intellectual Property Notice

This material and these concepts are the intellectual property of Coach U, Inc. You may not repackage or resell this program without express written authorization and royalty payment. The exception is that you may deliver this program to single individuals without authorization or fee. If you lead a workshop or develop or deliver a program to a group or company based on or including this material or these concepts, authorization and fees are required. You may make as many copies of this program as you wish, as long as you make no changes or deletions of any kind.

Tru Values Program

Your values are the behavior and activities to which you are naturally drawn. Values are who you really are. This includes things like:

- Creating
- Contributing
- Adventure
- Beauty
- Teaching
- Spirituality

The **Tru Values** program helps you to understand values and discern your top four values, and it puts you on a path to honoring them.

This three-phase, 25-step process can take up to two years to complete—not because it is difficult, but because you have to handle other aspects of life in order to be able to distinguish the subtlety of values and then reorient your life around them. This takes time. To honor your values is to give yourself the ultimate gift.

It is recommended that you work through the *Clean Sweep* and *NeedLess* programs prior to or concurrently with the *Tru Values* program. Your values are not as clear when clouded by unresolved matters and unmet needs. It is also recommended that you work with a professional coach trained in values work. You can do this on your own, but you will complete this program more quickly and more fully with a trained coach who has completed the process himself or herself.

Purpose of Program

The purpose of the Tru Values program is to help you to:

- Identify what your true values really are
- Create and complete a values expression project
- Reorient your life around expressing these values

What Are Tru Values?

Values are things you do or that you find very attractive. When engaged in these activities, you feel most like yourself: well, connected, excited, glowing, and effortless. We like these things, but most of us lead lives that do not grant us the chance to do just these things. We may be too busy with responsibilities, unresolved matters, chasing unmet needs, just getting by, and so on. In order to honor your Tru Values, you will have to substantially alter and enhance your life to get the room you need to engage in this ideal life.

Many of us spend our lives trying (consciously or not) to honor these Tru Values. We find ourselves getting disturbed or frustrated, bored or complacent, wishing and hoping to have a better life. This better life is, among other things, based on your Tru Values.

Will you give yourself the best gift ever? Embark on this program and don't stop until you reach 100 points. Your professional coach can assist you in more fully understanding the dynamic of values and the steps to have them expressed and honored.

Progress Chart

Date	Points (+/–)	Score

Tru Values Program 100-Point Checklist

	Top Four Values			
#	1. _____	2. _____	3. _____	4. _____
25				
24				
23				
22				
21				
20				
19				
18				
17				
16				
15				
14				

#	1. _____	2. _____	3. _____	4. _____
13				
12				
11				
10				
9				
8				
7				
6				
5				
4				
3				
2				
1				

Top Four Values

Give yourself credit as you get points on the 100-point program. Fill in columns from the bottom up.

Instructions

Please read these instructions twice, and read carefully to let the subtleties show themselves.

STEP 1: Select 10 Values.

Read the list of values and circle approximately 10 that resonate as a value for you. You are looking for a value, not a want, a should, a fantasy, or a wish. A value is a must for you to be yourself. Part of the first step is to tell the truth about what you actually value or love to do with your time. This may be the first time you have ever admitted this to yourself. Some of these you will know innately. Others require some straight looking. Please be willing to "try on" words you might normally skip over. These may be hidden values; if so, you may have one or more of the following reactions:

- "No, no, no; that would be too much fun."
- "That's a silly value; I should have a better one."
- "If that were true, I'd have to change my life a lot."
- You flush, blush, or shake when reading the word.

Got the idea? Now circle the 10 words that you believe to be Tru Values. Ask yourself: "If I had this, would I be naturally turned on, without effort?" (Work yes, struggle no.)

Please choose your four Tru Values and write them on the 100-point checklist where indicated.

Adventure	Risk	Thrill	Danger	Speculation
	Dare	Gamble	Endeavor	Quest
	Experiment	Exhilaration	Venture	The unknown
Beauty	Grace	Refinement	Elegance	Attractiveness
	Loveliness	Radiance	Magnificence	Gloriousness
	Taste			
To Catalyze	Impact	Move forward	Touch	Turn on
	Free others	Coach	Spark	Encourage
	Influence	Stimulate	Energize	Alter
To Contribute	Serve	Improve	Augment	Assist
	Endow	Strengthen	Facilitate	Minister to
	Grant	Provide	Foster	
To Create	Design	Invent	Synthesize	Imagination
	Ingenuity	Originality	Conceive	Plan
	Build	Perfect	Assemble	Inspire
To Discover	Learn	Detect	Perceive	Locate
	Realize	Uncover	Discern	Distinguish
	Observe			
To Feel	Emote	To experience	Sense	To glow
	To feel good	Be with	Energy flow	In touch with
	Sensations			
To Lead	Guide	Inspire	Influence	Cause
	Arouse	Enlist	Reign	Govern
	Rule	Persuade	Encourage	Model
Mastery	Expert	Rule field	Adept	Dominate field
	Superiority	Primacy	Preeminence	Greatest
	Best	Outdo	Set standards	Excellence
Pleasure	Have fun	Be hedonistic	Sex	Sensual
	Bliss	Be amused	Be entertained	Play games
	Sports			
To Relate	Be connected	Family	To unite	Part of community
	To nurture	Be linked	Be bonded	Be integrated
	Be with			
Be Sensitive	Tenderness	Touch	Perceive	Be present
	Empathize	Support	Respond	Show compassion
	See			

Be Spiritual	Be aware	Be accepting	Be awake	Relate with God
	Devoting	Holy	Honoring	Be passionate
	Religious			
To Teach	Educate	Instruct	Enlighten	Inform
	Prepare	Edify	Prime	Uplift
	Explain			
To Win	Prevail	Accomplish	Attain	Score
	Acquire	Win over	Triumph	Predominate
	Attract			

Step 2: Narrow your values to four.

We all value a little of everything listed on this page. But we want you to pick the four Tru Values from the ones you circled. You may wish to compare each of your 10 values with each of the others and ask yourself, "Now, do I really prefer X or Y? Which ones aren't that intriguing to me any more? Which ones, when honored, make the other ones not as exciting?"

Step 3: Create a life that honors and expresses your values.

Now that you have your Tru Values identified, you will want to create a way to have them all expressed, forever. This process has three parts, described in the following sections.

Honor your values.

When you honor your values, you honor your self or higher self. Values are those activities you naturally engage in when your life is in great shape. Until this time, you may have been expressing (e.g., doing) your values but not honoring them. To honor your values means to create and live your life in such a way that there is nothing in the way of your living your values. This means a life of integrity, free of addictions or attachments, with all needs being met, free of unresolved past experiences, with a full and supportive community—like an ideal life.

People engage in this values process as a way to get a great life. Look for examples of the kind of changes you can expect in step 7. Choose three of these changes to begin fully honoring your values.

Express your Tru Values through a project.

Now that you've cleared the decks and upgraded your life so your values can play, it is time to come up with a fun project that gives your values a showcase—a way to get stimulated and used, a way to show yourself that living your values is both possible and fulfilling. (Fulfillment is the experience of life one has when values are honored and expressed.)

This project shouldn't have any shoulds about it. Don't pick one that will drive you crazy, one that you are not ready for (but "should be"), one that you think you should want but really don't. Rather, design a project that lets you play big or play well, effortlessly. Examples are in step 11 on the last page of this section. Design a project that brings out your best, naturally. Don't do a project in order to get something out of it. Do it because you enjoy it.

Align your goals with your values.

After finishing your values expression project, you are ready for the final phase—aligning your life goals with your values. In other words, being at the place in life where you can afford to set only those goals that honor or express your values. This assumes you're close to 100 on the Clean Sweep and NeedLess programs. But wow, what a place to be in life! The alignment steps are:

- Make a list of your 10 goals for this year.
- Make a list of your top 10 values.
- Match the goals with the values.

Note: The objective is to only have values-based goals this year. If you have a goal that does not fit with one of your top 10 values, either adapt the goal to fit the value or get rid of it and come up with another. Don't adapt the value to the goal. And only have one goal per value. You are using your values as the reference point in your life—not your goals. And that is what makes this process so exciting!

Tru Values Program Checklist

Use this checklist to guide yourself through the program. Fill in the circle when you have *started* on the step. Fill in the square when you have *completed* the step. Fill in the appropriate box on the checklist provided when you have completed the step. Work these 25 steps in order.

Do this process for each of the four values you've chosen as Tru Values.

○ ❑ 1. Select the Tru Value, using the procedure described in step 1. Write in the value at the top of the checklist provided.

○ ❑ 2. Ask yourself, "Why is this value important enough to me to be a Tru Value?" Write down five specific reasons on a sheet of paper.

○ ❑ 3 Ask, "Who am I when I am this value? How do I act? What do I think about? What motivates me?" Write down five specific examples on a piece of paper.

○ ❑ 4. Ask, "Who am I not when I am this value? How do I behave? How do I feel about myself? About others? About life?" Write down five specific responses on a piece of paper.

○ ❑ 5. Ask, "How well am I honoring or expressing this value? What am I doing in my life that permits this value to be free enough to express itself?" Write down five specific ways that you are currently honoring your values.

○ ❑ 6. Ask, "Where am I not honoring or expressing this value? What I am doing that restricts, dishonors, or does not give my values the room and nourishment they need and deserve?" Write down five specific things you are doing that don't serve your values.

○ ❑ 7. Ask, "What three changes would I make in my life in order to fully honor and express this value?" Write down the three specific (and probably large) changes to make in the next 90 days. Examples of changes: change jobs, face and handle something tough, stop smoking, start fully communicating, let go of duties, get special training, let go of the future, let go of draining people.

○ ❑ 8. Make change #1—permanently.
○ ❑ 9. Make change #2—permanently.
○ ❑ 10. Make change #3—permanently.
○ ❑ 11. Ask, "What is the project or goal that I could design that would be a full expression of this value?" Come up with the project. Examples of projects:
  - Run the New York marathon
  - Make $1,000,000 this year
  - Write a book
  - Go parasailing in the Alps
  - Throw a huge party
  - Make yourself stunning
  - Help 1,000 people out
  - Invent a product or process
  - Master a subject or field
  - Climb Mt. Rainier
  - Develop a community
  - Be hedonistic
  - Get on a spiritual path
○ ❑ 12. Outline and milestone the project into seven phases. Give each phase an assessable result or milestone with a deadline.
○ ❑ 13. Begin the project; complete phase 1.
○ ❑ 14. Complete phase 2.
○ ❑ 15. Complete phase 3.
○ ❑ 16. Complete phase 4.
○ ❑ 17. Complete phase 5.
○ ❑ 18. Complete phase 6.
○ ❑ 19. Complete phase 7. Tie up loose ends.
○ ❑ 20. Celebrate significantly for completing your Tru Values expression project. You'll know what to do.
○ ❑ 21. Ask, "How must I now upgrade my life to have this value fully honored and expressed throughout it?" Come up with five substantial changes.
○ ❑ 22. Make these changes.
○ ❑ 23. Align your top 10 goals for this year with your top 10 values using the procedures discussed in step 3.
○ ❑ 24. Share this process with a friend and help them get started with it.
○ ❑ 25. Throw a party to celebrate your new life.

Intellectual Property Notice

This material and these concepts are the intellectual property of Coach U, Inc. You may not repackage or resell this program without express written authorization and royalty payment. The exception is that you may deliver this program to single individuals without authorization or fee. If you lead a workshop or develop or deliver a program to a group or company based on or including this material or these concepts, authorization and fees are required. You may make as many copies of this program as you wish, as long as you make no changes or deletions of any kind.

Reserve Index Program

Having a strong reserve in the six areas of your life is an advanced step in your personal development process. In fact, you are much more able to discover and share your unique gift when this reserve has been established.

The **Reserve Index** consists of 100 items that, when achieved, give you the inner strength you want because you then will have more than you need, personally and professionally.

The index is designed to be used in conjunction with the Reserve program or with your professional coach.

Benefits

On the lines provided, jot down specific benefits, results, and shifts that happened in your life because you handled an item in the Reserve Index.

Date   **Benefit**

_____   _____

_____   _____

_____   _____

_____   _____

_____   _____

_____   _____

_____   _____

_____   _____

_____   _____

_____   _____

Instructions

There are five steps to completing the Reserve Index.

Step 1: Answer each question.

If true, check the circle. Be rigorous; be a hard grader. If the statement is sometimes or usually true, please do not check the circle until the statement is virtually always true for you; you get no credit until it is really true. If the statement does not apply to you, check the circle. If the statement will never be true for you, check the circle. You get credit for it because it does not apply or will never happen. You may also change any statement to fit your situation better.

Step 2: Summarize each section.

Add up the number of checked circles for each of the six sections and write those amounts where indicated.

Step 3: Fill out the bonus section.

Please fill in the specific things or areas in which you do not currently have a reserve but know you really want one in. Select ones that are not mentioned in the other 90 choices.

Step 4: Color in the checklist provided.

If you have nine checks in the Time and Space section, for example, color in the bottom nine boxes of column A, and so on. Always work from the bottom up. The goal is to have all sections filled in. In the meantime, you have a current picture of how you are doing in each of the six areas.

Step 5: Keep playing until all boxes are filled in.

You can do it! This process may take 30 or 360 days, but you can achieve a perfect score on the Reserve Index. Use your coach or a friend to assist you. And check back once a year for maintenance.

Progress Chart

Date	Points (+/−)	Score

Reserve Index Program 100-Point Checklist

				Sections			
#	A	B	C	D	E	F	G
15							
14							
13							
12							
11							
10							
9							
8							
7							
6							
5							
4							
3							
2							
1							

Give yourself credit as you get points on the 100-point program. Fill in columns from the bottom up.

Special Note

If your total score starts out at 20 or 30 out of 100, don't worry about it. This is a rigorous list, and it takes time and training to reach 100.

We feel it is worth devoting time and energy to this process: Doing whatever it takes to be at 100 on this index strengthens you so you can afford (financially, personally, and professionally) to develop and share the unique and special gift you are.

A. Time and Space

Number of circles checked (15 max) _____

- ○ My gas tank is always at least half full.
- ○ I don't do errands, ever.
- ○ I am completely free of anything that binds me.
- ○ I am always 10 minutes early and never rushed.
- ○ My closets are empty of all that I don't need now.
- ○ I always wear a seat belt.
- ○ All my clothes are pressed or at the cleaners.
- ○ My three key boundaries are always honored.
- ○ The first and last 30 minutes of my day are the perfect way to arise and retire.
- ○ I don't get stopped or off track for more than one hour.
- ○ I am free of all addictions and attachments.
- ○ I have a daily routine that is a joy.
- ○ I use a time management system, and I do not miss appointments or forget things.
- ○ I do not tailgate, run yellow lights, or exceed the speed limit. I always let other cars in.
- ○ I do not do my own laundry or housework.

B. Love and Attraction

Number of circles checked (15 max) _____

- ○ No one in my life thinks I should change.
- ○ I received 25 cards on my last birthday.
- ○ My circle of 10 closest friends are fully supported and loved.
- ○ I grant everyone I know and everyone I've never met a lifetime of absolute forgiveness.

○ I have received 10 letters of gratefulness from friends or colleagues in the last 90 days.

○ I attract people rather than going after them.

○ I know the 10 things I want for others.

○ I speak straight, always and appropriately. I don't hold back—even on the little stuff.

○ I am a key part of a community of like-minded people.

○ I do not react to people; I have lots of space.

○ I treat everyone extremely well, from clerk to spouse.

○ I put my relationships far ahead of results.

○ I can afford to have others be right; they are.

○ I have no expectations (no hidden needs) of my friends and family—I expect nothing from them.

○ I've given a personal and extraordinary gift to my circle of 10 in the last six months.

C. Money and Freedom

Number of circles checked (15 max) _____

○ I always have $100 in my pocket that I never use.

○ I save or invest 20 percent of what I make each month.

○ I invest 5 percent of my revenue in my own training.

○ I have one year's reserve that I don't touch.

○ I have six months' worth of household and office supplies.

○ I charge more for my services than I think I am worth.

○ I am earning a stream of passive income.

○ I know how much I need to retire or be financially independent and am on that plan.

○ I have no credit card debt or short-term debt.

○ I make extra principal payments on my mortgage.

○ I keep at least $5,000 in my checking account.

○ I pay the full training tuition or donation prior to the deadline.

○ I tip 25 percent when the service was awful and tell the server why.

○ I tithe 10 percent to church, charity, friends, or those who have made me successful.

○ I buy the brands I want; I buy the best.

D. Energy and Vitality

Number of circles checked (15 max) _____

○ I get a massage or other body work done monthly.

○ My blood work shows all normal range results.

○ I eat only the foods that nourish me.
○ People remark weekly how well I look or how I glow.
○ I am never ill.
○ I wouldn't even think of tolerating anything, any time, and I am beyond suffering about stuff.
○ I consistently underpromise and overdeliver.
○ Adrenaline never courses through my veins.
○ My need #1 (_____) is fully satisfied.
○ My need #2 (_____) is fully satisfied.
○ My need #3 (_____) is fully satisfied.
○ My Clean Sweep score is 100 out of 100.
○ I take four relaxing vacations per year.
○ I print out my monthly personal or business financial statement by the 15th of the next month.
○ At the end of the business day, I am energized; work and play are the same.

E. Opportunities and Momentum

Number of circles checked (15 max) _____

○ I am at the center of a very strong network.
○ I look forward to each evening.
○ I can call someone for a quick $10,000 loan.
○ My vision is simple and being realized.
○ My three standards are clear and honored.
○ I have what's called the "edge."
○ I have more than enough time to focus solely on my passions.
○ My basic message is crystal clear to all I meet.
○ I discern and tell people who they are.
○ I make huge, strong requests that are accepted.
○ I initiate: I do not hope or wait, ever.
○ I have the ideal life.
○ I am not attached to any result.
○ I can afford to make a million mistakes.
○ People include me in business deals and opportunities.

F. Source and Power

Number of circles checked (15 max) _____

○ My #1 value (_____) is fully honored.
○ My #2 value (_____) is fully honored.
○ My #3 value (_____) is fully honored.
○ I always maintain a strong sense of inner peace.

○ I no longer have to prove myself; I am enough.
○ I am certain I am at choice about my entire life.
○ I honor and respond immediately to my inner voice.
○ I have a strong and personal theme for this year.
○ I am unafraid. I am confident.
○ I act based on desire, not consequence.
○ Nothing hooks me.
○ I self-create and self-manage.
○ I trust a higher power (or myself).
○ I am content with myself; I don't need anyone else to feel healthy or whole.
○ I completely trust my judgment but often ask for others' input.

G. Bonus 10

Number of circles checked (10 max) _____

○ I have more than enough _____.

○ I have more than enough _____.

○ I have more than enough _____.

○ I have more than enough _____.

○ I have more than enough _____.

○ I have more than enough _____.

○ I have more than enough _____.

○ I have more than enough _____.

○ I have more than enough _____.

○ I have more than enough _____.

Intellectual Property Notice

Super Reserve Program

Getting more than you need is the first step to sustainable success. Wise people have a reserve of things—such as time, money, supplies, capacity, love, people, opportunities, and so on. But a really wise person builds a super reserve of such things. What's the difference between a reserve and a super reserve? With a super reserve you don't just have more than enough—you have more than enough to free your mind up to focus on more creative and productive pursuits than mere survival. Remember, we are all programmed first and foremost to survive—not to prosper. So the Super Reserve process is more than conspicuous consumption or a Fort Knox type of stockpiling. Rather, it is the responsible, wise thing to do if you want to make the most of what you have. An inordinate amount of our personal energy or bandwidth is spent being concerned about surviving. A super reserve quiets that fear and provides us with enough resources to be our best.

The **Super Reserve** program consists of 100 items that, when achieved, give you the freedom you want because you then will have much more than you need, personally and professionally.

The program is designed to be used in conjunction with the Reserve program or with your professional coach.

Benefits

On the lines provided, jot down specific benefits, results, and shifts that happened in your life because you handled an item in the Super Reserve program.

Date   **Benefit**

_____   _____

_____   _____

_____   _____

_____   _____

_____   _____

_____   _____

Instructions

There are four steps to completing the Super Reserve program.

Step 1: Answer each question.

If true, check the circle. Be rigorous; be a hard grader. If the statement is sometimes or usually true, please do not check the circle until the statement is virtually always true for you; you get no credit until it is really true. If the statement does not apply to you, check the circle. If the statement will never be true for you, check the circle. You get credit for it because it does not apply or will never happen. You may also change any statement to fit your situation better.

Step 2: Summarize each section.

Add up the number of checked circles for each of the ten sections and write those amounts where indicated.

Step 3: Color in the checklist provided.

If you have nine checks in the Home and Comfort section, for example, color in the bottom nine boxes of column 1, and so on. Always work from the bottom up. The goal is to have all sections filled in. In the meantime, you have a current picture of how you are doing in each of the ten areas.

Step 5: Keep playing until all boxes are filled in.

You can do it! This process may take 30 or 360 days, but you can achieve a perfect score on the Reserve Index. Use your coach to assist you. And check back once a year for maintenance.

Progress Chart

Date	Points (+/–)	Score

Reserve Index Program 100-Point Checklist

	Sections									
#	1	2	3	4	5	6	7	8	9	10
10										
9										
8										
7										
6										
5										
4										
3										
2										
1										
2										
1										

Give yourself credit as you get points on the 100-point program. Fill in columns from the bottom up.

1. Home and Comfort
Number of circles checked (10 max) _____

- ○ My home has plenty of extra room.
- ○ I have two times as much storage as I need.
- ○ I do not run out of clean clothes.
- ○ I have cozy sheets and bedding.
- ○ I receive plenty of physical touch.
- ○ My home is always clean and orderly.
- ○ My home has plenty of heat and/or air conditioning.
- ○ I have plenty of eating and kitchen utensils.
- ○ I have a special place to curl up.
- ○ I like every room in my house.

2. Car and Vehicles
Number of circles checked (10 max) _____

- ○ I have high-quality jumper cables.
- ○ I have AAA-Plus or a similar service.
- ○ I have a cell phone handy if necessary.
- ○ I have $100 hidden in my car.
- ○ I fill up before reaching a quarter tank.
- ○ My car's battery is super-strong.
- ○ My car accelerates quickly when necessary.
- ○ My car has antilock brakes and/or airbags.
- ○ My car is rated safe in collisions.
- ○ I have flares, a blanket, water, and a spare tire in my car.

3. Financial
Number of circles checked (10 max) _____

- ○ I have $25,000 in savings or a money market account.
- ○ I pay my bills early.
- ○ Most of my bills are paid electronically.
- ○ I can do wire transfer by phone or personal computer.
- ○ I have $500 in extra cash at home.
- ○ I have no credit card debt.
- ○ I invest 5 percent per year to develop myself.
- ○ 25 percent of my income is passive.
- ○ I am properly compensated at work.
- ○ I am on a clear financial independence track.

4. Safety and Care
Number of circles checked (10 max) _____

- ○ I know what to do if I am mugged.
- ○ I stay away from places that scare me.
- ○ I avoid people who will drain me.
- ○ I have plenty of smoke detectors.
- ○ I always use seat belts.
- ○ My home has deadbolts and an alarm.
- ○ My car has a remote entry system or remote key fob.
- ○ My investments don't worry me.
- ○ I practice safe sex (or I am monogamous).
- ○ I am aware who is around me at all times.

5. Energy and Vitality
Number of circles checked (10 max) _____

○ My cholesterol count is healthy.

○ I am not tired; I get plenty of sleep.

○ I eat very healthful, fresh foods.

○ I drink eight glasses of water daily.

○ I exercise three times per week.

○ I have eliminated stress.

○ I take at least four vacations a year.

○ I have something to look forward to each morning.

○ I have something to look forward to each evening.

○ I don't use caffeine or drugs.

6. Opportunity and Skills
Number of circles checked (10 max) _____

○ I am online (have web access).

○ I have my own web page or web site.

○ I am extremely confident, with no fear.

○ I have 203 years' worth of interesting work or projects lined up.

○ I ask for more than I need at work.

○ I have incredibly good judgment.

○ I have developed a special skill set or knowledge that is in high demand.

○ I am part of a successful network.

○ I invest in my skills and network.

○ I can take an idea and leverage it.

7. Space and Time
Number of circles checked (10 max) _____

○ I am always 10 minutes early.

○ I underpromise, always.

○ I easily say no, even if tempted.

○ I end the day quietly, with no TV.

○ I always let cars squeeze in.

○ I have an assistant to handle personal or business stuff I'd rather not deal with.

○ I don't speed when driving.

○ I always keep one to two free hours a day.

○ Nothing in life is draining me.

○ I don't jump at every opportunity.

8. Calamity Protection
Number of circles checked (10 max) _____

○ I have a 12-volt flashlight plugged in the car.

○ I back up my computer weekly.

○ I store backups offsite, monthly.

○ I have a second internet service provider when needed.

○ I have a list of my credit cards and account numbers.

○ I have photocopies of my driver's license, passport, social security card, and birth certificate.

○ My will is current and accessible.

○ I have ample medical insurance.

○ I have ample car, home, and liability coverage.

○ If I die, my family will be financially okay.

9. Supplies and Equipment
Number of circles checked (10 max) _____

○ I have a six-month supply of toilet paper.

○ I have a one-year supply of postage.

○ I have a one-year supply of detergents.

○ I have a two-year supply of vacuum bags.

○ I have a one-month supply of underwear.

○ I have 56K, ISDN, or cable internet access.

○ My computer has a minimum of five gigs of storage.

○ My computer is faster than I need.

○ My tools are of the best quality

○ I use an ergonomic keyboard.

10. Relationships
Number of circles checked (10 max) _____

○ My children show their love.

○ My spouse shows his or her love.

○ My attorney is super-sharp.

○ I treat everyone with great respect.

○ I have no bad relationships.

○ I know who to call for any problem.

○ I have someone I can share anything with and ask for personal help.

○ I know five very successful people.

○ My emotional needs are fully met.

○ I have a relationship with God/a higher power.

Chapter 8

Attraction

This chapter covers the laws of attraction. You attract that which you put out to the universe. The concept is to naturally pull things toward you rather than pushing them toward you, floating downstream versus fighting the current. You will struggle less and life will become effortless when you implement these concepts. Your coachees will benefit tremendously from becoming attractive.

Included in this chapter are the main principles, changes to make, step-by-step programs, enhancement programs, and purpose worksheets.

The following sections are included in this chapter:

1. 28 Attraction Principles
2. Fundamental Changes to Becoming Irresistibly Attractive
3. The Zen of Attraction
4. Irresistible Attraction Program
5. 100 Smiles Program
6. What Makes You Happy?
7. Quality of Life 100
8. My Personal Mission Statement
9. Life Purpose Worksheet
10. Life Purpose, Business Mission, and Legacy
11. Personal Path Program

28 Attraction Principles

○ **Become incredibly selfish.**
Without you, there is nothing, and attraction isn't possible.

○ **Unhook yourself from the future.**
Attraction works in the present, not in the future.

○ **Overrespond to every event.**
By overresponding instead of overreacting, you evolve.

○ **Build a super reserve in every area.**
Having enough is not nearly enough.

○ **Add value for the joy of it.**
When you add value because you enjoy it, people are naturally attracted to you.

○ **Affect others profoundly.**
The more you touch others, the more attractive you'll be.

○ **Market your talents shamelessly.**
If you're embarrassed about what you do well, you won't be very attractive.

○ **Become irresistibly attractive to yourself.**
If you don't feel irresistibly attractive to yourself, you will not attract others.

○ **Get a fulfilling life, not just an impressive lifestyle.**
A great life is attractive; a lifestyle is usually seductive.

○ **Deliver twice what you promise.**
When you consistently deliver more than was expected, new customers are drawn to you.

○ **Create a vacuum, which pulls you forward.**
Being pulled forward is attractive; pushing forward is not.

○ **Eliminate delay.**
Time is expensive; thus, time is very unattractive.

○ **Get your personal needs met, once and for all.**
If you have unmet needs, you'll attract others with unmet needs.

○ **Thrive on the details.**
Subtleties, details and nuances are more attractive than the obvious.

○ **Tolerate nothing.**
When you put up with something, it costs you. These are expensive and thus unattractive.

○ **Show others how to please you.**
Don't make them guess.

○ **Endorse your worst weakness.**
When you can accept and honor the worst part of yourself, you are more accepting of others.

○ **Sensitize yourself.**
The more you feel, the more you'll notice and respond to the many opportunities in the present.

○ **Perfect your environment.**
The attraction Operating System (OS) is a sophisticated system, which requires a first-class environment.

○ **Develop more character than you need.**
Integrity is not enough to become irresistibly attractive.

○ **See how perfect the present really is.**
Especially when it is clearly not.

○ **Become unconditionally constructive.**
High levels of respect are very attractive.

○ **Orient exclusively around your values.**
When you spend your days doing what fulfills you, you attract.

○ **Simplify everything.**
Abandoning the nonessentials leaves more room.

○ **Master your craft.**
Being the best at what you do is the easiest way to become successful and attractive.

○ **Recognize and tell the truth.**
The truth is the most attractive thing of all, however, it requires skills and awareness.

○ **Have a vision.**
When you can see what's coming you don't need to create a future.

○ **Be more human.**
When you are genuine, you are attractive.

Fundamental Changes to Becoming Irresistibly Attractive

Almost anyone can learn to apply the attraction principles and benefit measurably. But what if you wanted to push the envelope of attraction in order to achieve the maximum possible result? What would you have to do differently in your life to become that attractive? To answer this question, we have outlined the emotional, intellectual, spiritual, and lifestyle changes we feel would be helpful to you if you have an interest in making the most of attraction. Remember, what follows is only suggested; you will have your own set of spaces to move through on the attraction path.

Completely give up the notion of a predesigned future.

In other words, literally give up goals and the striving for a particular future. One of the attraction principles is to unhook from the future. Get to a place where the future has absolutely no appeal, seductive or otherwise. It may be disorienting, to say the least, given that most of us have always been goal oriented and driven to succeed, produce, and contribute. Try to get to where you would rather dance from event to event than attempt to make something happen.

Eliminate the to-do list and automate or delegate everything.

In other words, eliminate meetings and obligations—everything that's about the future. This probably sounds extreme, but it works. Each day get up and do exactly what comes to mind to do. This is probably not practical—or wise—for most, but try to simplify your life to the point that it becomes normal. There may be a point in your life when you return to a more traditional lifestyle, but when you do, you will probably still maintain this sense of inner freedom and choice.

Eliminate the need for external validation.

Get rid of the need to be heard and appreciated for what you are doing or how special you are. Eliminate the need for someone to validate your thinking. In other words, don't be motivated by externals such as recognition, the opinions or support of others, the possibility of acknowledgement, or even fame. That need for validation may slip into a dependence on others for motivation. Don't be guided by what would sell or be popular or what specific people need from you. Stay in touch with what your market wants and needs, so you are not out of the loop, but be driven by what intrigues you most. Assume that whatever you do is not going to be commercially viable or even of interest. Talk about space!

Accept even the most unacceptable people.

Don't criticize or judge people because of their faults. Try to accept people for their strengths without faking it. Have enough space (and a strong enough reserve or level of protection internally) to handle people who may drive you crazy. Don't take people personally. One of the benefits of developing a strong personal foundation is that you can handle difficult people without cost to yourself. This comes from having the reserve enough to care and be generous. The next level in this area would be to actually enjoy such people.

Trust your whims, and experiment continuously.

Whims, ideas, thoughts, and plans may cost you (emotionally or financially) more than they benefit you. Allow yourself to experiment freely until you find the skill, phrase, or technique that actually works well for you. Be aware of any unconscious decision to get to know yourself and the world by deliberately making mistakes and seeing what happens. Make progress on understanding your whims better. Note that whims are different from intuition and inklings.

Learn from your environment, and evolve from what occurs.

The attraction principle of overresponding to every event is a key one. In other words, becoming a super-learner is key to attraction because it accelerates the development of your mind, body, and senses, and it keeps you in the present, experiencing life instead of studying about life or success. Some call this just-in-time learning, but we are talking about a level beyond that where you are always learning yet not for any reason (just-in-time learning is usually task or result oriented). Continual evolution can be more interesting than mastering a narrow set of skills. Both are excellent, however, many people focus on improvement or skills and do not get the evolutionary things.

Find totally different sources of stimulation for your life.

Attraction depends on synchronicity, which results from increased flow. And increased flow depends on both stimulation and the reduction of blocks or resistance. You get both when you put yourself in very different environments, hang out with a different type of person or group, or get into situations for which you have no objective other than to be surprised or stimulated. These little lasers zap parts of you that you cannot normally get to in your process of becoming resistance-free. Begin reading books in different genres or playing games that have no practical value. Try shaking up your stagnant thinking—and yourself—thus radically changing stimulations.

Experiment with the notion of "absence of."

Read and understand the attraction-related section on the Zen of attraction. It's simply a collection of 14 suggestions about what to stop doing in life. Most are pretty radical and not necessarily practical, but they will be effective for you along your own attraction path. And to take this a step further, learn the difference between *absence of* and *freedom from*. *Freedom from* usually means you are trying to get away from something; *absence of* connotes that there is nothing there to get away from any longer. It is a key distinction and essential in the process of learning attraction, given that reducing or eliminating blocks or resistance is a key part of becoming more attractive.

Abandon beliefs and opinions.

Try on the idea that beliefs and attraction are not compatible. Something or someone either is or is not at any given time. What does your belief or opinion about it have to do with anything? After all, aren't opinions a way to define yourself and get a buy-in (or argument) from others? Instead, ask questions that stimulate instead of trying to get people to agree with you.

Carve out your own reality and personal operating system (POS).

Most of us use a version of our parents' POS, or we have adopted a popular POS off the shelf, whether it is cultural, geographic, religious, or philosophical. Nothing is wrong with that; however, once you start working with attraction, you may find you will have to create your own POS in order to make the most of your life (and the principles). Most of us have never had a POS 101 course, so there is a learning curve involved, but it is worth the investment.

The Zen of Attraction

If less is more, then nothing is everything.

○ Promise nothing.
Just do what you most enjoy doing.

○ Sign nothing.
Just do whatever doesn't require a signature of any kind.

○ Offer nothing.
Just share what you have with those who express an interest in it.

○ Expect nothing.
Just enjoy what you already have; it's plenty.

○ Need nothing.
Just build up your reserves, and your needs will disappear.

○ Create nothing.
Just respond well to what comes to you.

○ Seduce no one.
Just enjoy people.

○ Adrenalize nothing.
Just add value and get excited about that.

○ Hype nothing.
Just let quality sell by itself.

○ Fix nothing.
Just heal yourself.

○ Plan nothing.
Just take the path of least resistance.

○ Learn nothing.
Just let your body absorb it all on your behalf.

○ Become no one.
Just be more of yourself.

○ Change nothing.
Just tell the truth, and things will change by themselves.

Irresistible Attraction Program

100 ways to make yourself irresistible to the right people and opportunities.

Instructions

There are three steps to completing the **Irresistible Attraction** program.

Step 1: Fill in the circles.

Give yourself credit when you have completed it or do this activity regularly. Add up the number of checked circles and keep a current tally in the progress chart.

Step 2: Color in the checklist provided.

If you have nine circles filled in for the Relating Skills to Master section, color in the bottom nine boxes of column A, and so on. Always work from the bottom up. The goal is to have the entire chart be filled in. In the meantime, you have a current picture of how you are doing in each of the four areas.

Step 3: Keep playing until all the boxes are filled in.

You can do it! Use your coach or a friend to assist you. And check back once a year to upgrade and track your progress.

Note: You may reword any of these questions to better suit your needs.

Benefits

On the lines provided, jot down specific benefits, results and shifts, which happened in your life because you completed an item in the Irresistible Attraction program.

Date:	Benefit

We call the Irresistible Attraction program a makeover for the inside. Yes, it helps to wear nice clothes in the colors that make you glow and to have your hair, eyes, skin, and body looking great. These do contribute to attracting others to you. However, once you've handled these cosmetic things, you need to go further in your makeover. That is, you need to go inside to shift things around, learn new communication skills, install healthy conditions in your environment, and include some new concepts. Altogether, these contribute to a person's higher development and make one attract those people, opportunities, and good stuff that we all want—and that some of us chase—and that few of us naturally attract.

This program is designed to be done with a professional coach who is trained in attraction work. Expect it to take about two years to reach 100 points.

Progress Chart

Date	Points (+/–)	Score

Irresistible Attraction Program 100-Point Checklist

#	Sections			
	A	B	C	D
25				
24				
23				
22				
21				
20				
19				
18				
17				
16				
15				
14				
13				
12				
11				
10				
9				
8				
7				
6				
5				
4				
3				
2				
1				

Give yourself credit as you get points on the 100-point program. Fill in columns from the bottom up.

A. Relating Skills to Master

Number of circles checked (25 max) _____

○ I don't just listen to or understand people: I really hear them; they have an experience of being gotten.

○ People get the clear feeling that I stand up for them, regardless of how they are feeling. I don't just love, support, or help them; I require their best.

○ When I have something to say, I phrase it so people can both hear it and benefit from it, forever—I speak in messages, not clichés, opinions, or possibilities.

○ I communicate fully in the moment. I don't hold back, wait until later, explain my feelings, censor my thoughts—I share them fully.

○ I can see faults in people, but whenever I do I accept them in that person.

○ I speak unconditionally constructively. I don't give constructive criticism or subtle digs or remind someone what they coulda, oughta, shoulda done. Regardless.

○ When I do a task or job, nothing about it comes back to bite me for at least five years—I do fully handle tasks of which I am proud. Good isn't enough.

○ I grant people the power, acknowledgement, and room they deserve and need; I am a big person. I don't try to take credit, diminish another, or hold back my praises. Yet I don't puff people up.

○ I see and want a lot for many people, and they can feel this. But I don't have to have it for them.

○ I don't just tell people I care, I show it, at least once per day. And I show it in a way that they would want me to, not the way I necessarily want to.

○ When I talk, I use the word *you* four times as often as the word *I*. And people appreciate this.

○ I am twice as interested (in the person, not just the information or news) than I am interesting.

○ I clearly reflect back to people who they are.

○ I can discern immediately if someone is good for me; if they are not, I exit. I don't go for losers, and I don't get seduced by the possibilities of what could happen or who they could be.

○ I am interdevelopmental with people: I am not codependent, dependent, or merely interdependent.

○ I can be with people.

○ I am grateful to and for others, and they feel it. This is not indebtedness, nor do I overwhelm or smother them with affection; nor am I merely thankful or appreciative—I am simply and purely grateful for who is in my life and how they help me be me.

○ I cause things to happen, not wait for them to happen.

○ Others model parts of their lives after mine.

○ Everything I do is a contribution.

○ I grant everyone I've met and not met a lifetime of forgiveness in advance.

○ I share those gifts that I can afford to give.

○ I always say just the right thing to others.

○ I show I care; I don't just talk about it.

○ I give the gifts that the other person really wants.

○ I put my needs first.

B. Conditions to Have in Your Life

Number of circles checked (25 max) _____

- ○ I have nothing unresolved or unfinished (90+ on Clean Sweep).
- ○ I am over any addictions and healthy and well.
- ○ I am a part of a full, successful, and happy community of people who love me as I am.
- ○ My needs are met! (90+ on NeedLess)
- ○ I have enough verbal facility to fully express my feelings, sensations, and problems.
- ○ I am able to want a tremendous amount but crave nothing.
- ○ My life is set up so I have really neat things, people or activities to look forward to all of the time.
- ○ I express my values (90+ on Tru Values).
- ○ I know where I am on my path of development, and I am moving forward effortlessly.
- ○ I have much more than I need (90+ on Reserve Index).
- ○ I get my source and power from outside myself.
- ○ I am virtually adrenaline free, and I catch myself immediately if I get caught up in something.
- ○ The goals I have turn me on, and that's enough for me.
- ○ My standards are clear, and they are high; they support me, yet I am not constrained by them.
- ○ I have accepted what is so and take actions from reality, rather than living in a world of hope or fantasy.
- ○ I have reached my professional stride, and my growth occurs naturally.
- ○ Physically, I am very, very well.
- ○ I have commitments that excite me.
- ○ I am leaving a legacy of which I am proud.
- ○ I am at 90+ on the Buff It Up! program.
- ○ I am at 75+ on the 100 Smiles program.
- ○ I have plenty of time. I am at 90+ on the Time Peace program.
- ○ I am really okay about and with myself.
- ○ I am no longer trying to "make it" or prove anything.
- ○ I am working on a special project that is personally and professionally fulfilling.

C. Concepts to Embrace and Get

Number of circles checked (25 max) _____

- ○ There is you and there is me, but we're really all one when it comes down to it.
- ○ People are absolutely perfect just as they are, even when it doesn't seem that way. And I make them right, because they are.
- ○ Others are mirrors of me. As I find them more attractive, I find myself even more so.

○ I attract people who are one step behind or one step ahead of me.

○ The universe never lies; things are perfect as they are. So don't fight it!

○ Responsibility is a privilege, not a duty or burden.

○ Love is something you deserve, not earn.

○ Making God right is the final step in personal development.

○ Having enough money is a responsibility of adulthood and essential to being irresistibly attractive—not because of how much you have, but because of how little it has you.

○ Nothing means anything, but things matter, and I know what matters most to me.

○ You have two parts—the ego and the self. It is the latter to whom other selves are attracted and the former to which other egos are attracted.

○ Everyone needs energy and motivation from some place and will do anything to keep the energy flowing. Your job is to choose your source of supply as if your life depended on it.

○ Struggling is for actors, not humans.

○ You already have all you need, but you may need to become aware of it all.

○ You are as big as the people with whom you associate. Upgrade, please.

○ Attempting to change people is fruitless, but you can help them become more of who they are.

○ When your needs are met, you can afford to be attractive.

○ Irresistible attraction is something that happens to you, not something you do, although you do cause it.

○ Attraction is when they come to you; seduction is when you get to them.

○ When you've made the choice to be fully alive for the rest of your life, you attract others who have made a similar choice.

○ When you are grateful for what you have, even if it seems like it's not enough, you get a whole lot more. It is a test!

○ It is okay to surrender to the counsel of friends. They know you.

○ The more attractive you are, the fewer people will be attracted to you, but what a group they are.

○ It is a skill to enjoy being fully engaged and participatory in life.

○ You are attractive, but not to everyone.

D. What I Don't Ever Do

Number of circles checked (25 max) _____

○ I don't gossip—that is, I virtually never speak about another person not present, sharing neither good news nor bad.

○ I simply do not tolerate anything or anyone. I am not uppity and obnoxious about it, but I either handle the situations fully or get the heck out.

○ I do not complain—rather, I turn all my complaints and petty disturbances into requests that get accepted.

○ I am through doing what I should, ought to, have to, could; I now fully choose each moment, person, and activity.

○ I don't fight the flow. Oh, I have courage and I am committed, and I can take a stand, but I will not hurt myself trying to prove something—I take the path of least resistance and I get there, effortlessly.

○ I don't allow people to cross my boundaries.

○ I don't let myself get into the position where I have to make a decision based on the consequences. I am insured and insulated from almost every problem.

○ I don't ignore anything someone says to me that doesn't sound right.

○ I don't wait; I respond immediately.

○ I don't fight. I smile, instruct, or walk away.

○ I don't try to get too close to people—either it is effortless or it's not worth it.

○ I don't let people manipulate or play games with me..

○ I don't say yes when I mean no.

○ I don't overpromise.

○ I don't try to puff someone else up, but I do speak with them in such a way that they feel good about themselves.

○ I don't abuse my body in any way.

○ I don't help people unless they are ready for it.

○ I don't live in hope someone will change; they won't as long as I need them to.

○ I don't process every thought I have; yet I don't blurt everything out either.

○ I am not invested in other people, although I do invest in them.

○ I don't get caught up in people's problems, even if I care deeply about them.

○ I don't expect anything from anyone.

○ I don't think my closest friends should meet all of my needs. I have these met by those who can.

○ I don't isolate; I am with those who care about me.

○ I don't hang with someone just to fill time; I fully enjoy them or I don't spend time with them. I don't tolerate anything less.

100 Smiles Program

There is a theory that goes like this: When a person has identified the 100 things that really make him or her smile, automatically, life finally becomes his or her own.

The **100 Smiles** program is the place to create and write down those things that really make a life for you. What type of things are these?

- Recreational activities
- Favorite pastimes
- Personal pleasures
- Exciting projects and endeavors

The objective of this program is to have you reorient your life to spend your time doing *only* these 100 things. And yes, you may have to upgrade or change your job or moneymaking work. One of the points here is to replace all the stuff that you don't like with the stuff you *love*. And this process helps you create a wonderful life.

Instructions

There are four steps to completing the 100 Smiles program.

Step 1: Write down 25 smile activities.

Record these in each of the four sections of the list provided.

Step 2: Fill in the circles.

Give yourself credit when you have completed it or do this activity regularly. Add up the number of checked circles, and keep a current tally at the top of each of the four sections.

Step 3: Color in the checklist provided.

If you have nine circles filled in for the With Myself section, color in the bottom nine boxes of column A, and so on. Always work from the bottom up. The goal is to have the entire chart filled in. In the meantime, you have a current picture of how you are doing in each of the four areas.

Step 4: Keep playing until all boxes are filled in.

You can do it! This process may take a year or two, but you can achieve a full smile! Use your coach or a friend to assist you. And check back once a year to upgrade and track your progress.

What Makes You Happy?

Fill in the information.

A. Indoors | Self	B. Indoors | Others	C. Out | Self
D. Out | Others	**E. Work | Self**	**F. Work | Others**
Other		

Why This Works

Just coming up with such a long list helps us define what we want and who we are.

Learning how to select things that make us smile automatically helps us tell the difference between wants/joys/fun and shoulds/have-tos/oughtas.

How to Create Your Smiles

Not Fully Articulated	**Fully Articulated**
Eating ice cream.	Sharing a hot fudge sundae on a warm summer evening, sitting on my deck after spending the day with Martha.

See the difference?

Here's the checklist for full articulation:

- Specific activity, using as many adjectives as possible
- With whom?
- Time of day or year
- Location
- Before or after what?

There are more you can include, but you get the picture. By fully articulating the event, situation, or activity, you are making it much more real and exciting. As a result, you are much more likely to go do more of it because it resonates. It is amazing.

Examples

What do you most enjoy doing alone? Reading, napping, writing, watching TV, painting, taking bubble baths, cleaning, cooking, watching videos, listening to music, singing, grooming, playing with the dog, journaling, making crafts, shopping, walking, exercising?

Exercise

Start by making a list of five things that make you smile.

Now, expand on one of the five things. Make it so perfect and appealing that you want to go out *right now* and go do it.

Now, can you imagine what your life would be like if you spent every waking hour *only doing things on that list*? Not possible, you say? *Wrong*. You can do it. So who would you have to be to simply be and do your 100 Smiles list? What commitments would you need to make? What changes would be necessary and appropriate?

Finally

It takes about one year to reorganize your life to be like this list. It is worth it, if you're in the right space for it.

Progress Chart

Date	Points (+/–)	Score

100 Smiles Program 100-Point Checklist

Sections				
#	A	B	C	D
25				
24				
23				
22				
21				
20				
19				
18				
17				
16				
15				
14				
13				
12				
11				
10				
9				
8				
7				
6				
5				
4				
3				
2				
1				

Give yourself credit as you get points on the 100-point program. Fill in columns from the bottom up.

A. With Myself

What do you most enjoy doing with yourself?

- ○ _____
- ○ _____
- ○ _____
- ○ _____
- ○ _____
- ○ _____
- ○ _____
- ○ _____
- ○ _____
- ○ _____
- ○ _____
- ○ _____
- ○ _____
- ○ _____
- ○ _____
- ○ _____
- ○ _____
- ○ _____
- ○ _____
- ○ _____
- ○ _____
- ○ _____
- ○ _____
- ○ _____
- ○ _____
- ○ _____
- ○ _____
- ○ _____
- ○ _____
- ○ _____
- ○ _____

B. With One Other

What do you most enjoy doing with one other person?

C. With a Group

What do you most enjoy doing with a group of friends or associates?

○ _____
○ _____
○ _____
○ _____
○ _____
○ _____
○ _____
○ _____
○ _____
○ _____
○ _____
○ _____
○ _____
○ _____
○ _____
○ _____
○ _____
○ _____
○ _____
○ _____
○ _____
○ _____
○ _____
○ _____
○ _____
○ _____
○ _____
○ _____
○ _____
○ _____
○ _____

D. Joys and Big Adventures with a Group

What really turns you on?

○ _____

○ _____

○ _____

○ _____

○ _____

○ _____

○ _____

○ _____

○ _____

○ _____

○ _____

○ _____

○ _____

○ _____

○ _____

○ _____

○ _____

○ _____

○ _____

○ _____

○ _____

○ _____

○ _____

○ _____

○ _____

○ _____

○ _____

○ _____

○ _____

○ _____

Quality of Life 100

How high is your quality of life currently? Take this test, and see how it ranks.

You get one point for each statement that is true for you.

	Family/Relationships		Career/Business
○	I am both pleased and content with my spouse/partner, or happy being single.	○	My work/career is both fulfilling and nourishing to me; I am not drained.
○	I have a circle of friends who I have a blast with, without effort.	○	I am on a positive career path that leads to increased opportunities and raises.
○	I am very close to my children. There is nothing in the way, nothing between us.	○	I am highly regarded for my expertise by my manager, clients, and/or colleagues.
○	I am part of a professional network that stimulates me intellectually and emotionally.	○	I work in the right industry or field; it has a bright future.
○	I have at least 20 friends and colleagues who live outside my country of residence.	○	My work is not my life, but it is a rich part of my life.
○	I am close to my parent(s), alive or not. There is nothing in the way, nothing between us.	○	My work environment brings out the very best in me because it is stimulating and/or supportive.
○	I have a best friend and treat him or her extremely well.	○	I look forward to going to work virtually every day.
○	I enjoy my family/extended family; we have worked through any dysfunction/past problems.	○	I work with the right people.
○	I get along well with my neighbors.	○	At the end of the day, I have as much energy as I did when I started the day; I am not drained.
○	I am loved by the people who mean the most to me.	○	The work I do helps to meet my intellectual, social, and/or emotional needs.
	____ section score		____ section score

	Money/Finances		Joy/Delight
○	I have at least a year's living expenses in the bank or money market fund.	○	I spend my leisure time totally enjoying my interests; I am never bored.
○	I don't have to work at financial success; money seems to find me with very little effort or pushing.	○	I have designed the perfect way to spend the last hour of my day.

Money/Finances		Joy/Delight	
○	I invest at least 10 percent of my income/earnings in my ability to increase/expand that income.	○	I am very, very happy.
○	When I buy something, I buy the best possible quality.	○	I have at least an hour a day that is exclusively for me, and I spend it in a chosen way.
○	I am financially knowledgeable—I know how money is made and lost.	○	I easily take delight in the smallest things.
○	I am on a financial independence track or am already there.	○	Weekends (or other days off) are a joy for me.
○	I have no financial stress of any kind in my life.	○	I look forward to getting up virtually every morning.
○	I do not carry credit card debt; I do not overspend.	○	I have designed—and am living—the perfect lifestyle for me right now.
○	I don't lose sleep over my investments.	○	I am able to stay present during the day; I don't lose myself to stress or adrenaline.
○	I make money because I add enough value to the people who need what I have.	○	My home brings me joy every time I walk inside.
____ section score		____ section score	

Effectiveness/Efficiency		Personal Foundation/Responsibility	
○	I don't spend time with anyone who bugs me or who is using me.	○	I love my home: its location, style, furnishings, light, feeling, and decor.
○	I have no problem asking for exactly what I want, from anyone.	○	I tolerate very, very little; I'm just not willing to.
○	Whatever can be automated is automated.	○	My wants have been satiated; there is little I want.
○	I reply to all e-mails as I read them; I don't maintain an inventory of unanswered e-mails.	○	There is nothing I am dreading or avoiding.
○	I know what my goals are, and I am eagerly and effectively making them a reality.	○	I have resolved the stresses and key issues of my upbringing and past events.
○	I have more than enough energy and vitality to get me through the day; I don't start dragging.	○	My boundaries are strong enough that people respect me, my needs, and what I want.
○	I have all of the right tools, equipment, computers, software, and peripherals that I need to work well.	○	I don't see a cloud on my future's horizon; it looks clear to me.

Effectiveness/Efficiency		Personal Foundation/ Responsibility	
○	Whatever can be delegated is delegated.	○	My personal needs have been satisfied; I am not driven or motivated by unmet needs.
○	I don't put things off; when it occurs to me, I do it, handle it, or have it done.	○	My personal values are clear, and my life is oriented around them.
○	I don't do errands.	○	I don't have a lot of unfinished projects, business, or hanging items; I am caught up.
____ section score		____ section score	

Personal Development And Evolution		Self-Care/Well-Being	
○	I could die this afternoon with no regrets.	○	I take at least four vacations a year.
○	There is nothing I am not facing head-on, nothing I am putting off dealing with.	○	My teeth and gums look great and are in top condition.
○	I have more than enough natural motivation, inspiration, and synergy in my life; I am not stuck.	○	I eat food for sustenance and pleasure, not for emotional comfort.
○	I have progressed beyond the notion of beliefs.	○	Whatever health problems I have, I am receiving proper, effective care for them.
○	I have learned to take the path of least resistance as I accomplish my goals.	○	I am not abusing my body with too much alcohol, television, caffeine, or drugs.
○	I am living my life, not the life that someone else designed for me or expected of me.	○	I reduce stress daily by meditating, taking a long bath, exercising, walking, or the like.
○	I attract success; I don't have to strive for it or chase it.	○	Life is easy; I have virtually no problems or unresolved matters affecting me.
○	I am evolving, not just improving, because I continually experiment.	○	I have more than enough time during my day.
○	I am at that place in life where I initiate and cause events, not wait for others or events to do so.	○	My body is in great shape.
○	I am beyond striving for success; I simply enjoy my life and focus on what fulfills me.	○	There is nothing I am doing that is messing up my mind or heart.
____ section score		____ section score	

	Happiness		Pleasure
○	Please write down the 10 things that make you the happiest, whether you currently have these things in your life or not. Check off each item that you do.	○	Please write down the 10 things that give you the greatest pleasure, whether you currently do these things in your life or not. Check off each item that you do.
○		○	
○		○	
○		○	
○		○	
○		○	
○		○	
○		○	
○		○	
○		○	
○		○	
	____ section score		____ section score

SCORING KEY

90–100	Awesome. Congratulations for having such a great life.
80–89	Excellent! Your score is very high—this is a tough test.
70–79	Very good. You're definitely on track for a high-quality life.
60–69	Pretty good. You are making progress, but there's work to be done.
50–59	Average score. Why not make your quality of life a priority and score 10 more points in the next month?
40–49	This is nothing to feel badly about, but you'll probably need to make some real changes to improve your life.
30–39	Weak. The questions are challenging, but not that challenging. What's up with you?
20–29	Okay, let's get serious. You have one lifetime. Why aren't you making the most of it?
10–19	What's this about? Is it a temporary condition or have you just not paid attention to your life yet?
0–9	Ouch! Why do you think your score is in this range? Could it be low self-esteem or emotional stress?

My Personal
Mission Statement

Read, understand, and complete the following.

Definition of Mission

The special duty or function for which someone is sent as a messenger or representative; and the special task or purpose for which a person is apparently destined in life; a calling.

Truth

My personal mission statement focuses on the special purpose I want to achieve in my life and the special approach I will take to achieve it. It is the consequence of my mission being achieved. It is a description of how the world will be after I've traveled through it.

Statement

I believe my unique mission is:

○ _____

Question

The fundamental life vision question is this:

If we were meeting back here on _____, and you were looking back over the preceding _____, what would have to have happened during those years for you to feel really good about yourself, your life, and the fulfillment of your personal vision?

○ _____
○ _____
○ _____
○ _____

Life Purpose Worksheet

Why are you alive?

What are you most proud of having accomplished at this point in your life?	
If you were financially able to retire one year from today, what would you begin working on to prepare for that?	
What would you most like the people at your funeral to say about you, specifically?	
Who in history do you admire most, and why?	
If you could solve a world problem, what would it be? Be very specific, please.	
What is the inkling you have of your purpose or vision?	
What is in the way of putting this ahead of what you are engaged in now?	
If it weren't important to have a life purpose, what would you most like to do in the next decade?	
List three possible life purposes.	1. 2. 3.

Life Purpose, Business Mission, and Legacy

Please respond to each question in the space provided. What is most important to you?

Life Purpose

What do you want for yourself, for others, and for life, personally? What is truly most important to you?

_____

_____

_____

Business Mission

What do you want, professionally, for your clients and others? Why do you do what you do? What do you offer that is unique and/or excites you?

_____

_____

_____

Legacy

What do you want to leave for others after you are gone? Be specific.

_____

_____

Personal Path Program

Personal Path is a self-paced personal development program for the individual who strongly desires a high quality of life and is willing to make the type and degree of changes that are usually required.

The program consists of 10 benchmarks or milestones in life—soft, yet very, very rich goals whose pursuit fundamentally shifts how participants relate to themselves, others, and their environment.

The 10 areas are:

        A. Inner peace
        B. Personal power
        C. Happiness and joy
        D. Spiritual bliss
        E. Grace and love
        F. Full satisfaction
        G. Natural balance
        H. Personal passion
        I. Vitality and wellness
        J. Fulfillment

This program is designed to be done concurrently with any other coaching program or goal you are working on.

Instructions

There are four steps to completing the **Personal Path** program.

Step 1: Answer each question.

If the statement is true, check the circle. If not, leave it blank until you've done what it takes. Be rigorous; be a hard grader. If the item does not apply or will never be true for you, fill it in anyway and give yourself credit. You may do this with up to five items. Feel free to rewrite or reword up to five of the items in this program to better suit you, your needs, and your life.

Step 2: Summarize each section.

Add up the number of checked circles for each of the 10 sections and write those amounts where indicated. Then add up all 10 sections and write the current total in the progress chart.

Step 3: Color in the checklist provided.

If you have five circles checked in the Inner Peace section, color in the bottom five boxes of column A, and so on. Always work from the bottom up. The goal is to have the entire chart filled in. This will indicate how strong your personal path is. In the meantime, you have a current picture of how you are doing in each of the 10 areas.

Step 4: Keep playing until all boxes are filled in.

This process takes between six months and five years, but you can do it! Use your coach or advisor to assist you. And check back quarterly for maintenance.

Progress Chart

Date	Points (+/−)	Score

Personal Path Program 100-Point Checklist

#	Sections									
	A	B	C	D	E	F	G	H	I	J
10										
9										
8										
7										
6										
5										
4										
3										
2										
1										

Give yourself credit as you get points on the 100-point program. Fill in columns from the bottom up.

A. Inner Peace

Inner peace is an inner calmness, a freedom from environmental hooks, an absence of disturbances or adrenaline, an inner knowing, a connection with one's spirit. You have a choice about whether to experience inner peace.

When experiencing inner peace, a person is
- Unhookable externally by circumstances or others
- Fully present and able to be with everyone, always
- Extremely gentle
- Accepting of all, including all of oneself

Until a person gets here, he or she is
- Easily disturbed by events, problems, or others
- Prone to create problems, crises, and disturbances for himself or herself
- Unable to relax, chill out, or fully enjoy life
- Prone to busy-ness, frantic-ness, rush, obsession, and preoccupation

The 10 Steps to Reach Inner Peace

Number of circles checked (10 max) _____

- ○ Have nothing unresolved as opposed to just having everything finished.
- ○ Surrender and accept what is so versus resisting, fighting.
- ○ Take full responsibility for how you react to others.
- ○ Become aware of and sensitive to feelings versus being blind or ignorant.
- ○ Tell the entire truth versus editing, censoring, lying or translating.
- ○ Distinguish between self and mind, ego, needs, or past experiences.
- ○ Immediately catch yourself when triggered by adrenaline.
- ○ Recognize and inquire into why your cage gets rattled.
- ○ Step over nothing, even the small stuff, yet don't fix others.
- ○ Reprioritize peace to be ahead of performance.

B. Personal Power

A powerful person has resources and knows how to use them. These resources include the people, skills, information, experience, abilities, and focuses that influence, cause, and create one's environment and results. We all have power available but must open ourselves to access it fully by being a conduit for power.

When experiencing personal power, a person
- Is able to accomplish a lot with little suffering
- Is able to create by using available resources

- Is results oriented but process sensitive
- Is always at cause, not at effect, and uses whatever power one has

Until a person gets here, he or she is
- Weak, at the mercy of circumstances and life
- Inconsistent in performance due to moods and low energy
- Frustrated at the length of time it takes to accomplish goals
- Controlling, pushy, too results oriented

10 Steps to Increase Personal Power

Number of circles checked (10 max) _____

- ○ Raise personal standards to reflect higher self-worth.
- ○ Empower others directly, recycling their power by listening.
- ○ Start being *for* others or results versus being *about* them.
- ○ Go for the quality, not quantity, of what you produce.
- ○ Master the phrasing you need to express yourself fully.
- ○ Have things be acceptable or unacceptable, not forever gray.
- ○ Initiate everything; wait for and follow no one.
- ○ Take many, many risks and experiment as much as possible.
- ○ Get to work, maintain momentum, be dedicated.
- ○ Read those books that inform and educate you well.

C. Happiness And Joy

Happiness and joy come from being who you want and having what you want. Happiness and joy are not mysteries; you can create these by being very, very selfish and by listening to your inner guide as opposed to society, culture, or shoulds, or being controlled by potential consequences.

When experiencing happiness and joy, a person
- Feels gratified and wants more of this
- Is doing exactly what he or she wants
- Is pleasure oriented and is willing to have more
- Is able to contribute well to others he or she cares about

Until a person gets here, he or she
- Experiences sadness and unhappiness
- Can't figure out how to be happy; happiness and joy are elusive
- Is stuck, miserable in the present, with no way out
- Doesn't even know what will make him or her truly happy

The 10 Steps to Become Happy and Joyful

Number of circles checked (10 max) _____

○ Figure out what does make you consistently happy.
○ Get your needs met so you can afford your wants.
○ Stop doing what you should do; do what you need or want to.
○ Restore your integrity to be at 100 percent.
○ Eliminate every single toleration and source of suffering.
○ Experience the difference between thoughts and feelings.
○ Become truly selfish, not egotistical.
○ Take what you need to be your best.
○ Become internally generative versus externally motivated.
○ Start creating a project that makes you feel very, very good.

D. Spiritual Bliss

Spiritual bliss comes from being totally connected with yourself, your soul, your body, and a higher power (meaning everyone). It is a high experience of life, rich with the subtleties and details that open one up to a quality of life unmatched by the trappings of the material or linear world.

When experiencing spiritual bliss, a person is
● Glowing with energy, love and caring, but not high
● Light, contributory, and being, yet fully responsible
● A part of a higher plane of existence
● Touching others in a profound way, measurable or not

Until a person gets here, he or she is
● Disconnected from healthy energy, chemically high
● Burdened by life's challenges, alone
● Fearful of possible consequences, defensive, right
● Trying too hard to project or create

The 10 Steps to Have Spiritual Bliss

Number of circles checked (10 max) _____

○ Identify the distinction between self and ego.
○ Take the path of least resistance versus forcing, fighting, or winning.
○ Develop a relationship with your self or a higher power.
○ Respond to as opposed to reacting to circumstances and others.
○ Keep yourself toxin free (chemical, adrenaline, stress).
○ Intuitively choose versus logically or linearly deciding.
○ Honor your inklings versus explaining, rationalizing, proving.
○ Clean out your Rolodex.

○ Dance with versus controlling others.
○ Take extreme self-care of every part of yourself.

E. Grace and Love

Grace and love come from having more than enough and from being able to give, receive, grant, attract, and enjoy yourself and others to a degree that it all becomes a flow of energy. Grace is saying yes to God; love is saying yes to yourself and others.

When experiencing grace and love, a person is
- Warm, friendly, easy with others
- Living effortlessly, rarely concerned, flowing smoothly
- People versus result oriented, gives a lot, without cost
- Building a reserve of time, money, energy, space

Until a person gets here, he or she is
- Critical, short, judgmental, measuring
- Alone, terminally unique, lots of effort for little return
- Needy, demanding, loud
- Childish, small, petty, not over self yet

The 10 Steps for Grace and Love

Number of circles checked (10 max) _____

○ Get more than you need, a reserve of everything.
○ Live very, very well, as opposed to just managing.
○ Start acknowledging others rather than complimenting them.
○ Get the who versus the what about other people.
○ Become charge neutral versus charged up or down.
○ Fully communicate, but get permission first.
○ Come from acceptance and compassion.
○ Condition change rather than forcing it.
○ Put relationships ahead of mere results.
○ Forgive and have compassion as opposed to merely understanding.

F. Full Satisfaction

One can become fully satisfied, which means that one is well taken care of emotionally, physically, spiritually, and intellectually. Becoming responsible is the process that creates the feeling of full satisfaction.

When fully satisfied, a person is

- Connected with abundance and grateful for what he or she has
- Selfish enough to get what he or she needs—as a first priority
- Operating with a very strong personal foundation
- Taking responsibility for what occurs in his or her space

Until a person gets here, he or she is

- Full of dissatisfaction, blame, complaints, disturbances
- Subject to neediness, pettiness, financial problems
- Trapped, restricted, imposed upon, externally prompted
- At the mercy of what he or she has not become responsible for

The 10 Steps to Get Fully Satisfied

Number of circles checked (10 max) _____

- ○ Understand that what you have, don't have, are, and are not, is perfect.
- ○ Understand and take care of core needs versus medicating or denying them.
- ○ Establish strong boundaries to protect the soul.
- ○ Respond to the current situation versus what was or will be.
- ○ Get on a path to be fully healed versus always seeing yourself as wounded and needing healing.
- ○ Do whatever it takes to get totally free; don't settle for temporary relief.
- ○ Understand the difference between adult, parent, and child.
- ○ Stop blaming yourself for what you didn't do.
- ○ Do only what you enjoy or must do for your integrity.
- ○ Fix or eliminate every source of dissatisfaction.

G. Natural Balance

Balance is a natural state that occurs when integrity is present. Balance is a barometer of this integrity. Humans are now just learning how to have it all and have balance. Balance is a life full of what is important to you.

When experiencing natural balance, one is

- Resilient because of a strong keel or foundation
- Consistently performing yet not at an emotional cost
- Enjoying the space created with balance
- Sharing one's gifts because nothing is being lost or used up

Until a person gets here, he or she

- Has up-and-down mood swings, is volatile, manic, and/or depressed
- Deliberately stresses self, pushes, feels that nothing is ever enough
- Can't get present, can't find home or self in the swirl
- Is full of reasons, excuses, evidence, and shoulds

The 10 Steps to Balance Well

Number of circles checked (10 max) _____

○ Start creating choices and solutions, not compromising.
○ Integrate all parts of your life rather than compartmentalizing activities.
○ Find out and fix what is causing the imbalance or problems.
○ Be very selective about who and what comes into your space—and how.
○ Underpromise, don't overpromise; don't stress yourself.
○ Identify your values and reorient goals around them.
○ Understand balance versus juggling, managing, or controlling.
○ Give yourself permission to eliminate all that causes unbalance.
○ Have no hidden costs that drag you down at work.
○ Recognize and eliminate adrenaline triggers before they run you.

H. Personal Passion

Passion adds spice to a spiritual life. Passion comes from a convergence of desire, dedication, and creation. Passion can be fully developed for oneself. It's healthy. People are passionate when they are truly contributing to others.

When being personally passionate, a person

● Is fully expressing himself or herself and being human
● Is working toward a vision, purpose, or meaning
● Is excited but not "on"
● Is coming from the soul, not the external projection

Until a person gets here, he or she experiences

● Frustration, boredom, regret
● Floundering, confusion, lack of direction
● Dilettantism
● Resistance to what turns him or her on

The 10 Steps to Be Personally Passionate

Number of circles checked (10 max) _____

○ Find out what most turns you on, then just do that.
○ Set huge goals that bring out your best.
○ Develop a compelling vision as opposed to having lots of ideas.
○ Start caring for others in a profound way.
○ Distinguish between passion and adrenaline.
○ Identify a theme to your life for the year that's ideal.
○ Start stating what you want rather than hoping for it.
○ Go for the excitement, not drama, in life.

- Design a contribution project that shares your gifts.
- Hang out with passionate people and learn from them.

I. Vitality and Wellness

Wellness is the basis for consistent creation, attraction, and love. Getting well and raising your standards of what wellness means to you requires a dedication to being your best.

When experiencing wellness, a person is
- Active, has plenty of energy
- Emotionally and physical available to others
- Attractive because he or she is responsible and can share energy
- Able to enjoy more of what he or she is doing; feeling good

Until a person arrives, he or she is
- Tired, lackluster
- Toxic to others, consuming space
- At the mercy of entropy
- Not creating or expressing himself or herself fully

The 10 Steps for Vitality and Wellness

Number of circles checked (10 max) _____

- ○ Develop a healthy morning routine instead of rushing.
- ○ Shift your day to be like you're on vacation.
- ○ Start using food for sustenance, not pleasure or reward.
- ○ Move your body aerobically several times per week.
- ○ Identify and stop all behaviors that cost you wellness.
- ○ Develop a reserve of energy.
- ○ Get all parts of your body fixed that are broken or blocked.
- ○ Communicate until you feel clear.
- ○ Discover and saturate yourself with what nurtures you.
- ○ Clean up every closet, room, and physical space so it's empty of clutter.

J. Fulfillment

Fulfillment comes from expressing yourself fully and feeling the impact this has on others and yourself. Basing your life on your Tru Values is the place to start experiencing fulfillment. Fulfillment is the inner reward for living your life this way.

When experiencing fulfillment, a person is
- Creating something
- Full, proud, pleased
- Engaged and enjoying it
- Profoundly impactful

Until a person gets here, he or she is
- Bored
- Looking for the meaning of life
- Making lots of decisions
- Making lots of changes

The 10 Steps to Be Fulfilled

Number of circles checked (10 max) _____

- ○ Start coming from the *is* versus shoulds, coulds, oughtas, wants.
- ○ Do the maximum.
- ○ Have a vision or project that leaves the legacy you want.
- ○ Do what comes naturally to you.
- ○ Master something, anything, but experience being the best at it.
- ○ Learn the difference between accomplishments and results.
- ○ Honor your inner feelings, desires, and inklings completely.
- ○ Build something rather than randomly creating.
- ○ Hang out with people who are fulfilled or well on their path to being so.
- ○ Make the most of what you already have.

Intellectual Property Notice

This material and these concepts are the intellectual property of Coach U, Inc. You may not repackage or resell this program without express written authorization and royalty payment. The exception is that you may deliver this program to single individuals without authorization or fee. If you lead a workshop or develop or deliver a program to a group or company based on or including this material or these concepts, authorization and fees are required. You may make as many copies of this program as you wish, as long as you make no changes or deletions of any kind.

Chapter 9

Perfect Life

In this chapter we will explore the concept of having a perfect life. Can this be done? We believe so. This is about your coachees taking their lives to the next level and creating the lives they truly desire. By taking everything up a notch, they will raise the bar on the quality of their lives.

You will find information on improving and perfecting their lives along with concepts and programs that will enhance their development in this area. By implementing the learning in this area, they can dramatically improve their lives.

The following sections are included in this chapter:

1. The 12 Areas of a Perfect Life
2. The Zen of Perfect
3. The Benefits of Having a Perfect Life
4. How to Have a Perfect Life
5. Background Changes to Make
6. "Absence Of" 100
7. Abundance Of
8. Time Peace Program
9. Sports, Recreational Activities, and Hobbies
10. My Perfect Day
11. Annual Life Planner
12. 100 Steps to Becoming a Class Act
13. Class Act 100 Program
14. Buff It Up! Program

The 12 Areas of a Perfect Life

- ○ Love—relationships and family
- ○ Freedom—money and financial independence
- ○ Happiness—pleasure and joy
- ○ Vitality—self-care and energy
- ○ Richness—lifestyle and quality of life
- ○ Ease—personal operating system and approach to life
- ○ Success—business and career
- ○ Connectivity—community and networks
- ○ Advancement—evolution and development
- ○ Grace—awareness and spirituality
- ○ Synergy—communication and collaboration skills
- ○ Self-expression—creativity and experimentation

The Zen of Perfect

○ What is, is perfect—
And you can perfect it.

○ What isn't perfect, is perfect—
Because there is something to learn.

○ You are perfect—
Even when you are not.

○ Others are perfect—
Especially when you are not.

○ Life is perfect—
But only when you see that it is.

○ Weaknesses are perfect—
Their perfection is simply unrecognized.

○ Your strengths are perfect—
So continue to perfect them.

○ What already is perfect, is perfect—
Leave it alone.

○ Tragedies are perfect—
We just can't see their perfection yet.

○ Perfect is perfect—
Make perfect an art form.

The Benefits of Having a Perfect Life

○ You feel terrific almost all of the time—
Without being artificially high.

○ You have virtually no problems or conflicts—
They just seem to disappear.

○ Your sources of energy are very clean and, thus, sustainable—
And you need far less energy to flourish.

○ You have ample outlets and opportunities—
For your creativity to flourish.

○ You're engaged in life as it unfolds today, not as it unfolded yesterday—
So you attract the best people to you naturally.

○ Everyone else will naturally leave you alone—
You more easily respond to change.

○ You can afford to be flexible—
Your life comes easier because it is fully integrated.

○ Work is play—people are love—ideas are money—
You operate on a higher plane, thus avoiding the common turbulence of life.

○ You lose the urge to strive—
Striving is expensive.

○ People love you—you love them—
There is nothing in the way of the natural exchange of love.

○ Each day feels like a fresh canvas—
Life becomes an experiment that you totally enjoy.

○ Blocks and limitations disappear—
You no longer need them to protect you.

How to Have a Perfect Life

○ Know how you measure success—
Start living your life by design.

○ Abandon perfectionism—
Replace perfectionism with pride.

○ Accept, then perfect, what isn't perfect—
Acceptance is the first step toward perfection.

○ Enjoy an absence of personal problems—
Life's too short for problems of any kind—become a problem-free zone.

○ Automate the business of your life—
Don't you have better things to do?

○ Upgrade your personal and professional network—
People bring you the best opportunities in life.

○ Seriously invest in a special skill set—
The more you can deliver, the more you can earn.

○ Have whims worth following—
Perfection occurs as you respond to what tugs at you.

○ Perfect your self-care—
A perfect life isn't sustainable without advanced self-care.

○ Lighten your footprint—
Need less—be more.

○ Evolve your sources of energy—
Design advanced sources of motivation.

○ Raise your standards—reduce your expectations—
This raises you above the muck of life into the realm of the perfect.

Background Changes to Make

This section focuses on changes you may want to make to better position yourself for success and fulfillment.

This is a list of 10 fundamental or background changes that people often make in order to improve the quality of their lives and to become even more successful. This type of list is important because it contains strategies and approaches that can do as much for you as a direct effort to reach your goals. Think of this list as an investment in you, which pays off in the long term.

○	**Strengthen your personal foundation.** Just as a skyscraper needs a deep and strong foundation to support its weight and to withstand the environmental stresses affecting it (heat, cold, gravity, wind, earthquakes), so do we need a strong foundation, which we call a personal foundation. Your personal foundation includes extensive boundaries; high levels of integrity; high standards; resolution of the past; a strong community, network, and family; a healthy reserve of time, space, opportunities, money, and energy; an absence of tolerations; personal needs that are completely satisfied; and values that are being expressed. If any of these areas need attention, your coach can help you with them.
○	**Learn the attraction approach to living.** There is an easier way to live, and that is to attract the best people, opportunities, love, energy, and money to you by making yourself irresistibly attractive. And how does one do that? By learning and applying the attraction principles. Many clients try hard to be successful and get frustrated by how long it takes and the stress involved, because they are using an outdated approach to success that does not work any longer. The attraction approach is a low-cost, high-return method.
○	**Let go of the future as a focal point.** Most of us are driven by the future instead of being inspired by the present. In other words, we focus on the future (a goal, a lifestyle, an outcome) and, like a tractor beam, we're on it—but at what cost to us and to our present? One of the things that is really challenging is to change your relationship with the future (and thus with time itself). The future will take care of itself if you take care of what is in the present. Obviously, you are hiring a coach to reach goals and make improvements, so do not give up on goals, but we believe that the number of opportunities available all around you are more accessible if you let go of the future and simply overrespond to the present.
○	**Come to understand—and respect—what motivates you.** There are literally hundreds of things and feelings that motivate us, but we don't often know what these are or how they work. We all know about fear, greed, love, and pleasure as motivators, but each of us also has several other motivators that drive us, whether we want them to or not. Part of the coaching process is to come to understand how you are wired and what motivates you. While it is true that most people have a sense of this already, few have the awareness of all that is occurring. This increased awareness (which a coach can help you expand) will give you more self-control and help you design an emotional (intangible) and physical (tangible) environment that brings out your best.

Trust your whims, and experiment continuously.

There is nothing wrong with making logical and rational decisions. Given the right data with an intelligent analysis, you probably buy into something. But as time progresses, it is important to note that we are being forced to embrace chaos and learn how to make decisions based on an increased number of variables and a decreased number of cause-and-effect relationships. In other words, what used to work in decision making works less and less today. Better to develop your instinct, inklings, and intuition into an art form rather than slipping into the familiar comfort of making merely logical choices.

Learn from your environment, and evolve from what occurs.

Most of us have been trained to control or override our environment in order to get something done. But consider the possibility of responding (and overresponding) to what is already occurring, much like an Aikido master who uses the energy of the attacker and redirects it to get what he wants, instead of resisting, fighting, or overcoming it. So the next time something bad happens, don't just overcome it: Surrender to it, see the perfection in it, and learn from it quickly.

Find healthy sources of stimulation for your life.

Most of us are overstimulated or stimulated by things that are not very healthy. Television, news, movies, cities, sights, events, and even certain people can overstimulate you, leading to stress, manic states, and exhaustion. Stimulation is fun, but each of us has an optimal level of it, yet we do not always know what that level is. The point here is to calm your life down to the point of near boredom and to find ways to enjoy the simple things.

Spend as much time cleaning house as you do building an addition.

Metaphorically, anyway. The idea here is that it's easier to build more after you have perfected what you have. And for most of us, simplification is one of the ways to perfect what we have, given that most of us have too much (goals, projects, pressure, responsibilities, roles, etc.). So try reducing and perfecting while you are adding and building rather than just working hard to add, build, or create more.

Let go of beliefs and opinions.

Most of us have lots of beliefs and opinions about things (and won't mind getting in others' faces about them). Let go so you have almost no beliefs or opinions about people, things, or yourself. Something or someone either is or is not at any given time. What does belief or opinion about it have to do with anything? After all, aren't opinions a way to define yourself and get a buy-in (or argument) from others? Ask questions that stimulate rather than trying to get people to agree with you. It's too expensive! It's not that beliefs or opinions are bad, just that they slow you down.

Carve out your own reality and personal operating system (POS).

Most of us use a version of our parents' POS or have adopted a popular POS off the shelf, whether it is cultural, geographic, religious, or philosophical. Nothing is wrong with that, but one of the things that you now get to do is to create your own POS in order to make the most of your life. Most of us have never had a POS 101 course so there is a learning curve involved, but it is worth the investment. The point is that you get to decide how your life is going to work and what tools you are going to use to make the most of it. Formulas will work less and less. A custom-tailored POS is becoming a necessity.

"Absence Of" 100

Identify the area of your life or business you wish to focus on for your "absence of" project or the project that is large enough in scope to warrant 100 items to be in "absence of." Then write in the 100 items to be in absence of and check off each one as it is completed.

		Item	Resource or Support Needed
1.	○		
2.	○		
3.	○		
4.	○		
5.	○		
6.	○		
7.	○		
8.	○		
9.	○		
10.	○		
11.	○		
12.	○		
13.	○		
14.	○		
15.	○		
16.	○		
17.	○		
18.	○		
19.	○		
20.	○		
21.	○		
22.	○		
23.	○		
24.	○		
25.	○		

		Item	Resource or Support Needed
26.	○		
27.	○		
28.	○		
29.	○		
30.	○		
31.	○		
32.	○		
33.	○		
34.	○		
35.	○		
36.	○		
37.	○		
38.	○		
39.	○		
40.	○		
41.	○		
42.	○		
43.	○		
44.	○		
45.	○		
46.	○		
47.	○		
48.	○		
49.	○		
50.	○		
51.	○		
52.	○		
53.	○		
54.	○		
55.	○		

		Item	Resource or Support Needed
56.	○		
57.	○		
58.	○		
59.	○		
60.	○		
61.	○		
62.	○		
63.	○		
64.	○		
65.	○		
66.	○		
67.	○		
68.	○		
69.	○		
70.	○		
71.	○		
72.	○		
73.	○		
74.	○		
75.	○		
76.	○		
77.	○		
78.	○		
79.	○		
80.	○		
81.	○		
82.	○		
83.	○		
84.	○		
85.	○		

		Item	Resource or Support Needed
86.	○		
87.	○		
88.	○		
89.	○		
90.	○		
91.	○		
92.	○		
93.	○		
94.	○		
95.	○		
96.	○		
97.	○		
98.	○		
99.	○		
100.	○		

Abundance Of

For you to be perfect, what are the 25 things you would need to have an abundance of?

What are the specific feelings, resources, opportunities, environments, support systems, areas of knowledge, skill sets, competencies, relationships, and networks you would need to be a perfect person, without struggling to be one?

	Notes
1.	
2.	
3.	
4.	
5.	
6.	
7.	
8.	
9.	
10.	
11.	
12.	
13.	
14.	
15.	
16.	
17.	
18.	
19.	
20.	
21.	
22.	
23.	
24.	
25.	

Would support be helpful?

Crafting and creating yourself as a perfect person is a lot more fun when you can focus with a friend, partner, colleague, or professional coach. Especially important is how you identify and articulate each of your 25 elements. Properly phrased, each element will excite and naturally motivate you. Poorly phrased, you may feel pressure to perform, or the items may become just more shoulds or coulds in your life.

Time Peace Program

This section focuses on 100 ways to save time, create time, and have more than enough time. And to do so peacefully.

Instructions

There are three steps to completing the **Time Peace** program.

Step 1: Fill in the circles.

Give yourself credit when you have completed it or do this activity regularly. Add up the number of checked circles and keep a current tally in the progress chart.

Step 2: Color in the checklist provided.

If you have nine circles filled in for the Distinctions to Identify and Embrace section, color in the bottom nine boxes of column A, and so on. Always work from the bottom up. The goal is to have the entire chart filled in. In the meantime, you have a current picture of how you are doing in each of the four areas.

Step 3: Keep playing until all boxes are filled in.

You can do it! This process may take a year or two, but you can achieve a reserve of time. Use your coach or a friend to assist you. Check back once a year to upgrade and track your progress.

Note: You may reword any of these questions to better suit your needs.

Benefits

On the lines provided, jot down specific benefits, results, and shifts that happened in your life because you completed an item in the Time Peace program.

Date	Benefit

Progress Chart

Date	Points (+/−)	Score

Time Peace Program 100-Point Checklist

#	Sections			
	A	B	C	D
25				
24				
23				
22				
21				
20				
19				
18				
17				
16				
15				
14				
13				
12				
11				
10				
9				
8				
7				

	Sections			
#	A	B	C	D
6				
5				
4				
3				
2				
1				

Give yourself credit as you get points on the 100-point program. Fill in columns from the bottom up.

A. Distinctions to Identify and Embrace

Peace requires a deeper sense of yourself to the point that you stop having concerns or worries. To get to this rich place, one needs to learn and understand more about what time is, how it works, and how to relate with it properly. Following the principles given here will accelerate you toward peace and having plenty of time.

Number of circles checked (25 max) _____

- ○ Time is a tool that is exclusively mine to play with.
- ○ How I spend my time will give me 80 percent of the fulfillment I desire.
- ○ Time is a gift when I grant myself to others.
- ○ Time is elastic. I can stretch it or compress it.
- ○ Time has been used as a weapon to suppress, conform, and standardize human existence.
- ○ Time is a limited reference point from which to view being.
- ○ Time is not manageable, but my choices and actions are.
- ○ Time is not a thing; it is merely a reflection of how I am being.
- ○ Time is a function of the mind; space is a function of being.
- ○ I have far more time than I need.
- ○ Time is a flow; I can't get more of it, but I can do more with it.
- ○ Lack of time is a resistance or emotional problem.
- ○ One has enough time when one is doing what matters rather than doing what means something.
- ○ The more powerful and able I become, the bigger my boundaries need to be.
- ○ Time has no consequences. However, not being responsible for what I need does have consequences.
- ○ My relationships are more important than my results.
- ○ Miracles and discontinuous results are natural, and they happen to me.
- ○ Good timing occurs naturally when you've mastered this thing called time.

- Success comes from applying yourself and from luck. Luck is a matter of timing. Timing is a matter of attraction. Attraction is a matter of reserve. Reserve is a matter of selfishness. Selfishness is a matter of extreme self-care. Self-care is a matter of a strong personal foundation. A strong personal foundation comes from applying yourself to yourself. Applying yourself takes time. Time takes commitment.
- Cutting out 50 percent of what you should do grants time.
- There is plenty of time for what you're ready for.
- Time is not a function of the clock. Time is a way to describe one's space, not one's schedule.
- Having a reserve of time is a lifestyle.
- One's good judgment is often enhanced with space.
- Coming from eternity grants one lots of time.

B. Habits and Conditions to Install in Your Life

Having time and peace usually calls for a change in routine, priorities, and lifestyle. One may have to radically change one's habits and conditions just to free the pendulum, and it may whack itself on the opposite side of the case before finding its natural center of balance. It's worth the risk, but make sure you have the money, space, and time to shift your relationship with time and peace.

Number of circles checked (25 max) _____

- I am always early. I leave early, I arrive early, I return earlier than I said I would.
- I keep my word 99 percent of time, but I don't panic or rush or use adrenaline when I can't. But I do revoke promises and give early warning if I must.
- I've made a commitment to value my self and my time.
- I am above 90 on the Reserve program.
- I budget time to handle the problems caused by entropy.
- I have all the time I want.
- My three key boundaries are simply never crossed.
- I have at least one free hour each day.
- I put my needs ahead of another's wants, needs, or problems.
- I take the path of least resistance, and then I fully apply myself. I row gently downstream.
- I have all the tools, information, relationships, and resources to be extremely productive, naturally.
- My gas tank is never less than half full.
- I do not speed or tailgate; I am not in a hurry.
- I use a time management system so that I don't have to remember anything.
- I am at 90 or above on the Clean Sweep program.
- I am 90 or above on the NeedLess program.
- I am 90 or above on the Tru Values program.
- I know the top three things I will accomplish this month.
- I know the top three things I will accomplish this year.
- I have four vacations scheduled this year and am excited about each of them.

○ I've let go of the past. It was; I am.

○ I integrate my activities so I have time enough for all of the ones I really care about.

○ I have and enjoy a routine of 10 daily habits that keep me well.

○ I've made the authentic choice to have life be effortless, and it shows.

○ I've set a financial value on my professional time, and I get it or know why I chose not to receive it.

C. Personal Skills to Practice and Master

In addition to changing habits, one can benefit by developing or strengthening interpersonal and life management skills, a number of which are listed here.

Number of circles checked (25 max) _____

○ When emergencies happen, I schedule them in.

○ I ask for exactly what I want, not what I think I can get.

○ I naturally educate my environment so that all that comes to me is exactly what I want or is something better.

○ I stop people when they say or do something that doesn't sound straight to me or if it affects our relationship.

○ I fully handle matters; everything I touch does not come back to bite me for at least five years.

○ I can leverage my time—through efficiency, leverage, and timing—to produce miraculous results in record time, consistently.

○ I am a master at saying no even when I should or could say yes.

○ I promise about 50 percent of what I know I will deliver.

○ I know how to fully resolve or accept something, even though it is not finished yet.

○ I can think and dance three-dimensionally; I no longer use the linear approach.

○ I am at cause; I self-manage.

○ I know how to condition and position results, rather than forcing or managing them.

○ I am an excellent problem solver.

○ I know how to plan my time well.

○ I respond to people's problems or opportunities; I don't react to them. They are not mine.

○ I know how to prioritize, so I get what's most important to me done first.

○ I know where my juice comes from, and I am facile at getting it and having a supply of it.

○ I have the phrasing, distinctions, and vocabulary I need to avoid chatter.

○ I know my required degree of integrity, and I am skilled enough to keep myself there. If I slip, I regain my footing within a day.

○ I manage and maintain my reserve of time and protect it from encroaching ideas, commitments, obligations, wants, and shoulds. I value that reserve.

○ Each day I work on the goal, project, need, or skill that will give me a real future, not just incremental progress.

○ I can sense people who will waste my time or take my energy from a distance and I take steps to avoid, manage, or educate them.

○ I get things done in less than half the time it used to take me. I don't drag things out unless I want to.

○ I take all the time I need so that the tasks I touch are finished completely and don't unravel later.

○ Time is my friend and resource.

D. What to Stop Doing Forever

To have time and peace, one usually needs to give up some behaviors or routines. During this process, you may feel irritability, freedom, boredom, confusion, a sense of loss, or rushes of energy. Just remember, one usually needs to pass though the gates of boredom to enter the garden of peace. Be willing to be bored and work through that.

Number of circles checked (25 max) _____

○ I have completely stopped doing things that I should, could, or ought to do, yet I am still fully responsible.

○ I don't even think about doing things I should, could, or ought to do. My mind doesn't wrestle with stuff anymore.

○ I don't do errands, ever.

○ I don't do my own laundry or housework.

○ I don't wait to handle problems, I RAH them: recognize, anticipate, and handle.

○ I don't do important stuff alone anymore.

○ I don't tolerate anything from anyone, and people still like and love me.

○ I don't create problems or dramas in my life anymore.

○ I do not tailgate, speed, cut it close with pedestrians, or run yellow lights. I always let the other person in.

○ I don't offer. I let people ask first.

○ I don't gossip or spread talk about others, good or bad. I talk about the person with whom I am speaking.

○ I don't hang around with people who diminish me or give me a hard time.

○ I don't do things in order to get things. I go for the ultimate goal, not the ones I think I should have to get first.

○ I don't set goals that I should; I set goals that I want.

○ I don't take on other people's problems, even if they are seemingly critical ones.

○ I don't diddle; rather, I take time to be fully unscheduled so I can feel free.

○ I don't beat a dead horse, even if it should be able to get up. I cut my losses and move on to plan B, which I always have.

○ I don't "do" adrenaline any longer. I'm over it!

○ I don't hang out with associates or friends who are adrenaline addicts.

○ I don't "do" good ideas any longer; I do what has meaning to me.

○ I don't get my energy from causing accountability deferment tactics, overcoming problems, or beating deadlines.

○ I am not defined by what I do, so I don't have to do more to be more. I am who I am, and I am happy about that.

○ I don't "do" emergencies. They are a source of accountability deferment tactics.

○ I don't try to change people, but I do extend boundaries.

○ I am not rushing through this program.

Sports, Recreational Activities, and Hobbies

Looking for something fun? Start here.

Aerobatics
Aerobics
Aikido
Amateur archaeology
Amateur/ham radio
Antiquing
Aquariums
Archery
Arm wrestling
Art collecting
Astrology
Astronomy
ATVing
Auto racing
Backgammon
Badminton
Baking
Ballet
Ballooning
Ballroom dancing
Baseball
Basket making
Basketball
Batik
Baton twirling
Beachcombing
Beading
Beanie baby collect-
   ing
Beekeeping
Belly dancing
Biathlon
Bicycling
Bike racing
Billiards
Bird watching
Blimping
Boating
Bobsledding
Bocci
Bonsai
Bowling
Box making
Boxing
Bridge
Bunko

Calligraphy
Camping
Canasta
Canoeing
Capoeira
Car racing
Cards
Casino
Ceramics
Checkers
Chess
Choi Kwang-Do
Civil War reenacting
Climbing
Clubs
Collecting
Coloring
Comic books
Computer games
Cooking
Country dancing
Crafts
Cribbage
Cricket
Crocheting
Croquet
Cross-country skiing
Cross-stitch
Crossword puzzles
Curling
Danball
Darts
Deep sea fishing
Dining in
Dining out
Diving
Dog field training
Dogsledding
Doll collecting
Doll making
Dressage
Driving
Dune buggying
Egg art
Embroidery
Fencing

Field hockey
Fishing
Flamenco dancing
Flower arranging
Fly fishing
Folk dancing
Football
Foot massage
Fox hunting
Furniture refinishing
Gambling
Garage sales
Gardening
Geneology
Glass blowing
Golf
Gourmet cooking
Gun collecting
Gymnastics
Hacky sack
Handball
Handcrafted jewelry
Handspinning
Handwriting analysis
Hang gliding
Hiking
Hockey
Home repair
Home brewing
Horse racing
Horseback riding
Hunting
Ice skating
Jai alai
Jazz dancing
Jogging
Judo
Juggling
Jujitsu
Karate
Kayaking
Kendo
Kickboxing
Kit car building
Kiting
Knitting

Kung Fu
Lacrosse
Leather work
Lottery playing
Lowrider building
Luging
Magic
Magazines
Making love
Massage
Metal working
Miniature golf
Miniatures
Model aircraft
Model boats
Model cars
Model trains
Modern dancing
Monopoly
Motocross
Motorcycle racing
Motorcycle riding
Mountain biking
Mountain climbing
Movies
Mud wrestling
Museums
Needlepoint
Numerology
Off-road cycling
Opera
Orienteering
Origami
Painting
Paragliding
Parcheesi
Philately
Photography
Pictionary
Pinocle
Playing instrument
Poetry
Poker
Polo
Pool
Pottery

Potting
Prospecting
Puppetry
Puzzles
Quilting
Racing pigeons
Racquetball
Radio boats
Radio-controlled cars
Radio planes
Rafting
Reading
Restoring autos
Rock climbing
Rockets
Rocks, gems
Rodeo
Roller coasters
Rollerblading
Rook
Rounders
Rowing
Rubber stamping
Rug hooking
Rugby
Running
RVing

Salsa dancing
Sambaing
Scottish dancing
Scrabble
Scrapbooking
Scrimshaw
Scuba diving
Sculpting
Sewing
Sex
Shell craft
Shopping
Skateboarding
Skeet shooting
Skydiving
Sledding
Slot cars
Snooker
Snorkelling
Snow skiing
Snowboarding
Snowmobiling
Soap making
Soaring
Soccer
Softball
Speed skating

Spelunking
Square dancing
Squash
Stamp collecting
Stickers
Sumo wrestling
Sunbathing
Surfing
Swimming
Swing dancing
Symphony
Table tennis
Taekwondo
Tai chi
Talking on the phone
Talk shows
Tango dancing
Tanning
Tap dancing
Target shooting
Tatting
Telemarketing
Tennis
Theater
Theme park
Tie-dying
Tobogganning

Tole painting
Trap shooting
Traveling
Treasure hunting
Triathlon
Ventriloquism
Videos
Volleyball
Volunteering
Walking
Water parks
Water polo
Water skiing
Watercolor painting
Weaving
Weight lifting
Weight training
Whale watching
Windsurfing
Woodworking
Writing
Writing letters
Yahtzee
Zoo

My Perfect Day

What are the 25 elements of your perfect day?

Who would be in your perfect day? What would you do together? What would you enjoy doing alone? What activities or rituals would comprise your perfect day? What feelings would you experience? What would occur? What matters most to you during your day? Tip: Include only those people, activities, and experiences that are truly perfect for you—no shoulds, coulds, woulds, or musts. This is your perfect day—in this lifetime. As each item becomes a natural and consistent part of your day, fill in the preceding circle.

	Notes
1.	
2.	
3.	
4.	
5.	
6.	
7.	
8.	
9.	
10.	
11.	
12.	
13.	
14.	
15.	
16.	
17.	
18.	
19.	
20.	
21.	
22.	

	Notes
○ 23.	
○ 24.	
○ 25.	

Would Support Be Helpful?

Crafting and creating yourself as a perfect person is a lot more fun when you can focus with a friend, partner, colleague, or professional coach. Especially important is how you identify and articulate each of your 25 elements. Properly phrased, each element would excite and naturally motivate you. Poorly phrased, you may feel pressure to perform, or the items become just more shoulds or coulds in your life.

Annual Life Planner

Complete the following lists.

Five Key Goals	
1.	
2.	
3.	
4.	
5.	
Five People to Get Closer To	
1.	
2.	
3.	
4.	
5.	
Five New Skills to Learn	
1.	
2.	
3.	
4.	
5.	
Five Problems to Resolve	
1.	
2.	
3.	
4.	
5.	
Five Fabulous Adventures	
1.	
2.	
3.	
4.	
5.	
Five Things to Let Go Of	
1.	
2.	
3.	
4.	
5.	

100 Steps to Becoming a Class Act

Are you a class act? Here's a checklist of the qualities, behaviors, and character traits that many would say comprise a class act. Work with your professional coach to accelerate your progress along this path.

1. Honor
The core of yourself

- ○ Fair
- ○ Conviction
- ○ Courage
- ○ Truthful
- ○ Moral
- ○ Loyal
- ○ Accountable
- ○ Responsible
- ○ Committed
- ○ Diligent

2. Integrity
What you stand on

- ○ Honest
- ○ Well
- ○ Prudent
- ○ Thrifty
- ○ Simple
- ○ Orderly
- ○ Detail-oriented
- ○ Needs met
- ○ Punctual
- ○ Balanced

3. Style
How well you express yourself

- ○ Excellence
- ○ Trusting
- ○ Polished
- ○ Clean
- ○ Well-dressed
- ○ Gracious
- ○ Appropriate
- ○ Passionate
- ○ Consistent
- ○ Resilient

4. Caring
How well you treat others

- ○ Respectful
- ○ Available
- ○ Concerned
- ○ Tender
- ○ Tolerant
- ○ Sharing
- ○ Kind
- ○ Patient
- ○ Generous
- ○ Hospitable

5. Effectiveness
How smart you operate

○ Bandwidth/absorption rate

○ Vision

○ Mastery

○ Productive

○ Accomplished

○ Causal/initiating

○ Enrolling

○ Investing

○ Effective

○ Practical

6. Self
How you feel within

○ Confident

○ Secure

○ Content

○ Integrated

○ Self-caring

○ Self-motivated

○ Capacity

○ Mature

○ Capable

○ Harmonious

7. Openness
How you relate with the world

○ Accepting

○ Intuitive

○ Aware

○ Willing

○ Adventurous

○ Spiritual

○ Visual

○ Present-oriented

○ Creative

○ Flexible

8. Delivery
How well you perform

○ Win-win

○ Results-oriented

○ Proactive

○ Adds value

○ Underpromises

○ Interdevelopmental

○ Adaptive

○ Innovative

○ Direct

○ Resourceful

9. **Life Skills**
   Your personal tools

   ○ Loving

   ○ Clever

   ○ Hip

   ○ Light

   ○ Humorous

   ○ Diplomatic

   ○ Savvy

   ○ Generous

   ○ Wise

   ○ Perspective

10. **Communication**
    How well you come across

    ○ Tone

    ○ Dance

    ○ Articulate

    ○ Clear

    ○ Appreciative

    ○ Congratulatory

    ○ Constructive

    ○ Encouraging

    ○ Friendly

    ○ Expressive

Class Act 100 Program

One of the highest compliments an individual can receive is to be called a person of character—a class act.

This program is designed to help you understand where you are along this path and to give you ideas for areas worth developing.

The **Class Act 100** program includes a list of 100 character traits, life skills, special qualities, and personal practices that will help you to both become and feel like a class act, naturally.

We suggest you work with a coach trained in this process.

Instructions

There are four steps to completing the Class Act 100 program.

Step 1: Read each statement and fill in the appropriate circle.

Check the left circle if the statement is *sometimes* true, the middle circle if the statement is *often* true, the right circle if the statement is *always* true.

Note: As you progress, feel free to fill in all of the circles on the left side, so when you get to 100 items that are *always* true, all three circles for each statement are filled in.

Step 2: Add up your circles.

After you've filled in the appropriate circles, add up the number of right-hand circles (always true) for each of the 10 sections and write your "count" on the line provided.

Step 3: Fill in checklist boxes.

After you've written down your score for each section, fill in the boxes of the checklist provided to match the summary number at the end of each section. Fill in the boxes from the bottom up.

Step 4: Each month, come back and update your progress and scores.

Most people who take this profile score 20–50 the first time out and add three to five points per month.

Progress Chart

Date	Points (+/–)	Score

Class Act 100 Program 100-Point Checklist

#	Sections									
	A	B	C	D	E	F	G	H	I	J
10										
9										
8										
7										
6										
5										
4										
3										
2										
1										

Give yourself credit as you get points from the 100-point program. Fill in columns from the bottom up.

A. Honor

Number of circles checked (10 max) _____

S = **S**ometimes
O = **O**ften
A = **A**lways

S	O	A	
○	○	○	**Fair** I do only what's right and just.
○	○	○	**Conviction** I clearly know what I believe in, and I am steadfast.
○	○	○	**Courage** I have ample inner strength.
○	○	○	**Truthful** I have not lied in at least a year, nor have I been deceptive in any of my dealings.
○	○	○	**Moral** I live my life according to my moral code.
○	○	○	**Loyal** I stand by my family, friends, and others to whom I am committed.
○	○	○	**Accountable** I keep my word 99 percent of the time.
○	○	○	**Responsible** I can always be counted on to meet agreed-upon expectations.
○	○	○	**Committed** My actions demonstrate my commitment, which is obvious to others.
○	○	○	**Diligent** I do not waver until the ribbon is tied on whatever I am involved with.

B. Integrity

Number of circles checked (10 max) _____

S = **S**ometimes
O = **O**ften
A = **A**lways

S	O	A	
○	○	○	**Honest** I always deal fairly; I am not sneaky.
○	○	○	**Well** I am in optimum emotional, spiritual, and physical condition.
○	○	○	**Prudent** I have and use excellent judgment in all of my actions.

○	○	○	**Thrifty**	I save 10–30 percent of my net earnings.
○	○	○	**Simple**	I live an honest, simple, easy life.
○	○	○	**Orderly**	I am neat, tidy, and orderly.
○	○	○	**Detail-oriented**	I understand that God is in the details.
○	○	○	**Needs met**	I know what my personal needs are, and I am up front about getting them met.
○	○	○	**Punctual**	I am on time 98 percent of the time.
○	○	○	**Balanced**	I am juggling nothing.

C. Personal Style

Number of circles checked (10 max) _____

S = **S**ometimes
O = **O**ften
A = **A**lways

S	O	A		
○	○	○	**Excellence**	I only buy and deliver quality.
○	○	○	**Trusting**	I handle my dealings with others on the basis that people are trustworthy.
○	○	○	**Polished**	I come across as polished.
○	○	○	**Clean**	I maintain the highest standard of personal hygiene.
○	○	○	**Well-dressed**	I always look exceptionally good, even if very casual.
○	○	○	**Gracious**	I am always charming and warm, and I always offer appropriate courtesies.
○	○	○	**Appropriate**	I am sensitive to timing.
○	○	○	**Passionate**	It's clear to all what I feel strongly about and what I most enjoy or believe in.
○	○	○	**Consistent**	People know what to expect from me. I am predictable when it matters.
○	○	○	**Resilient**	I bounce back from adversity quickly (in 2 to 48 hours) and/or willingly. I recover.

D. Caring

Number of circles checked (10 max) _____

S = **S**ometimes
O = **O**ften
A = **A**lways

S	O	A	
○	○	○	**Respectful** I don't violate any aspect of another person, animal, or object.
○	○	○	**Available** I am very willing to help.
○	○	○	**Concerned** I take an interest in others.
○	○	○	**Tender** I am lovingly considerate and highly respectful.
○	○	○	**Tolerant** I welcome diversity because it expands me emotionally and spiritually.
○	○	○	**Sharing** I do not hoard. I'm not stingy; I give.
○	○	○	**Kind** I don't hurt people or animals; I don't kill insects.
○	○	○	**Patient** I can easily wait, no problem.
○	○	○	**Generous** I err on the side of generosity.
○	○	○	**Hospitable** I make people feel comfortable in my home or my space.

E. Caring

Number of circles checked (10 max) _____

S = **S**ometimes
O = **O**ften
A = **A**lways

S	O	A	
○	○	○	**Bandwidth/absorption** I easily handle or assimilate lots of input from any source.
○	○	○	**Vision** I see clearly what is possible for people and am oriented around that.
○	○	○	**Mastery** I am at the top of my game at work.
○	○	○	**Productive** I easily get more done in a day than most people get done in a week.

○ ○ ○ Accomplished
I have a track record of doing well and contributing to life.

○ ○ ○ Causal/initiating
I create my own path and do not wait for others to direct me.

○ ○ ○ Interest
I can easily help others make choices about what they really want.

○ ○ ○ Investing
I consciously invest in people, concepts, equipment, and opportunities.

○ ○ ○ Effective
What I work on gets done.

○ ○ ○ Practical
I have excellent common sense.

F. Self

Number of circles checked (10 max) _____

S = **S**ometimes
O = **O**ften
A = **A**lways

S   O   A

○ ○ ○ Confident
I feel confident, from the inside.

○ ○ ○ Secure
I am safe. I fear almost nothing.

○ ○ ○ Content
I am very satisfied with myself and my life.

○ ○ ○ Integrated
I don't lead separate lives; all of my goals work together to forward me.

○ ○ ○ Self-caring
I take better care of myself than anyone I know.

○ ○ ○ Self-motivated
I don't rely on others or on potential consequences to motivate me.

○ ○ ○ Capacity
I can handle all that life brings.

○ ○ ○ Compassionate
I naturally forgive and am always understanding of others' mistakes.

○ ○ ○ Mature
I never behave childishly.

○ ○ ○ Capable
I have found my strengths and have developed them fully.

G. Openness

Number of circles checked (10 max) _____

S = **S**ometimes
O = **O**ften
A = **A**lways

S	O	A	
○	○	○	**Accepting** I don't resist what is so. I let people be who they are. I embrace.
○	○	○	**Intuitive** I listen to my hunches and that little voice inside. I trust myself.
○	○	○	**Aware** I understand what awareness is, and I am on the path of becoming more aware.
○	○	○	**Willing** I am always willing to try or to help.
○	○	○	**Adventurous** I actively seek new people, ideas, activities, and projects. I go for it.
○	○	○	**Spiritual** I value the notion of a higher plane or being. I get that we're all connected.
○	○	○	**Visual** I see all of what's around me, and I fully respond to it.
○	○	○	**Present-oriented** Life is occurring right now. I live here, not yesterday, or tomorrow.
○	○	○	**Creative** Great ideas just come to me; I don't have to create them.
○	○	○	**Flexible** I adjust quickly and readily.

H. Delivery

Number of circles checked (10 max) _____

S = **S**ometimes
O = **O**ften
A = **A**lways

S	O	A	
○	○	○	**Win-win** Everyone I work with wins as much as I do. Win-win is my approach to life.
○	○	○	**Results** I produce and deliver results.
○	○	○	**Proactive** I anticipate needs and act early.

○ ○ ○ Adds value
I seek to willingly share my talents, gifts, and resources with everyone.

○ ○ ○ Underpromises
I deliver more than promised.

○ ○ ○ Interdevelopmental
I learn as much from others as they learn from me. We both grow.

○ ○ ○ Adaptive
I quickly adapt to new situations, ideas, and technology, thus offering more.

○ ○ ○ Innovative
I continually experiment and make things better.

○ ○ ○ Direct
I am up-front and candid, always.

○ ○ ○ Resourceful
I can pull solutions out of a hat.

I. Life Skills

Number of circles checked (10 max) _____

S = **S**ometimes
O = **O**ften
A = **A**lways

S	O	A

○ ○ ○ Loving
I rejoice in my love of, and the love I receive from, others.

○ ○ ○ Quick
I make the most of opportunities in order to accomplish my objectives.

○ ○ ○ Authentic
I have absolutely no attitude or pretense. I have nothing to sell or prove.

○ ○ ○ Light
Things matter to me, but I am not burdened by people, situations, or life.

○ ○ ○ Humorous
I see the humor in almost anything.

○ ○ ○ Diplomatic
I seek to build relationships, even if takes an investment of time.

○ ○ ○ Savvy
I have street smarts and understand what motivates people.

○ ○ ○ Generous
When in doubt, I share what I have.

○ ○ ○ Wisdom
I am very wise. I've learned well.

○ ○ ○ Perspective
I can always see the forest for the trees. I always see the bigger picture.

J. Communication

Number of circles checked (10 max) _____

S = **S**ometimes
O = **O**ften
A = **A**lways

S	O	A	
○	○	○	**Tone** I speak in warm, clear tones.
○	○	○	**Dance** I can speak and hear, simultaneously.
○	○	○	**Articulate** I clearly state what I want to say.
○	○	○	**Clear** I speak simply. I am easily understood.
○	○	○	**Appreciative** I thank people and I am sincere.
○	○	○	**Congratulatory** I am truly excited for the success of others, and I congratulate them.
○	○	○	**Constructive** I reinforce the positives of a person; I don't criticize.
○	○	○	**Encouraging** People need encouragement, and I am unstinting in my support.
○	○	○	**Friendly** I like people and let them know it.
○	○	○	**Expressive** My spirit, love, emotions, and excitement come across when I communicate.

Buff It Up! Program

Buff = Perfection + Personal Style

The **Buff It Up!** program is a self-paced personal development program for the individual who wants—and is ready—to have it all and have it all right now.

The Buff It Up! program targets 10 areas of your life, as listed.

This worksheet is designed to be used in conjunction with a coach trained to deliver this program. Also, many people find that this program is more realistic after they've completed the Personal Foundation Program.

The 10 areas on which you will be working are:

        A. My body
        B. My spirit
        C. My heart
        D. My self-care
        E. My home
        F. My work
        G. My quality of life
        H. My finances
        I. My family and friends
        J. My magic

Note: This is a very rigorous program. Take it one piece at a time. Your first score may be less than 10 or 20. Do not worry. You'll get to 70, 80, or 90+ sooner than you may think. Once started, the personal buff process carries its own momentum.

Instructions

There are four steps to completing the Buff It Up! program.

Step 1: Answer each question.

If the statement is true, check the circle. If not, leave it blank until you've done what it takes. Be rigorous; be a hard grader. If the item does not apply or will never be true for you, check it and give yourself credit. You may do this with up to five items. Feel free to rewrite or reword up to five of the items in this program to better suit you, your needs, and your life.

Step 2: Summarize each section.

Add up the number of checked circles for each of the 10 sections and write those amounts where indicated.

Step 3: Color in the checklist provided.

If you have five circles filled in the My Body section, for example, color in the bottom five boxes of column A, and so on. Always work from the bottom up. The goal is to have the entire chart filled in. In the meantime, you have a current picture of how you are doing in each of the 10 areas.

Step 4: Keep playing until all boxes are filled in.

This process can take between six months and five years. Use your coach or advisor to assist you, and check back quarterly for maintenance. Also, please note that if any of the categories don't fit with you, cross them out and fill in what does work for you. Most of all, have fun with this!

Progress Chart

Date	Points (+/−)	Score

Buff It Up! Program 100-Point Checklist

					Sections					
#	A	B	C	D	E	F	G	H	I	J
10										
9										
8										
7										
6										
5										
4										
3										
2										
1										

Give yourself credit as you get points from the 100-point program. Fill in columns from the bottom up.

A. My Body

Number of circles checked (10 max) _____

○ My hair is the color, shape, style, and cut that I most love.
○ My skin is toned, clear, and glowing.
○ My eyes shine and are the color I most want.
○ My teeth look great; the color and shape are as I want them.
○ I eat only the foods that my body works best with.
○ I only eat fresh, healthy, and nourishing foods.
○ My fingernails and toenails look perfect and healthy.
○ My posture is great: I stand tall and walk gracefully.
○ I look 10 years younger than I am. I age slowly.
○ I have all the sex I want, and it's great and healthy for both of us.

B. My Spirit

Number of circles checked (10 max) _____

- ○ I see the beauty in everything and everyone.
- ○ I listen more than I speak.
- ○ I simply do not get sick.
- ○ I am well connected to spirit, which is my energy source.
- ○ Nothing breaks around me.
- ○ I believe it's possible to get 100 on this without struggling.
- ○ I never raise my voice.
- ○ I walk around feeling overwhelmingly grateful.
- ○ I grasp concepts and ideas quickly; there are no blocks.
- ○ I feel very connected with others.

C. My Heart

Number of circles checked (10 max) _____

- ○ I only have happy, loving dreams.
- ○ Every friend I have makes me feel great, all of the time.
- ○ I simply do not have negative thoughts.
- ○ All of my emotional needs are fully taken care of, always.
- ○ I have virtually no concerns, problems, or worries.
- ○ I am light-hearted and delightful to be with.
- ○ I have plenty of love for everyone.
- ○ I protect myself from people who are needy or insensitive.
- ○ I always ask for exactly what I need, before I need it.
- ○ I am fully developed and mature: I no longer react.

D. My Self-Care

Number of circles checked (10 max) _____

- ○ I have a facial weekly.
- ○ I have a massage weekly.
- ○ I have my hair trimmed or styled at least monthly.
- ○ I treat myself better than anyone I know.
- ○ I've had my colors done, and my clothes make me look great.
- ○ I only wear natural fibers.
- ○ My phone has a nice ring to it.

○ I only wear shined, attractive, and well-heeled shoes.
○ I only drink clean water.
○ I have my car cleaned professionally, biweekly.

E. My Home

Number of circles checked (10 max) _____

○ I sleep on 300-thread count sheets or Egyptian cotton.
○ I love the view from my home.
○ I have the right amount of natural lighting in my home.
○ I love the geographic area in which I live.
○ There are no environmental toxins in my home.
○ My furniture is exactly the way I want it.
○ I always have fresh flowers in my home.
○ I feel safe, loved, and inspired in my home.
○ My home is professionally cleaned weekly.
○ I have beautiful art on my walls.

F. My Work

Number of circles checked (10 max) _____

○ My work, quite simply, is play. I have no hassles at work.
○ My work is a full expression of my top four Tru Values.
○ My files are perfectly neat and orderly.
○ I am working on a fulfilling, creative project right now.
○ The people I work with respect me and support my work.
○ I love my office or work area.
○ I have every piece of equipment I need to do a great job.
○ I am well trained and am amazingly productive.
○ I am well regarded in my field.
○ I do my job better than anyone I know in my locale.

G. My Quality of Life

Number of circles checked (10 max) _____

○ I don't do errands.
○ I work out at least three days per week and love it.

○ I have more than enough time to do what I want.
○ If I wear jewelry, it's only the finest quality.
○ Adversity and suffering are foreign concepts to me.
○ Every day feels fresh and new; nothing is carried over.
○ I am adrenaline-free.
○ I have 95+ on the Reserve Index.
○ I am proud of the life I lead.
○ I want for nothing.

H. My Finances

Number of circles checked (10 max) _____

○ I have $100,000 in savings or liquid investments.
○ I earn at least $100 per hour for my time.
○ I have insurance to protect me from what might harm me.
○ My taxes are professionally prepared by someone I trust.
○ I understand investments fully and am well invested.
○ Money is just a detail in my life.
○ I give 10 percent of what I make in time or cash to those I love.
○ I am saving at least 20 percent of what I make each month.
○ My net income is increasing at least 10 percent per year.
○ I have no money blocks; I live the idea of abundance.

I. My Family and Friends

Number of circles checked (10 max) _____

○ I am admired and respected by my family.
○ I know all the people I need to know.
○ Everyone around me is fulfilled.
○ I don't spend time with anyone who disturbs me.
○ I love my parents and appreciate what they've done for me.
○ My friends and family go out of their way to show their love.
○ I treat my children and/or siblings very, very well.
○ I protect myself from family and friends who aren't nice to me.
○ I've stopped looking for new friends. I have plenty!
○ I remember and celebrate my family and friends' birthdays.

J. My Magic

Number of circles checked (10 max) _____

- ○ I seem to be getting points on this program without trying.
- ○ I am a perfectionist, but not compulsive about it.
- ○ People who come into my life seem to be ready for me.
- ○ Everything I need consistently comes to me.
- ○ My plants never die.
- ○ People are always great to me.
- ○ When I want something, I always get it, easily.
- ○ Animals and children are drawn to me.
- ○ Life is easy for me.
- ○ I love this personal perfection program.

Chapter 10

Personal Evolution

This chapter will continue your coachees' personal evolution and take everything they have learned up to this point to the next level. It will continue their growth and development as people.

Included is information on evolving, ways to evolve, and how to know you are evolving. There are lists, assessments, and programs to support the coachee in this continued growth.

The following sections are included in this chapter:

1. 100 Ways to Know You're Evolving
2. 100 Key Distinctions to Fully Understand and Evolve Into
3. 21 Evolutionary Practices
4. Evolutionary Progressions
5. Evolutionary Progressions: 100 Three-Step Developments
6. Extreme Self-Care Program
7. 101 Relationship Questions: Ways to Know You're Evolving

100 Ways to Know You're Evolving

1. Relating

- ○ I can say no easily and kindly, without feeling funny about it.
- ○ Negative and cynical people have disappeared from my life.
- ○ I am surrounded by people who are in touch with themselves.
- ○ I can be with anyone without feeling uncomfortable or reacting to them.
- ○ I let people evolve me instead of resisting them.
- ○ I find myself having upgraded levels of conversation everywhere I go.
- ○ My boundaries are extensive, yet people are close to me.
- ○ I find myself connecting with others in new ways.
- ○ Most of my relationships are interdevelopmental, not just interdependent.

2. Learning

- ○ I honor my relationships enough to ignore nothing.
- ○ I no longer feel compelled to learn, yet I find that I'm continually learning on a profound level.
- ○ I synthesize all that occurs and use it to my advantage.
- ○ I am so sensitive to my environment that I notice, embrace, integrate, and assimilate even the slightest change.
- ○ I can give simple language to the most complex issues.
- ○ I stay fully caught up with technology.
- ○ Discovering the truth of something is a joy for me.
- ○ I have extended my intelligence by connecting with people who can use it.
- ○ I constantly experiment with the gifts I have.
- ○ I follow my whims instead of disregarding them as impractical or unwise.
- ○ The unknown has become a doorway, not a cliff.

3. Effectiveness

○ I no longer feel the need to fix or improve myself or others.

○ I don't look for things to motivate me; getting up in the morning is all I need.

○ Synchronicity (fortuitous timing) has become the norm. It occurs so frequently that it's easy to accomplish things.

○ Being important, admired, or impressive has become irrelevant.

○ I always use synergy, whether with others or alone.

○ I am skilled at creating environments that facilitate what I want to do.

○ I am inspired by people, possibilities, or events, instead of being motivated by factors or situations.

○ I attract instead of selling or pushing.

○ I can do much more with a lot less.

○ I am able to experience (and harvest) energy from almost every person, event, object, and environment.

4. You

○ I feel inner peace almost all of the time.

○ My needs are quiet because they are so well met.

○ I am willing to go back to foundational work whenever it is needed instead of thinking I've evolved beyond that.

○ I wouldn't even think of being inauthentic.

○ I've gotten over myself in every possible way, yet I honor my self, my needs, and my soul.

○ I have nothing left to prove.

○ I've developed my own personal operating system (POS).

○ I am shameless.

○ I enjoy being a work in progress, yet I am complete as well.

○ My behavior is increasingly becoming an expression of my evolving true self.

5. Living

○ My evolution is a by-product of living a creative life, not an objective to reach.

○ Traditions are a choice, not a habit or obligation.

○ I get what I want, without having to push or exploit to get it.

○ Possibility is my currency because I'm living in reality.

○ Living life has become an art form.

○ Creativity has become a way of life.

○ I easily ask for exceptions and special treatment whenever I need them.

○ I live ecologically because I respect nature.

○ I am taking better and better care of myself because evolving calls me to, without forcing myself to.

○ I love my life.

6. Flow

○ I have progressed beyond freedom and now maintain an "absence of."

○ I accept the inevitable variations in the rhythm, rate, and quality of my evolutionary experiences.

○ I can give generously because I have reserves.

○ Time is irrelevant because I am in the flow.

○ I live in harmony with the physical universe.

○ Fear doesn't stop me for very long.

○ I am quite comfortable outside of my comfort zone.

○ I can respond fully to surprising developments because I have enough space and reserves in my life.

○ I've stopped resisting.

○ Grace is present in all that I do.

7. Thinking

- ○ I'd rather trust my intuition and be wrong than trust my mind and always be right.

- ○ Whatever happens, I know there is always another way of looking at it.

- ○ I am aware that every problem has multiple solutions.

- ○ Apparent contradictions aren't.

- ○ I grasp and embrace complex ideas within several minutes.

- ○ I have a regular source of information and ideas outside of my usual network, so my thinking stays fresh, global, and innovative.

- ○ My brain, mind, and spirit have found a common language to communicate with.

- ○ I find it easy to integrate seemingly unconnected or random events.

- ○ I'd rather adopt a new paradigm than push myself in the current one.

- ○ I have all of the language I need to express all that I am feeling and seeing.

8. Skill sets

- ○ My ability to respond to new information is increasing exponentially.

- ○ Mutating doesn't scare me.

- ○ I've stopped trying to evolve, and yet I evolve.

- ○ I have become a conduit as well as a source.

- ○ I've mastered the cyberskills.

- ○ My body guides me in my decisions during the day.

- ○ I find developing my skills to be an increasingly enjoyable process, even with the inevitable learning curve.

- ○ I've become super-conductive—reducing the energy I need by 90 percent.

- ○ I've simplified everything because I enjoy things that way.

- ○ Uncertainty is not a problem.

9. Perspective

○ I don't mind losing who I used to be even if I was terrific.

○ I view the world as an interrelated web—everything is connected, especially in nature.

○ I see that flow is a seemingly chaotic web of events, not a linear path.

○ I have come to accept the inevitable element of chaos inherent in the evolutionary process.

○ When facing a big problem, I can increase the context enough to create a strategy for quick resolution.

○ When I see that a paradigm does not work in a particular area, I look for a new paradigm that does.

○ I see the subtle distinctions in every situation that show me the opportunity that is always there.

○ I read and view a wide enough variety of magazines, books, and movies to stimulate my thinking, feeling, and awareness.

○ I laugh at my own expectations when they arise.

○ I laugh at my own humanness. It's funny.

10. Orientation

○ I've become the host of a thriving network and evolve as I learn new ways to serve them.

○ Success has become a feeling, not an outcome.

○ I have chosen to evolve myself, not just develop myself.

○ I have become strength based, not power based.

○ I've chosen my sources of energy, and they are effective for me.

○ I'm not afraid to have a perfect life, even if it means making significant changes.

○ I can easily change my assumptions; they are disposable.

○ I've shifted from a hunger for knowledge to a desire to learn.

○ My definition of success continues to change.

○ The past and future have become mostly irrelevant given the richness of the present.

100 Key Distinctions to Fully Understand and Evolve Into

Distinctions are word pair comparisons where one word is stronger or more evolved than the other. In the examples provided, the first word of the pair is the more evolved of the two. The value of distinctions is that they highlight an often subtle difference between two fairly similar words. This difference is more than semantic—it's evolutionary. In other words, as you learn distinctions, you start to gravitate to and orient around the stronger of the pair.

If you know the difference, put an X in the preceding box. If you know the difference and your life is fully oriented around the first of the word pair, then fill in the box. The goal is to have all 100 boxes filled in.

1. 1–10

○ Accept versus justify

○ Accomplishments versus results

○ Adding value versus adding more

○ Assimilation versus integration

○ Assist versus help

○ Attain versus achieve

○ Attract versus seduce

○ Authentic versus genuine

○ Awareness versus knowledge

○ Balance versus juggle

2. 11–20

○ Buff versus excellence

○ Build versus create

○ Capillary system versus promotion machine

○ Cellular learning versus acquire knowledge

○ Centers of influence (COI) versus network

○ Character versus personality

○ Charge neutral versus charge up/down

○ Choice versus decision

○ Coach versus consult

○ Coach versus help

3. 21–30

- Compassion versus empathy
- Competence versus experience
- Complete versus finished
- Condition versus force

- Confidence versus arrogance
- Constructive versus comparative
- Cooperation versus competition
- Courage versus bravado
- Deliver versus do
- Desire versus compulsion

4. 31–40

- Discern versus judge
- Distinction versus definition
- Do versus say
- Distinguished distinction versus ignorance
- Effective versus efficient
- Emotional cost versus financial cost
- Enroll versus sell
- Eternity versus purpose
- Evolve versus learn
- Experiment versus test

5. 41–50

- Expertise versus experience
- Extensive versus inadequate boundaries
- Extreme self-care versus just enough
- Feel versus think

- Feeling versus emotional reaction
- Financial independence versus savings
- Flow versus momentum
- For versus about
- Freedom versus relief
- Fulfillment versus satisfaction

6. 51–60

- Generosity versus giving
- Get versus understand

- Healed versus healing
- High standards versus self-righteousness
- Honor versus protect
- Inform versus promote

- Initiate versus respond
- Inkling versus evidence
- Inspire versus motivate
- Integrated versus compartmentalized

7. 61–70

○ Integrity versus morality

○ Interdevelopmental versus interdependent

○ Intuition versus instinct

○ Language versus articulate

○ Life design versus life plan

○ Life versus lifestyle

○ Market talents versus market self

○ Mastery versus expert

○ Material versus important

○ Matter versus mean something

8. 71–80

○ Meme versus gene

○ Model versus description

○ Model versus expert

○ Need versus want

○ Overrespond versus overreact

○ Path versus circle

○ Personal versus personable

○ Possibility versus pipe dream

○ Present versus future

○ Pull goals versus push goals

9. 81–90

○ Ready versus able

○ Relationship versus result

○ Reserve versus reserves

○ Restore versus recover

○ Self-worth versus self-esteem

○ Selfish versus needy

○ Sensitize versus sensitive

○ Shift versus change behavior

○ Simplify versus eradicate

○ Solution versus answer

10. 91–100

○ Space versus time

○ Standards versus boundaries

○ Surrender versus accept

○ Toleration-free zone versus intolerant

○ Truth versus facts

○ Underpromise versus overdeliver

○ Values versus morals

○ Vision versus goal

○ Who versus What

○ You versus roles

21 Evolutionary Practices

Personal evolution is distinct from personal development. When you evolve, you alter. When you develop, you become more of who you are. Both are excellent approaches to a rich and fulfilling life, but they are different enough that a coach should know which is occurring with his or her clients. Want to evolve yourself? Here's what to do.

○ Surround yourself with new ideas instead of recycling your beliefs:
Beliefs can limit your ability to experience life as it unfolds.

○ Seek out chaos whenever you can:
The unexpected is necessary for survival in a rapidly changing world.

○ Let your environments do most of your evolutionary work for you:
Evolution occurs as you respond to the stimuli of such environments.

○ Use tolerations to evolve how you operate:
Every single thing you are putting up with is an opportunity waiting to be leveraged.

○ Constantly experiment until you do so naturally and effortlessly:
You may need to alter your relationship with risk in order to enjoy experimentation.

○ Spend more time in nature:
Nature nourishes and calibrates our natural systems.

○ Become the host of a thriving network:
Let your network evolve as you invent clever ways to serve them.

○ Continuously integrate all aspects of your life:
Integration evolves you from being needlessly complicated to being richly complex.

○ Invest in your virtual environments, not just your physical environments:
Life is becoming more virtual.

○ Actively choose and design your sources of energy:
You can then operate at a higher, more effective frequency.

○ Become superconductive:
Reduce the energy you consume by 90 percent by reducing your resistance to yourself, life, and events.

○ Master the evolving cyberskills:
Extend your intelligence by connecting with everyone and utilizing all aspects of the internet.

○ Surround yourself with people who are eagerly evolving:
They spark you and you spark them. Evolution occurs naturally.

○ Stop resisting:
Assimilate events the first time they occur. Synchronicity doesn't occur very often when you are fighting flow.

○ Choose a goal or vision that is bigger than you are:
Be pulled forward by it instead of pushing yourself.

○ Get over yourself in every possible way:
Release the cultural, mimetic, and ego binds that keep you who you've been.

○ Get to know every element of who you are and how you operate:
This process of discovery and integration provides you with the awareness you need to handle whatever comes up in life so that you don't get waylaid by it.

○ Take your gifts very, very seriously:
Design your life to fully develop and express them. Gifts are the levers of evolution.

○ Emotionally heal, completely:
Healing maximizes your emotional IQ and increases the rate at which you learn.

○ Follow your whims:
Whims are messages; develop the skill to read them.

○ Make what you don't know more interesting than what you do know:
Enjoy learning more than teaching.

Evolutionary Progressions

In this section are 100 three-step evolutionary progressions. Read through each of these and fill in the box, diamond, or circle that precedes the level that you are at in each of the 100 areas of life. If the progression does not apply to you, fill in the circle. If you are not sure what a term means, move left until you find a term that you are clear on and fill in that box or diamond (and ask your coach). Then add up your total score. A box is one point, a diamond is worth two points, and a circle will give you three points. Maximum points are 300. Anything above 200 points is very good. Over 250 is excellent! Check back monthly to update your score.

☐ Relief	◇ Freedom	○ Absence of
☐ Appreciation	◇ Gratitude	○ Acceptance
☐ Do	◇ Deliver	○ Accomplish
☐ Idea	◇ Expression	○ Art
☐ Accept	◇ Integrate	○ Assimilate
☐ Seduction	◇ Promotion	○ Attraction
☐ Honest	◇ Genuine	○ Authentic
☐ Revenue	◇ Passive revenue	○ Automated revenue
☐ Assumptions	◇ Beliefs	○ Believe
☐ Pleasure	◇ Joy	○ Bliss
☐ Movement	◇ Improvement	○ Breakthrough
☐ Sympathy	◇ Empathy	○ Caring
☐ Revenue	◇ Net profit	○ Cash flow
☐ Initiate	◇ Generate	○ Cause
☐ Cognitive	◇ Experiential	○ Cellular learning
☐ Morals	◇ Ethics	○ Character
☐ Obligation	◇ Responsibility	○ Choice
☐ Training	◇ Mentoring	○ Coaching
☐ Debate	◇ Discuss	○ Collaborate
☐ Vocabulary	◇ Language	○ Communication
☐ End	◇ Finish	○ Complete
☐ Attentive	◇ Present	○ Connected
☐ Knowledge	◇ Awareness	○ Consciousness

☐ Competition	◇ Cooperation	◯ Coopetition
☐ Discover	◇ Synthesize	◯ Create
☐ Satisfy	◇ Please	◯ Delight
☐ Want	◇ Commitment	◯ Desire
☐ Definition	◇ Comparison	◯ Distinction
☐ Promise	◇ Underpromise	◯ Don't promise
☐ Efficient	◇ Productive	◯ Effective
☐ Integrated	◇ Balanced	◯ Effortless
☐ Flow	◇ Connection	◯ Energy
☐ Support	◇ Structure	◯ Environment
☐ Juggle	◇ Balance	◯ Equilibrium
☐ Time	◇ Space	◯ Eternity
☐ Grow	◇ Develop	◯ Evolve
☐ Change	◇ Shift	◯ Evolve
☐ Help	◇ Assist	◯ Expand
☐ Product	◇ Service	◯ Experience economy
☐ Listen	◇ Hear	◯ Experience
☐ Course	◇ Confidence	◯ Fearlessness
☐ Integration	◇ Responsiveness	◯ Flow
☐ Accept	◇ Understand	◯ Forgive
☐ Product	◇ Brand	◯ Franchise
☐ Gratification	◇ Satisfaction	◯ Fulfillment
☐ Listen	◇ Hear	◯ Get
☐ Understand	◇ Accept	◯ Get
☐ Style	◇ Refinement	◯ Grace
☐ Balance	◇ Peace	◯ Harmony
☐ Wantingness	◇ Deservingness	◯ Havingness
☐ Know	◇ Feel	◯ Inkle
☐ Evidence	◇ Intuition	◯ Inkling
☐ Manager	◇ Guide	◯ Inspire
☐ Challenged	◇ Motivated	◯ Inspired

☐	Honesty	◇	Responsibility	○	Integrity
☐	Interdependent	◇	Interdevelopmental	○	Intermagical
☐	Experiment	◇	Innovate	○	Invent
☐	Teaching	◇	Facilitating	○	Learning
☐	Acquire information	◇	Study	○	Learn
☐	Contribution	◇	Value added	○	Legacy
☐	Competent	◇	Expert	○	Master
☐	Competence	◇	Expertise	○	Mastery
☐	Content	◇	Context	○	Meaning
☐	Idea	◇	Opinion	○	Message
☐	Intermediate	◇	Advanced	○	Metz-level
☐	Plan	◇	System	○	Model
☐	Want	◇	Focus	○	Occurrence
☐	Expense	◇	Investment	○	Opportunity cost
☐	SOP	◇	MO	○	OS (operating system)
☐	React	◇	Respond	○	Overrespond
☐	Position	◇	Perspective	○	Paradigm
☐	Network	◇	Community	○	Partners
☐	Perfectionism	◇	Perfection	○	Perfect
☐	Future	◇	Eternity	○	Present
☐	Notion	◇	Concept	○	Principle
☐	Interesting	◇	Intriguing	○	Profound
☐	Decide	◇	Choose	○	Respond
☐	Open	◇	Flexible	○	Responsive
☐	Egotistical	◇	Human	○	Selfish
☐	Ego	◇	Humanity	○	Self
☐	Search	◇	Experiment	○	Serendipity
☐	Symptom	◇	Cause	○	Source
☐	Boundaries	◇	Requirements	○	Standards
☐	Do	◇	Be	○	State
☐	Assist	◇	Empower	○	Strengthen

☐ Sufficiency	◇ Reserves	○ Super-reserves
☐ Timing	◇ Positioning	○ Synchronicity
☐ Plan	◇ Strategy	○ System
☐ Improve	◇ Reinvent	○ Transform
☐ Tangible	◇ Intangible	○ Transparent
☐ Integrated	◇ Automated	○ Transparent
☐ Hope	◇ Faith	○ Trust
☐ Interpretation	◇ Reality	○ Truth
☐ Facts	◇ Context	○ Truth
☐ Features	◇ Benefits	○ Value
☐ Wants	◇ Needs	○ Values
☐ CEO	◇ Leader	○ Visionary
☐ Purpose	◇ Mission	○ Vision
☐ Reserves	◇ Financial Independence	○ Wealth
☐ Information	◇ Knowledge	○ Wisdom

Evolutionary Progressions: 100 Three-Step Developments

What are these?

Evolutionary progressions are the next evolutionary progression of distinctions. Distinctions, as you probably know, are two generally synonymous words, one of which is a bit more evolved than the other, like *power* and *strength*, where strength is more evolved as a way of living than power is.

Using These Progressions

You would share a progression from this list with a client who was in the middle of a transition, developmental process, and/or evolution—for example, a client who's a busy networker but doesn't seem to benefit financially from those efforts. In this case you would want to introduce the following evolutionary progression:

Network > Community > Partnerships

The client is obviously getting stuck at the networking stage.

Performance

- ○ Dedication > Motivation > Inspiration
- ○ Do > Deliver > Accomplish
- ○ Efficiency > Productivity > Effectiveness
- ○ Goal > Objective > Outcome
- ○ Improve > Excel > Attain
- ○ Objective > Strategy > Model
- ○ Organized > Systematized > Automated
- ○ Plan > Strategy > Model
- ○ Seduction > Promotion > Attraction
- ○ Underpromise > Satisfy > Overdeliver

Learning

- Surrender > Endorse > Integrate
- Accept > Integrate > Assimilate
- Acquire information > Feel > Learn
- Awareness > Comprehension > Acceptance
- Competence > Expertise > Mastery
- Feel > Get > Know
- Intellectual > Experiential > Cellular learning
- Listen > Experience > Evolve
- Information > Context > Understanding
- Sensations > Language > Awareness

Oneself

- Boundaries > Standards > Safety
- Capacity > Bandwidth > Flow
- Confidence > Fearlessness > Edge
- Ego > Humanity > Self
- Honesty > Integrity > Wholeness
- Morals > Ethics > Character
- Obligation > Duty > Responsibility
- Personality > Qualities > Character
- Purpose > Role > Mission
- Self-care > Selfullness > Selfishness

Behavior

- Attention > Focus > Presence
- Courageous > Shameless > Fearless
- Compulsion > Need > Desire
- Experiment > Innovate > Evolve
- Power > Development > Strength
- Recover > Restore > Strengthen
- Style > Effortlessness > Grace
- Vitality > Energy > Spirit
- Preference > Compulsion > Addiction
- Risk > Threat > Fear

Relating

- Attentive > Present > Responsive
- Connect > Interact > Dance
- Connect > Synthesize > Create
- Honest > Genuine > Authentic
- Interdependent > Interdevelopmental > Intermagical

- Network > Community > Partnerships
- Succumb > Surrender > Trust
- Touching > Impactful > Profound
- Trust > Compatibility > Bond
- Empathy > Forgiveness > Compassion

Communicate and Relate

- Control > Manager > Coach
- Help > Assist> Empower
- Hint > Suggest > Request
- Linear > Intuitive > Laser coaching
- Suggest > Advise > Recommend
- Support > Advise > Coach
- Accurate > Informative > Constructive
- Ask > Challenge > Inspire
- Language > Connection > Communication
- Listen > Hear > Get

Time, Space, and Events

- Cause > Effect > Chaos
- Complex > Simple > Transparent
- Forever > Eternity > Present
- Synchronicity > Serendipity > Magic
- Tangible > Intangible > Space
- Time > Space > Vacuum
- Increase > Critical mass > Combustion
- Ended > Finished > Complete
- React > Respond > Overrespond
- Relief > Freedom > Absence of

Information

- Content > Context > Meaning
- Facts > Truth > Understanding
- Important > Key > Pivotal
- Information > Knowledge > Expertise
- Interpretation > Reality > Truth
- Assess > Measure > Compare
- Notion > Concept > Theory
- Position > Perspective > Paradigm
- Facts > Truths > Messages
- Definition > Description > Distinction

Personal Development

- ○ Basic > Advanced > Meta
- ○ Believe in > Commit to > Stand for
- ○ Change > Shift > Evolve
- ○ Clean Sweep > Personal Foundation > Attraction
- ○ Condition > Sensitize > Experience
- ○ Improvement > Empowerment > Breakthrough
- ○ Innovate > Revolutionize > Reinvent
- ○ Awareness > Intelligence > Wisdom
- ○ Perspective > Context > Paradigm
- ○ Reinvention > Transformation > Evolution

Business

- ○ Capital > Investment > Return
- ○ Cash flow > Profit > Dividends
- ○ CEO > Leader > Visionary
- ○ Company traditions > Practices > Culture
- ○ Features > Benefits > Value
- ○ Genre > Niche > Specialty
- ○ Product > Brand > Franchise
- ○ Sell > Enroll > Attract
- ○ Trade > Business > Economy
- ○ Objectives > Business Plan > Budget

Extreme Self-Care Program

Instructions

There are four steps to completing the **Extreme Self-Care** program.

Step 1: Answer each question.

Give yourself credit for completing each item. Be a tough grader. Don't go for the points—go for the truth. However, if the item does not fit for you or doesn't apply, or if you don't agree with it, please just reword or change the item so it does work for you.

Step 2: Summarize each section.

Add up the number of checked circles in each of the 10 sections and write those amounts where indicated. Then add up all 10 sections and write the current total in the progress chart. The maximum score is 100.

Step 3: Color in the checklist.

If you have nine checks filled in under the Stress Elimination section, for example, color in the bottom nine boxes of column A of the checklist, and so on. Or you can fill in the boxes that match the statement you get credit for.

Step 4: Keep playing until all boxes are filled in.

You can do it! This process may take 30 or 360 days, but you can achieve a perfect score on the Extreme Self-Care program. Use your coach or a friend to assist you. And update once a year.

Progress Chart

Date	Points (+/−)	Score

Extreme Self-Care Program 100-Point Checklist

Sections										
#	A	B	C	D	E	F	G	H	I	J
10										
9										
8										
7										
6										
5										
4										
3										
2										
1										

Give yourself credit as you get points from the 100-point program. Fill in columns from the bottom up.

Living in today's world places many demands on your body, mind, heart, and spirit. The purpose of this program is to guide you as you focus on yourself in order to strengthen your balance, wellness, and quality of life. The key word in the program title is *extreme*. Everyone has his or her own way of working this program, so please adapt it to meet your needs.

The Extreme Self-Care program consists of 100 items that, when completed, will likely result in emotional and physical balance for you.

The 10 areas of the program are:

A. Stress elimination
B. Environment and family
C. Pleasure
D. Health and emotional balance
E. Special care items
F. Support and experts
G. Ingestion
H. Appearance
I. Sustainability
J. Daily rituals

A. Stress Elimination

Note that the section title is Stress *Elimination*, not Stress Reduction.

Number of circles checked (10 max) _____

○ If my job, business, or profession is harming me and I can't seem to make it completely stress-free, I have quit, have sold it, or am changing professions.
○ I have made a list of the 10 promises that I have made to others that are causing me stress, even if it's stress that I can handle.
○ I have revoked all 10 of these promises and have worked something else out.
○ I have identified the three primary sources (people, roles, others' expectations) of my current stress.
○ I have completely eliminated these three items.
○ I have cut out most volunteer activities, unless they directly support all of my life.
○ I have a house cleaner.
○ Someone else runs my errands.
○ All bills, paperwork, and administrative tasks have been outsourced and are electronically handled and/or I have an assistant who handles everything administratively, automatically.
○ Any legal, tax, or financial clouds or problems have been completely resolved.

B. Environment and Family

We are such a product of our environment, and we have the option of designing and educating our environment(s) to be exactly what's best for us.

Number of circles checked (10 max) _____

- ○ I live in a nurturing home environment.
- ○ My computer is backed up weekly.
- ○ My pets (if any) add energy to my life.
- ○ My spouse (if any) adds energy to my life.
- ○ My children (if any) add energy to my life.
- ○ There is absolutely no clutter or messes in or around my home or office.
- ○ Everything is fully and properly organized and filed in my home and office. (Everything!)
- ○ I'm fully aware of every aspect of my physical environment and draw energy from it.
- ○ I fully respond to my environment. If something goes wrong, I quickly learn from the experience and immediately grow.
- ○ If I don't like something, I fix it, now.

C. Pleasure

You know what makes you feel great, so please write down your 10 favorite personal, whimsical, intellectual, and entertainment pleasures here.

Number of circles checked (10 max) _____

- ○ _____
- ○ _____
- ○ _____
- ○ _____
- ○ _____
- ○ _____
- ○ _____
- ○ _____
- ○ _____
- ○ _____

D. Health and Emotional Balance

The list below contains physical and emotional wellness steps

Number of circles checked (10 max) _____

- ○ I have "given up" the future; I am living in the here and now, and I am not chasing anything.
- ○ I have a complete physical exam every one to three years.
- ○ I have had a complete blood work up and discussed the results with a licensed nutritionist.
- ○ I exercise three to seven times a week for at least 30 minutes, even if I have to hire a trainer to keep me on track.
- ○ If I react to others or to problems, I have gotten to the source of the emotional reaction.
- ○ I have excellent posture, I move naturally, and my body is well balanced and integrated.
- ○ If I am not eating perfectly, I have arranged nutritionally correct prepared food to be delivered twice weekly.
- ○ I am calm. I am adrenaline-free.
- ○ I have arranged to be lovingly touched or held several times per week, each time for as long as I need it.
- ○ I know what motivates me.

E. Special Care Items

On the lines provided, please write in the special needs or wants that you have that you haven't seen elsewhere in this program. Use your imagination and, of course, be very, very selfish.

Number of circles checked (10 max) _____

- ○ _____
- ○ _____
- ○ _____
- ○ _____
- ○ _____
- ○ _____
- ○ _____
- ○ _____
- ○ _____
- ○ _____

F. Support and Experts

Extreme self-care is made possible by the investment you make in all areas of your life and also the investment you make in the services of experts.

Number of circles checked (10 max) _____

- ○ I am working with a personal coach who has a track record of helping others practice extreme self-care and who walks the talk.
- ○ I have worked with a chiropractor or similar practitioner who has removed any energy blocks.
- ○ I have been Rolfed or have undergone a similar treatment.
- ○ If needed or beneficial, I am in therapy with an expert in my area of primary concern.
- ○ I have been to a dermatologist and had the skin on every part of my body thoroughly examined.
- ○ I have a supportive relationship with God (or my personal equivalent).
- ○ I am expertly massaged twice a month.
- ○ I have a friend or family member who is always a source of unconditional support and love for me.
- ○ If I have money concerns or problems, I have worked them out completely, using an expert or team of experts.
- ○ I have a Rolodex of 100 experts that I can call on for assistance (see the Team 100 checklist for a list of 100 experts).

G. Ingestion

Open mouth, insert extreme self-care.

Number of circles checked (10 max) _____

- ○ I drink at least half a gallon of spring water each day.
- ○ I take time-release Vitamin C (500–1,000 mg) daily, if recommended.
- ○ I take odorless garlic daily.
- ○ I do not smoke.
- ○ I rarely drink alcohol or use drugs.
- ○ I do not use caffeine.
- ○ I have eliminated most meat and dairy products (if medically appropriate for me) from my diet.
- ○ I take a nutritionist-recommended multivitamin daily.
- ○ I rarely eat sugar.
- ○ I treat my body like the temple that it is.

H. Appearance

Extreme self-care includes the outside part of you, not just the inside.

Number of circles checked (10 max) _____

- ○ I have tossed every single article of clothing that does not make me look great.
- ○ My hair is styled and/or colored exactly as I most like it.
- ○ I have my nails professionally manicured.
- ○ I have had my colors done, and my wardrobe colors flatter my skin tone.
- ○ If I want or need hair removed, I am seeing a licensed electrolysis expert (or similar practitioner).
- ○ I've had a hair transplant/weave or a similar procedure if I am sensitive about the amount of hair I have.
- ○ I have (or give myself) facials at least monthly.
- ○ I wear only great shoes.
- ○ My body is in excellent shape, toned and exercised regularly. I am proud of my body.
- ○ My teeth look great, and I smile broadly at every opportunity.

I. Sustainability

Part of the extreme self-care process is to integrate the changes that you are making so that they become natural behavior for you, not just a temporary effort.

Number of circles checked (10 max) _____

- ○ I am working on the Personal Foundation program (available from Coach U Inc.).
- ○ I am working on the Irresistible Attraction program (available from Coach U Inc.).
- ○ I've gotten my needs met completely.
- ○ I have restructured my finances (cut expenses, increased income) so that I have absolutely no financial concerns and money does not drive my decisions.
- ○ I have worked through all of my parent/sibling/upbringing issues in therapy. I am not living according to, or being blindly guided by, the past.
- ○ I have resolved and healed from whatever damage that was done to me prior to today.
- ○ I say no easily.
- ○ As a part of the extreme self-care process, I have radically raised my personal standards.
- ○ Everyone around me is on a similar extreme self-care track. No one is sabotaging my efforts or me.
- ○ I know what my strengths are, and I have installed support systems to do for me what I can't, won't, or don't do for myself.

J. Daily Rituals

Extreme self-care is a daily process, not just a one-time program.

Number of circles checked (10 max) _____

- ○ I stretch daily.
- ○ I have a relaxing pre-bedtime ritual (reading, music, touch, etc.) so I fall asleep with a smile on my face.
- ○ I floss well, twice daily.
- ○ My routine upon rising is nourishing and deliberate; it's not influenced by pressure.
- ○ I make sure that my days are spent doing what I most want to do, not what I should be doing or what others expect of me.
- ○ I underpromise, consistently—I don't get caught up in the performance or catch-up trap.
- ○ I have something wonderful to look forward to each evening.
- ○ I have specially identified time just for me in my schedule.
- ○ I am physically active each day.
- ○ I don't lose touch with myself during the day.

101 Relationship Questions: Ways to Know You're Evolving

The following are 101 questions for you and your spouse or partner to ask each other.

1. Communication

○ When you get home from work, what are the three things you would like me to do or say in the first several minutes?

○ How will you tell me that you've changed your responses to any of these questions?

○ What do I say that makes you the most uncomfortable when we are alone together?

○ What do I say that makes you the most uncomfortable when we are together in public?

○ What are you tolerating about the way we speak with each other?

○ What about my voice or communication style makes you want to spend more time with me?

○ What about my voice or communication style makes you want to spend less time with me?

○ How do you feel about arguing or fighting?

○ What should I never say to you, even in anger or frustration?

○ What will I have to say or do to get your attention when I've not been able to?

2. Our Happiness

○ How much space or time do we need apart during the day? Week? Month? Year?

○ How long are we in this relationship for?

○ What will keep us happily together?

○ What need of yours will I never be able to fill or satisfy?

○ Why is that?

○ What kind of memories do we want to create together?

○ What do you expect from me that you really should be expecting of yourself?

○ What has held you back, intimacy-wise, in your personal relationships?

○ Who do we know who has the kind of intimacy that we most want?

○ How much room or license do we have to ask each other to change?

○ What changes do you think I'll need to make in order for you to be really happy?

452

3. Our Relationship

○ What will be the early warning signs that our relationship is in trouble?

○ How will we know if our relationship is over?

○ What activities and common interests can we develop that will bring us closer together?

○ What are you willing to do with or for me that you haven't been willing to do in any previous relationship?

○ What are your feelings about monogamy at this stage of our relationship? Is it possible that that will change over the next 10 years?

○ Why are we in this relationship in the first place?

○ Where will we be in this relationship five years from now?

○ What's the biggest lesson you can learn from me?

○ What's the biggest lesson I can learn from you?

○ What about our relationship will evolve us both?

4. Our Reactions

○ What is going to set you off?

○ What can you say to me before this happens?

○ What do you do when you feel hurt by me?

○ How will I be able to be forgiven when I've done something that really hurts you?

○ What will ruin our relationship?

○ Which of my weaknesses have you totally accepted and no longer have a problem with?

○ Who do I remind you of? Is that okay?

○ What are three concerns you have about my emotional or psychological state or personality?

○ What habits do I have that are upsetting you?

5. What Happens If ...

○ What will you do when you feel tempted sexually by another person?

○ What do we do if one of us wants sex and the other one does not?

○ What will you say—or not say—if you cheat on me?

○ What happens if we can't agree on something important that involves both of us?

○ How can we get both of our needs met when we want different things on a particular day?

○ What do we do if both of us are having a bad day?

○ What happens if we're upset with each other before we go to sleep?

○ What happens if one of us needs more space than the other?

○ What happens if I can't stand someone who becomes a close friend or associate of yours?

○ What happens if I get discouraged about our relationship?

6. Touching (nonsexual)

○ What kind of touch or demonstration best says "I love you" to you?

○ What are the three parts of your body that you most like touched? How?

○ What are the three parts of your body that you most like massaged?

○ How close do you like to sit when eating together?

○ How "touchy" do you like to be with me?

○ How "touchy" do you want me to be with you?

○ How do you feel about public displays of affection?

○ Where should I *not* touch you? Why?

○ How should I touch you differently?

○ How will you tell me when you need to not be touched for a little while?

7. Preventing Problems

○ What could I do that will cause you to pull away from me?

○ What's our code word to use during a conversation or argument when one of is getting hurt and a time out is needed?

○ What can we do to avoid arguing or fighting entirely? Is it possible?

○ When we argue, how will you take responsibility for your part of the problem?

○ What about our living situation is likely to give us a recurring problem?

○ What about our personalities is likely to give us a recurring problem?

○ What about our financial situation is likely to give us a recurring problem?

○ What about our children is likely to give us a recurring problem?

○ What about our parents or family is likely to give us a recurring problem?

○ What about our work is likely to give us a recurring problem?

8. Sexual Discovery

○ What is the ideal way for me to start the sexual process?

○ What five things work well for you as an aphrodisiac?

○ How will we let each other know what we want sexually?

○ How much time do you usually need to warm up?

○ Do you prefer sex in the evening? Morning? Daytime? Any time?

○ How many days between sex will be too long?

○ How long should sex take, from beginning to end?

○ Do you like to talk during sex (dirty or conversational)?

○ Besides the bedroom, is there any place else in the house that you like to have sex?

○ What's the biggest sexual turnoff for you?

9. Sexual Preferences

O Would you like to be more aggressive or dominant with me, sexually?

O What do you think I like most in our lovemaking?

O What were the hottest sexual experiences you've ever had?

O How important is hot sex to you in our relationship?

O If I said you could do anything to me, what would that be?

O What about my personality is sexy to you?

O Which sexual positions or acts are off limits forever and ever?

O Which sexual positions or acts are off limits, at least for now?

O What is a fantasy of yours that I probably will never be able to fulfill?

O What should I say or not say during your orgasm?

10. Sexual Activities

O What are the five most sexually sensitive areas of your body?

O Is there something you really like to do sexually that you're afraid I won't like or will think less of you for liking?

O What are the five things you like most about my body? Why?

O What drives you wild?

O What fantasy would you like to act out with me?

O If we did the same thing each time for sex, what would you want that to be?

O What do you most want to do after we've had sex?

O What are your favorite sexual positions and activities?

O What's the kinkiest thing we'll probably ever do together?

11. And ...

O What's the most sacred part of you?

www.coachinc.com

Part 3
Business Coaching

Chapter 11

Business Coaching

This chapter targets the business world from sole proprietors to corporations and includes information, forms, and programs relating to businesses or organizations. They can be used for your client's business or within corporations. Not all will be applicable to all situations; however, feel free to adapt them to suit your needs.

The information is laid out in such a way as to provide introductory material, programs to work through for skill awareness and growth, business forms, tracking sheets, and checklists. You may wish to pass them on to your coachees.

The following sections are included in this chapter:

1. The Coach Approach: An Introduction to Coaching in the Organization
2. Coach Manager/Staff Excellence Program
3. Communication Faults: 100 Communication Mistakes People Make
4. Certified Communicator Program
5. Biz Whiz Success Program
6. Professional Practice Checklist
7. New Business Start-Up Program
8. Business Mission Statement
9. Business Budget
10. The Friday Checklist
11. Annual Goals Chart
12. Internet Marketing 100
13. Web Site 100: Design and Functional Elements of a Terrific Web Site
14. E-Tip Broadcasting: 100 Steps to Setting Up a Successful E-News or E-Tip Broadcast

The Coach Approach: An Introduction to Coaching in the Organization

Read and understand the following.

The Reasons Organizations Are Adopting a Coach Approach

In the aftermath of downsizing and outsourcing, a new approach to working with people to achieve business results is essential.

- The pace of business has changed.
- Business is global, and there is a need for greater inclusiveness and valuing of diversity in order for businesses to be competitive.
- Coaching can help eliminate a culture of fear and paternalism.
- Today, technology does not provide a competitive advantage; people do.
- The employment contract has changed, and individuals are now more responsible for managing their own development and career advancement.

What Coaching Is

- Creating a trusting and collaborative environment in which personal development and performance improvement occur
- Having a respectful conversation that focuses on the person being coached
- A positive style of relating that can be utilized anywhere, any time
- A means of helping people achieve extraordinary performance
- A way of being with another individual that promotes reflection, self-discovery, and openness to taking more effective actions

What Coaching Is Not

- Directing, controlling, or manipulating others according to the coach's agenda.
- Having all the answers and solving problems for others.
- Being judgmental or punitive.
- Coaching without mutual understanding and agreement.
- Counseling or therapy.

What a Coach Does

- Models integrity and high standards for others.
- Establishes collaborative relationships based on trust.
- Treats others with respect, always using language that is constructive.
- Tells the truth in a way that enables others to hear it and grow as a result.
- Provides objectivity.
- Promotes discovery of possibilities, solutions, and alternatives.
- Supports others to stretch beyond their current capabilities.
- Assists others to look honestly at gaps in their attitudes or behaviors that decrease their interpersonal effectiveness.

How Coaching Benefits the Organization

- It is applicable to individuals and teams throughout the organization.
- It uses a common language that everyone can relate to.
- It complements other quality improvement processes.
- Its results are measurable and sustainable.
- It promotes focused discussions tied to the achievement of business results.
- It promotes development of new skills in the organization.
- It fosters future-oriented thinking.

How Coaching Benefits Individuals

- It emphasizes the unique potential of individuals.
- It provides a structure and a process for individual development.
- It uses language that is grounded in respect for people and their capabilities.
- It establishes the focus on the person being coached.
- It promotes personal discovery and self responsibility for solving problems.
- It fosters the development of high levels of self-confidence and mastery.

- It forms a basis for planning for career advancement.
- It provides a model for personal leadership development.

Why a Coaching Conversation Is More Likely to Achieve Results

- There's a purpose and focus to the conversation.
- The structure of the coaching conversation helps both the coach and the client to stay on track.
- The structure of the conversation fosters heightened attention and new awareness.
- The coaching conversation creates a safe space in which present limitations or challenges can be examined and acted upon.
- Boundaries and time frames for agreed-upon actions are established.
- Accountability is built into the structure and process of the coaching conversation.

Coach Manager/Staff Excellence Program

We've identified the 100 key skills, behaviors, and styles of the highly effective manager in the new millennium. This program is helpful in the following ways:

Management
- To shift the company culture
- To get everyone on the same track

Managers
- As a blueprint for staff training
- As a way to foster and develop teams

Staff
- To strengthen interpersonal skills
- To accelerate their career paths

The 10 areas on which to focus are:

    A. Personal balance
    B. High productivity
    C. Self-management
    D. Communication
    E. Healthy boundaries
    F. Quality work
    G. Take initiative
    H. Manage up
    I. Teamwork
    J. Career path

Instructions

There are four steps to completing the **Coach Manager/Staff Excellence** program.

Step 1: Answer each question.

If the statement is true, check the circle. If not, leave it blank until you've done what it takes. Be rigorous; be a hard grader. If the item does not apply or will never be true for you, check it anyway.

Give yourself credit. (You may do this with up to five items.) Feel free to rewrite or reword up to five of the items in this program to better suit you, your needs, and your life.

Step 2: Summarize each section.

Add up the number of checked circles for each of the 10 sections and write those amounts where indicated. Then add up all 10 sections and write the current total in the progress chart.

Step 3: Color in the checklist provided.

If you have five squares filled in the Personal Balance section, color in the bottom five boxes of column A, and so on. Always work from the bottom up. The goal is to have the entire chart filled in. This will indicate how strong you are as a coach manager. In the meantime, you have a current picture of how you are doing in each of the 10 areas.

Step 4: Keep playing until all boxes are filled in.

This process takes between six months–five years, but you can do it. Use your coach or advisor to assist you, and check back quarterly for maintenance.

Note: This is a checklist and outline of the skills and style that staff in the corporate environment can benefit from. This program is designed to be delivered by a coach trained and licensed by Coach U. This program is owned exclusively by Coach U and any adaptation or corporate use requires licensing and royalty payment. Single individuals may use this program, however, for their own professional development, with no licensing required.

Progress Chart

Date	Points (+/−)	Score

Coach Manager Program 100-Point Checklist

					Sections					
#	A	B	C	D	E	F	G	H	I	J
10										
9										
8										
7										
6										
5										
4										
3										
2										
1										

Give yourself credit as you get points from the 100-point program. Fill in columns from the bottom up.

A. Personal Balance

Number of circles checked (10 max) _____
A great manager starts with a strong person. Are you in good physical and emotional shape? Do you know who you are, what you most want, and where you are along your path of development? If not, use a coach to get this stuff handled.

- ○ I have a rewarding life outside of work.
- ○ I have a coach who is developing me personally.
- ○ I don't try to get love or personal needs met at work.
- ○ I tell the truth to myself; I don't kid myself.
- ○ I know my top Tru Values and set goals around these.
- ○ I have a very strong personal foundation.
- ○ My personal life rarely gets in the way of my work life.
- ○ I know where I am along the path of development.
- ○ My body is in excellent shape.
- ○ I am emotionally well.

B. High Productivity

Number of circles checked (10 max) _____
High productivity is not a mystery; it simply requires a commitment and the tools, training, and resources to make it happen, naturally.

- ○ I am 100 percent current, with no inventory of unfinished tasks or jobs.
- ○ I prioritize well and delegate everything I can.
- ○ I have all the equipment I need to be fully productive.
- ○ I have had all the training I need to be very productive.
- ○ I know my goals and I reach them consistently.
- ○ I can access all information quickly; my files are perfect!
- ○ My work area is spotless and orderly.
- ○ I've mastered my job and I enjoy it; there are no crises.
- ○ I have or use an agenda for meetings, yet I am flexible.
- ○ I'm fully automated (computer, fax, e-mail, systems).

C. Self-Management

Number of circles checked (10 max) _____
If you don't manage yourself, how do you expect to manage anyone else? Here's a list of 10 ways to keep yourself on track.

- ○ I'm always on time and ready for meetings; no rushing.
- ○ I've mastered time management. It all gets done well.
- ○ I dress well, am well groomed, and like the way I look.
- ○ I am very, very willing to grow and change.
- ○ I know my limits, and I underpromise consistently.
- ○ I'm almost always in a good mood, naturally.
- ○ I anticipate or respond immediately to problems.
- ○ I do it, delegate it, reject it, or dump it.
- ○ I go out of my work area for lunch and breaks.
- ○ If I find myself getting stopped or blocked, I ask for help.

D. Communication

Number of circles checked (10 max) _____

We know who people are by the way they communicate and relate with us. Here's an advanced list of skills.

○ I am unconditionally constructive whenever I speak.
○ I speak "charge neutral" versus up or down.
○ I remain criticism-free even when I correct others.
○ I have tremendous amounts of compassion for others.
○ I make my points quickly and powerfully: I "message."
○ I don't gossip. Period.
○ I always come from a positive place that is solution oriented.
○ I prepare for rather than forcing change.
○ I am direct, yet not obnoxious, in my speaking style.
○ I listen and discern *exactly* what another person is saying.

E. Healthy Boundaries

Number of circles checked (10 max) _____

Everyone wants and needs things from you. But you become a victim unless you protect yourself. Every company needs managers with strong boundaries. Don't be afraid to develop yours.

○ I take responsibility for failure, but I do not blame or shame.
○ I don't get caught up in any adrenaline or deadline rushes.
○ I don't answer the phone when I'm focused.
○ I don't let others dump on or be disrespectful to me.
○ I say no when I need to without putting people off.
○ I don't volunteer unless my work is caught up and perfect.
○ I don't tolerate very much or suffer at work.
○ I am honest with my manager regarding my workload.
○ I think about and evaluate requests before I respond.
○ I finish my work and leave on time almost every night.

F. Quality Work

Number of circles checked (10 max) _____

100 percent is now barely enough.

○ I do accurate work; things don't come back to bite me.
○ I am very proud of everything I touch and accomplish.

○ My personal standards are very, very high.
○ I come in early and under budget on my projects and tasks.
○ I continually improve and innovate on work I do.
○ I have a policy to continuously add value to products or services.
○ I am committed to the highest quality work and continued improvement.
○ I expect, foster, and even require the best from everyone.
○ I do accurate work; I don't make errors.
○ I suggest ways to create new products or services.

G. Take Initiative

Number of circles checked (10 max) _____
Companies desperately need managers to take initiative and become "intrapreneurs" so the firm can continue to create and stay ahead of the curve. This takes practice and willingness.

○ I solve problems quickly and easily; then I prevent them.
○ I am fearless: I can ask anyone for everything I need.
○ I don't wait: I act immediately.
○ I always speak up when I see a problem or possibility.
○ I don't get involved in projects that get me off track.
○ I take out "insurance" when I take a risk. I'm not foolish.
○ I take at least one big risk a week.
○ When I feel scared, I reach out to get support or confidence.
○ I am willing to make mistakes.
○ I trust and respond to my intuition, instinct, or gut.

H. Manage Up

Number of circles checked (10 max) _____
It's okay to help your manager to manage you better. This process is called managing up. Here are 10 ways.

○ I empower my manager to manage me well.
○ I keep my manager fully informed, especially of bad news.
○ I have weekly meetings with my manager to report and learn.
○ I relate to my manager as more of a great coach.
○ I make strong requests of my manager so I produce well.
○ I don't compete or react to my manager. We're equals.
○ I immediately give my manager problems I cannot solve.
○ I brief my manager well—with data, options, and recommendations.
○ I put myself in my manager's shoes and manage from there.
○ Regardless, I always stay in full communication with my manager.

I. Teamwork

Number of circles checked (10 max) _____
Nothing worth doing is worth doing alone. Teams are the answer.

- ○ I know how to be a great team player, and I am.
- ○ The team is set up to maximize strengths, not weaknesses.
- ○ I am a collaborator versus a competitor; I go for win-win.
- ○ I'm a straight shooter, very real and honest with others.
- ○ I focus on people and results, not just results.
- ○ I use the team as my resource instead of waiting for the team to help.
- ○ We are a team, not a support group. Everyone plays hard.
- ○ We get along well and respect our individual needs.
- ○ We only work on projects that warrant a team.
- ○ Every team member has a buddy or single partner.

J. Career Path

Number of circles checked (10 max) _____
Either you're designing your career or the circumstances are.

- ○ I am well connected with those who can advance me.
- ○ I am not afraid to get noticed and to shine.
- ○ I understand my firm's politics and flow with them rather than fighting them.
- ○ I'm up to speed on the development of my industry.
- ○ I am respected as a model, productive employee.
- ○ I have a clear plan for my career path.
- ○ I look for big ways to improve my company.
- ○ I know what it takes to get ahead, and I do that honorably.
- ○ I contribute to the culture of my firm.
- ○ I know and support my firm's mission, values, and goals.

Intellectual Property Notice

Communication Faults: 100 Communication Mistakes People Make

What mistakes are you making when you open your mouth? Here are 100 common communication faults. Use this checklist to strengthen your effectiveness or as part of your professional development. As you use this list, you will discover that each item leads to a person's heart and soul. If one's eyes are mirrors of the soul, communication is a mirror of the mind.

1. Lack of Credibility

○ Overpromises results or benefits

○ Overstates facts; hypes

○ Lies, misrepresents; is dishonest

○ Sneaky, not forthright

○ Eager to please, needs approval

○ Pretentious, tries to impress

○ Sounds needy, desperate

○ Insincere-sounding; not real

○ BS-er, full of it, full of themselves

○ Justifies, overexplains

2. Disrespectful

○ Critical, harsh, judgmental

○ Insensitive, no compassion

○ One-ups, downplays efforts

○ Ignores what was said

○ Patronizes, parents

○ Sexist, bigoted, intolerant

○ Digs, undermines, barbs

○ Inappropriate comments or humor

○ Stingy with praise or support

○ Hard sell; tries to convince or trick

3. Disrupts Flow

- ○ Too positive; pushes mood
- ○ Too fast, adrenalized, pushes mood
- ○ Half-duplex (can't hear when speaking)
- ○ Inattentive, easily distracted
- ○ Information-reactive (responds only to information, not person or feelings)
- ○ Literal, can't get gist easily
- ○ Keeps making point even after other person got it
- ○ Responds with non sequiturs
- ○ Interrogates, peppers with questions
- ○ Overly concerned, too significant

4. Lack of Clarity

- ○ Trite, boring, old, useless
- ○ Pat answers or quotes, walking cliché
- ○ Confusing, overly complicated
- ○ Vague, rambles, repetitive
- ○ Mishears, mislabels, assumes
- ○ Consumes information versus assimilating it
- ○ Dogmatic, righteous, singular
- ○ Linear, two-dimensional, flat information
- ○ Overloads with too much information
- ○ Too quick with advice

5. No Warmth

- ○ Cold, icy
- ○ No personality, flat, no fizz
- ○ Measured, controlled
- ○ Suspicious, distrusting
- ○ Negative, jaded, acerbic
- ○ Quickly points out flaws
- ○ Rigid
- ○ Highly technical language
- ○ Analytical; logic without feelings
- ○ Judges, labels, compartmentalizes

6. Weak Listener

- ○ Listens too hard
- ○ Listens only for the familiar; misses subtlety
- ○ Can't multiprocess (can only hear one idea, subject, or problem at a time)
- ○ Listens ignorantly (not sure what to listen for)
- ○ Doesn't echo (person doesn't feel heard)
- ○ Always preparing a response; misses what is being said
- ○ Reacts negatively, stops listening
- ○ Interrupts too much
- ○ Corrects too much

7. Poor Speaker

- ○ Doesn't condition or contextualize
- ○ Uses jargon or boilerplate
- ○ Uses generic, nonspecific language
- ○ Has inadequate vocabulary
- ○ Doesn't know distinctions
- ○ Ignorant, uninformed about life or subject
- ○ Mostly I/me oriented
- ○ Oblivious to or unaware of people's reactions
- ○ Numb, unaware of own feelings
- ○ Steps over or ignores key clues

8. Wrong Focus

- ○ Symptoms-oriented (versus source)
- ○ Problem-centric (versus source)
- ○ Past-oriented (versus present)
- ○ Future-oriented (versus present)
- ○ Consequence-oriented
- ○ Old-fashioned (versus current thinking)
- ○ Hearsay, gossip (versus fact)
- ○ Theoretical (versus practical)
- ○ Tactical (versus strategic)

9. Ineffective Style

- ○ Oblique, hinting (versus direct)
- ○ Slow, plodding (versus quick)
- ○ Draining (consumes space or energy)
- ○ Coach versus consult
- ○ Coach versus help
- ○ Matter versus mean something
- ○ Intense, overeager, too "on"
- ○ Speaks too slowly
- ○ Speaks too quickly
- ○ Bossy, domineering, controlling
- ○ Sugary sweet; puffery
- ○ Broadcasts, lectures, speaks at
- ○ Talks more than listens

10. Annoying Voice or Tone

- ○ Feeble, weak, doesn't reach or affect
- ○ Loud, booming, overpowering
- ○ Nasal, grating
- ○ High pitch, squeaky
- ○ Hesitant, tentative, unsure
- ○ Heavy breather, spitter
- ○ Shrill
- ○ Whiny
- ○ Negative, doomsday tone
- ○ Heavily significant, overacting

Certified Communicator Program

1.	How well do you come across?				
	These are how others would likely describe your communication style.				
1.	Loud	1	2	3	Quiet
2.	Fast/slow	1	2	3	Natural
3.	Charged up/down	1	2	3	Neutral
4.	Complain	1	2	3	Pleased
5.	Flat	1	2	3	Expressive
6.	Speak at	1	2	3	Share with
7.	Heavy/significant	1	2	3	Light
8.	Know-it-all	1	2	3	Simple
9.	Suspicious	1	2	3	Friendly/trusting
10.	Rigid	1	2	3	Flexible

2.	How well do you listen?				
	How well do you hear what is being said, and not said?				
11.	Listens hard	1	2	3	Be with
12.	Hears info/facts	1	2	3	Hear it all
13.	Waits for evidence	1	2	3	Trust inklings
14.	Acquires info	1	2	3	Learn
15.	Listens passively	1	2	3	Knows what to listen for
16.	Prepares response	1	2	3	Hears the person
17.	Doubting	1	2	3	Accepting
18.	Interrupts	1	2	3	Prompts
19.	One thing at a time	1	2	3	Can handle multiple inputs
20.	Hears 10–90%	1	2	3	Hears 90–100%

3.	How well do you articulate?				
	How well are you understood?				
21.	Talks at	1	2	3	Contextualizes
22.	Lectures	1	2	3	Educates
23.	Rambles	1	2	3	Succinct
24.	Clichés	1	2	3	Messages
25.	Jargon	1	2	3	English
26.	Rote	1	2	3	Personalizes
27.	General terms	1	2	3	Specific terms
28.	Holds back	1	2	3	Says it all
29.	Convoluted	1	2	3	Clear
30.	Limited vocabulary	1	2	3	Extensive vocabulary

4.	What do you converse about?			
	What do you focus on and talk about with others?			
31.	Symptoms	1	2	3	Source of the problem
32.	The negative	1	2	3	The positive
33.	The past	1	2	3	The present/how things are
34.	Coulds and shoulds	1	2	3	What you really want
35.	Reactions	1	2	3	Chosen responses
36.	Swaps info	1	2	3	Dances
37.	Responds to facts	1	2	3	Gets the gist
38.	The What	1	2	3	The Who
39.	Facts	1	2	3	Concepts
40.	Others	1	2	3	Yourselves

5.	How well do you converse?			
	How often do you have fluid, two-way conversations?			
41.	Repeats/echos	1	2	3	Improves phrasing
42.	Reactive	1	2	3	Responsive
43.	Speak (half-duplex)	1	2	3	Speak and listen (full participation)
44.	Unaware of mood	1	2	3	Matches mood
45.	Distracted	1	2	3	Attentive
46.	Confrontive	1	2	3	Evoking
47.	Delayed response	1	2	3	Immediate response
48.	Adds a spin	1	2	3	Adds no spin
49.	Nonsequitur	1	2	3	Tracks/follows
50.	Pepper with questions				Clarifies what was said

6.	How authentic do you sound?			
	How real are you, and how real do you sound?			
51.	Pretentious	1	2	3	Real
52.	Puffs up people	1	2	3	Is accurate with praise
53.	Sneaky	1	2	3	Forthright, forthcoming
54.	Dishonest	1	2	3	Completely honest
55.	Overstates	1	2	3	Accurately states
56.	Performs	1	2	3	Relates
57.	Knows it all	1	2	3	Seeks to learn
58.	Is affected	1	2	3	Real
59.	Full of it	1	2	3	Legitimate
60.	Not genuine/insincere	1	2	3	Genuine

7.	How big are you?				
	How flexible, respectful, and generous are you?				
61.	Critical	1	2	3	Constructive
62.	Excludes people	1	2	3	Includes people
63.	One-ups	1	2	3	Endorses
64.	Disrespectful	1	2	3	Respectful
65.	Result-driven	1	2	3	Person-oriented
66.	Judges	1	2	3	Tolerant
67.	Pushes agenda	1	2	3	Shares your views
68.	"On"	1	2	3	Not "on"
69.	Rigid	1	2	3	Open
70.	Digs	1	2	3	Builds a person up

8.	How mature are you?				
	What does your communication style tell others about you?				
71.	Hesitant	1	2	3	Confident
72.	Fearful	1	2	3	Goes for it
73.	Speaks haltingly	1	2	3	Fluid
74.	Repeats/mimics	1	2	3	Synthesizes
75.	Gossips	1	2	3	Doesn't gossip
76.	Childish	1	2	3	Adult
77.	Blames	1	2	3	Owns
78.	Clueless	1	2	3	Speaks with wisdom
79.	Speaks from theory	1	2	3	Speaks from experience
80.	Righteous	1	2	3	Compassionately accurate

9.	How free are you of communication blocks?				
	What's holding back your effectiveness as a communicator?				
81.	Compulsive talker	1	2	3	Listens more than talks
82.	Personally needy	1	2	3	Has plenty, a reserve
83.	Adrenalined/up	1	2	3	Present
84.	Ignorant	1	2	3	Informed/educated
85.	Toxic personality	1	2	3	Clean and healthy
86.	Attached to past	1	2	3	Creating a future
87.	Stressed	1	2	3	Calm
88.	Unconscious	1	2	3	Conscious/aware
89.	Blind spots	1	2	3	360-degree view
90.	Conspiratorial	1	2	3	Cooperative

10.	How effective are you?				
	How good are you at producing results?				
91.	Hints at	1	2	3	Asks directly
92.	Silent/says little	1	2	3	Speaks up/requests
93.	Dealing in past	1	2	3	Dealing in the present
94.	Immediate gratification	1	2	3	Long-term investor
95.	Win-oriented	1	2	3	Win-win oriented
96.	Problem-oriented	1	2	3	Solution-oriented
97.	Book knowledge	1	2	3	Street smarts
98.	Shares a goal	1	2	3	Inspires with a vision
99.	Bounces around	1	2	3	Sees/gets right to problem
100.	Talks about stuff	1	2	3	Is "for" stuff

Biz Whiz
Success Program

We've identified the 100 key factors to consistent business success and profitability and grouped these into 10 distinct areas:

A. Service excellence
B. Staff management
C. Planning and strategies
D. Sales management
E. Productivity
F. High profits *now*
G. Empowered leadership
H. Trends and ratios
I. CEO personal balance
J. Accounting and taxes

Congratulations for taking this one! .

Instructions

There are four steps to completing the **Biz Whiz** success program.

Step 1: Answer each question.

If the statement is true, check the circle. If not, leave it blank until you've done what it takes for it to be checked. Be rigorous; be a hard grader.

Step 2: Summarize each section.

Add up the number of checked circles for each of the 10 sections and write those amounts where indicated. Then add up all 10 sections and write the current total in the progress chart.

Step 3: Color in the checklist provided.

If you have five checks in the Service Excellence section, color in the bottom five boxes of column A, and so on. Always work from the bottom up. The goal is to have the entire chart filled in. This will indicate that you are managing your company well. In the meantime, you have a current picture of how you are doing in each of the 10 areas.

Step 4: Keep playing until all boxes are filled in.

This process may take 30 or 360 days, but you can do it! Use your coach or advisor to assist you. And check back quarterly for maintenance.

Progress Chart

Date	Points (+/−)	Score

Biz Whiz Success Program 100-Point Checklist

#	Sections									
	A	B	C	D	E	F	G	H	I	J
10										
9										
8										
7										
6										
5										
4										
3										
2										
1										

Give yourself credit as you get points from the 100-point program. Fill in columns from the bottom up.

A. Service Excellence

Number of circles checked (10 max) _____

- ○ The firm has an objective system to quantitatively measure customer satisfaction.
- ○ Quarterly meetings with key clients are conducted and changes made to improve service better.
- ○ The standards and philosophies of your organization are known and enhanced.
- ○ The staff learns from every mistake or client loss.
- ○ Service standards are written and are very high.
- ○ A total quality management (TQM) program has been created and implemented.
- ○ Value is continuously being added to products and services, whether or not customer asks for it.
- ○ Service and requirements are fulfilled in record time, far faster than the customer expected.
- ○ The firm has a strong reputation for being the best in delivering service.
- ○ The firm knows what the customers want and need even before they do.

B. Staff Management

Number of circles checked (10 max) _____

- ○ Staff accountabilities are written and clear.
- ○ Quarterly employee reviews are conducted.
- ○ Staff members report to managers automatically.
- ○ All staff members know what their contribution is.
- ○ Each employee is in the job that uses his or her strengths; there is no suffering or mismatches.
- ○ Consequences are imposed for nonperformance.
- ○ Every employee is fully competent and skilled; there are no weak links or drag-me-downs. Every manager is qualified by experience, education, loyalty, motivation, and competence.
- ○ No one is coasting or being carried by the firm.
- ○ Everything has a deadline or promised completion date, and the employee and manager manage this.
- ○ Staff members want to come to work and are well taken care of at work.

C. Planning and Strategies

Number of circles checked (10 max) _____

○ The firm has a business plan that sets forth the strategic and operational objectives and programs for the year.

○ Quarterly planning sessions are conducted with managers and staff.

○ The market for the company's product or service is good or excellent.

○ The business plan is being used, measured against, and updated at least quarterly.

○ Well-sourced sales projections are used to establish inventory and personnel and cash requirements.

○ The firm is going in a single direction, and every major decision supports that direction.

○ The company has more than sufficient resources to meet its short-range objectives.

○ Adequate cash is always available for emergencies.

○ The firm has the right consultant, coach, banker, accountant, attorney, and other advisors to guide it properly.

○ The company is not dependent on a single supplier.

D. Sales Management

Number of circles checked (10 max) _____

○ Sales are being carried out only by those who can really sell. There are no extra bodies in the sales department.

○ Salespeople are managed daily or weekly on results, and the source of less-than-quota results is known.

○ Every salesperson has a daily quota and meets or exceeds this quota, regardless.

○ Salespeoples' compensation is adequate.

○ The sales staff is a team working on a daily goal together. Awards are given.

○ Unit sales volume is increasing.

○ The sales staff prepares sales projections, and its performance against the forecast is monitored frequently.

○ The sales staff is motivated, productive, and excited about its success.

○ The sales department maintains an attractive visual display of group and individual sales.

○ The sales department staff is supported well by every other department and is cheered on.

E. High Productivity

Number of circles checked (10 max) _____

- ○ All paperwork is touched only once.
- ○ Operations are fully computerized.
- ○ Very, very few problems occur in any department. Any problems are handled immediately and the source is eliminated. The firm is a problem-free zone.
- ○ A single individual has responsibility for the day-to-day operating decisions.
- ○ The staff does very accurate work; nothing is thrown together or substandard.
- ○ The staff works hard and intelligently, with no duplication.
- ○ Decisions are pushed down as far as possible.
- ○ Every meeting accomplishes something specific.
- ○ Staff members communicate everything that is getting in the way of their productivity and know how to make their requirements known without complaining.
- ○ Staff members have the equipment and training they need to *double* their productivity.

F. High Profits Now

Number of circles checked (10 max) _____

- ○ The firm's profits are very, very high at a very conservative level of sales, or a whole lot is being sold.
- ○ Profitability is not an issue or a problem in the firm.
- ○ Staff and plants are being utilized at 80 percent plus.
- ○ Break-even levels are low.
- ○ Services and/or products are packaged so that they produce a stream of income, not just a one-time sale.
- ○ The company is profit driven, not merely revenue driven.
- ○ Budget variances are recorded, analyzed, and managed.
- ○ Individual responsibilities for achieving financial goals are clearly defined.
- ○ The firm is one of the leaders in the market.
- ○ The firm's pricing policy is not tied to the market leaders.

G. Empowered Leadership

Number of circles checked (10 max) _____

- ○ The CEO has a strong vision, and others have bought into it.
- ○ The firm has a simple mission statement.

- ○ The firm's culture is cooperative rather than adversarial.
- ○ The firm has very large goals, and everyone is excited about reaching these goals.
- ○ The CEO frequently interacts with employees at all levels.
- ○ The CEO initiates huge requirements.
- ○ The CEO is developing leaders, not just managers.
- ○ Staff members are proud of the high-quality work they do.
- ○ The firm is customer sensitive and customer driven.
- ○ The staff is proud of its role in the success of the firm.

H. Trends and Ratios

Number of circles checked (10 max) _____

- ○ Debt service as a percentage of gross profit decreased last year.
- ○ The ratio of the company's total debt to equity decreased last year.
- ○ All accounts receivable are being collected according to standards (average collection period is less than 150 percent of customer payment policy).
- ○ General and administrative expenses are decreasing as a percentage of net sales.
- ○ Profit margins have increased for core products or services over the last three years.
- ○ No one customer accounts for more than 25 percent of total sales or receivables.
- ○ Sales are consistent and increasing.
- ○ Management turnover is less than 20 percent per year.
- ○ Inventory turnover is high.
- ○ Customer satisfaction and repeat buying are increasing.

I. CEO Personal Balance

Number of circles checked (10 max) _____

- ○ The CEO has more time than he or she needs because everything is so well done or delegated.
- ○ The CEO has a right-hand person or executive assistant who handles every detail so the CEO has space.
- ○ The CEO has a strong, happy, and healthy personal life with lots of physical activity and pleasure, so work is just work and not his or her life.
- ○ The CEO is adrenaline free.
- ○ The CEO is putting aside plenty of funds with which to become financially independent.
- ○ The company is always in good enough shape to sell.

○ The CEO has a strong personal foundation.
○ The CEO enjoys creating blockbuster results for the firm.
○ The CEO does his or her 10 daily personal habits consistently.
○ The CEO is proud of himself or herself as a human and as CEO.

J. Accounting and Taxes

Number of circles checked (10 max) _____

○ Bank reconciliations are complete and up to date.
○ All income, sales, and property taxes are filed, paid, and current.
○ All bills are routinely paid on time.
○ Payroll is automated, accurate, and effortless.
○ Inventory procedures are in effect that insure an accurate account of usable inventory at the end of each month.
○ The accounts payable ledger is current and includes all bills and purchase orders.
○ The firm is current with loan payments and is in conformance with all loan agreements.
○ Accounting department is well run.
○ Financial statements are done by the 15th of the month.
○ Each department gets the reports it needs and uses.

What Else?

Please write down the additional things your firm needs to be successful. Check them off when they have been completed.

_____

_____

_____

_____

_____

_____

_____

Intellectual Property Notice

This material and these concepts are the intellectual property of Coach U, Inc. You may not repackage or resell this program without express written authorization and royalty payment. The exception is that you may deliver this program to single individuals without authorization or fee. If you lead a workshop or develop or deliver a program to a group or company based on or including this material or these concepts, authorization and fees are required. You may make as many copies of this program as you wish, as long as you make no changes or deletions of any kind.

Professional Practice Checklist

We've identified the 100 key factors in building and maintaining a full, rewarding, and profitable professional practice, and we've grouped them into 10 distinct areas.

- A. Strong client relationship
- B. Service, value, and excellence
- C. A cost-free practice
- D. Referral generation
- E. High productivity
- F. Practice management
- G. Empowered clients
- H. Personal balance
- I. Accounting and profitability
- J. Potpourri

This program works for all types of professionals and small business owners.

Instructions

There are four steps to completing the **Professional Practice Checklist.**

Step 1: Answer each question.

If the statement is true, check the circle. If not, leave it blank until you've done what it takes for it to be a full *yes*. Be rigorous; be a hard grader. If the statement does not apply or will never be true for you, check it and give yourself credit.

Step 2: Summarize each section.

Add up the number of circles for each of the 10 sections and write those amounts where indicated. Then add up all 10 sections and write the current total in the box on the progress chart.

Step 3: Color in the checklist provided.

If you have five checks in the Strong Client Relationship section, color in the bottom five boxes of column A, and so on. Always work from the bottom up. The goal is to have the entire chart filled in. This will indicate that you are managing your practice well. In the meantime, you have a current picture of how you are doing in each of the 10 areas.

Step 4: Keep playing until all boxes are filled in.

This process may take 30 or 360 days, but you can do it! Use your coach or advisor to assist you. And check back quarterly for maintenance.

Progress Chart

Date	Points (+/−)	Score

Professional Practice 100-Point Checklist

#	Sections									
#	A	B	C	D	E	F	G	H	I	J
10										
9										
8										
7										
6										
5										
4										
3										
2										
1										
2										
1										

Give yourself credit as you get points from the 100-point program. Fill in columns from the bottom up.

A. Strong Client Relationship

Number of circles checked (10 max) _____

Clients hire a professional because of his or her reputation or availability; they stay with the professional because of the service they receive and because of the relationship that both parties create. Here's how to do more of this.

- ○ I am ahead of my clients: I know what is next for them, and they know that I know this.
- ○ I tell my clients what I want for them.
- ○ There is virtually complete trust between my clients and me. They tell me everything that I need to know to be able to help them professionally.
- ○ I do extra things for my clients regularly.
- ○ I am proud of my clients and enjoy their company.
- ○ I don't put up with much from my clients.
- ○ My clients bring out my best work, consistently.
- ○ I work only with the clients who are right for me and who are ready for my services.
- ○ I show the good client how to be a great client.
- ○ My clients bring out my best and keep me developing myself.

B. Service, Value, and Excellence

Number of circles checked (10 max) _____

The professional must continuously add value to the client and to the relationship in order to stay competitive. With the growing number of people entering your field, you cannot afford not to be innovative or less than fully client oriented. Here are benchmarks for providing value.

- ○ I use an objective system to quantitatively assess my clients' satisfaction with my services.
- ○ I conduct quarterly meetings with key clients and make changes to serve them better.
- ○ I've Identified moments of truth for my organization and enhanced my practice accordingly.
- ○ I make three changes or upgrades each time I lose a client or make a mistake with a client.
- ○ Service standards are written and are very high.
- ○ I have and operate from a simple mission statement.
- ○ I continuously add value to products and services, whether the client asks for it or not.
- ○ I fulfill service and requests in record time, far faster than the clients expect.
- ○ I have a strong reputation for being the best in delivering service in my field.
- ○ I know what my clients want and need even before they do.

C. A Cost-Free Practice

Number of circles checked (10 max) _____

Every practice has high hidden costs—emotional costs—that limit the quality of service provided and keep the practice at less than full. In fact, there is a direct relationship between the size of the practice and the number of costs that the professional experiences. Use this list to identify and eliminate all of these costs.

- ○ My clients do not violate my personal and professional boundaries.
- ○ I do not gossip about my clients, ever.
- ○ My clients almost always do what they promise.
- ○ My clients give me credit for the part I play in their success.
- ○ My clients consistently keep their appointments.
- ○ I don't work outside of my best daily schedule.
- ○ My clients do not complain or blame; rather, they create, request, or problem solve, and they use me as a resource to accomplish this.
- ○ I do not count on willpower to do the things I know I should do in my practice. I have a supportive coach or partner to support me in completing these things.
- ○ I have not overpromised results or hinted that I could accomplish more than I absolutely know I really can with one hand tied behind my back. In other words, I have underpromised.
- ○ None of my clients dig at, demean, or fight me.

D. Referral Generation

Number of circles checked (10 max) _____

The best clients often come from referrals. Generating a flow of these referrals requires a strategy and a plan. Here are 10 elements of most successful referral plans.

- ○ My clients know that I want more business.
- ○ I have strong relationships with at least 5–10 centers of influence who are currently sending me referrals.
- ○ All of my clients know all of what I offer.
- ○ All of my clients know the types of clients I am looking for.
- ○ I thank the source of every single referral.
- ○ I give my clients or centers of influence an incentive for sending me new business.
- ○ I have a way for prospective clients to get to know me, try out my services, or get started on a smaller scale.
- ○ I send out a monthly or quarterly newsletter, brochure, or announcement about my services.
- ○ I have written material, such as a card or brochure, that my clients or I can give to others.
- ○ My clients know what happens when someone they refer calls or comes in, so they feel more confident about sending referrals.

E. High Productivity

Number of circles checked (10 max) _____

Billable time is the financial engine of any practice, which means that anything that gets in the way of this is very, very expensive. Start increasing productivity by doing everything on this list so you can bill more!

- ○ I touch my paperwork only once.
- ○ Operations are fully computerized.
- ○ Very, very few problems occur anywhere. If they do, they are handled immediately and the source is eliminated. My practice is a problem-free zone.
- ○ A single individual has responsibility for the day-to-day operating decisions.
- ○ My staff and I do very accurate work; nothing is thrown together or sub-standard.
- ○ There is no part of my client procedures or process that costs me physical or emotional wellness. I have found a way to effectively delegate.
- ○ I do no paperwork or procedures that are unbillable.
- ○ Every meeting accomplishes something specific.
- ○ My staff communicates everything that is getting in the way of its being productive and knows how to make a request without complaining.
- ○ Staff members have the equipment and training they need to double their productivity.

F. Practice Management

Number of circles checked (10 max) _____

The professional must operate in a supportive, cost-free environment, which means that every staff person is an integral part of a winning team. Here's what to do to make this happen.

- ○ Staff accountabilities are written and clear.
- ○ I conduct quarterly employee reviews.
- ○ My staff members live to support me, and they go out of their way to make my job easier—even effortless.
- ○ I have the right accountant, banker, attorney, coach, and other advisers, who add to my profitability.
- ○ Each employee is in the job that uses his or her strengths; there is no suffering or mismatches.
- ○ Consequences are imposed for nonperformance.
- ○ Every employee is fully competent and skilled and is qualified by experience, education, loyalty, motivation, and competence, with no weak links or drag-me downs.
- ○ I have a business plan, which I refer to monthly.
- ○ Everything has a deadline or promised completion date, and the employee and manager manage this.
- ○ This staff wants to come to work and is well taken care of at work.

G. Empowered Clients

Number of circles checked (10 max) _____
Clients need empowerment to be their best—for themselves and to be with you powerfully. You can show them how by raising your standards, establishing extensive boundaries, and showing them how to get the most from your services and the relationship. Here are 10 ways.

○ My clients know the benefits they are receiving from the services they are getting.
○ My clients add to my reputation. I work with no one who will make me look bad or damage my reputation.
○ My clients send me referrals for more business.
○ My clients will be able to pay increasing fees.
○ My clients are responsible for their own needs and results in their personal and business lives. They use me appropriately, yet they are not too dependent on me, nor do they blindly follow my advice.
○ My clients use me as a partner and not just as a technician to fix or handle something. We have a healthy relationship.
○ My clients have a recurring need for my services.
○ My clients always pay their bills on time. Money is rarely an issue between us.
○ Every client respects my advice and expertise and gives me the room I need to do an extraordinary job.
○ My clients look for ways to help me because they care.

H. Personal Balance

Number of circles checked (10 max) _____
The quality of the professional's work and the success of the practice depend heavily on how high the professional maintains his or her wellness—physically, emotionally, mentally, and spiritually.

○ I have more time than I need because everything is so well done or delegated.
○ I have a right-hand person or executive assistant who handles every detail so I have space.
○ I have a strong, happy, and healthy personal life with lots of physical activity and pleasure, so work is just work and not my life.
○ I am adrenaline free.
○ I put aside plenty of funds with which to become financially independent early in life.
○ The practice is in good enough shape to sell.
○ I have a very strong personal foundation.
○ I enjoy creating blockbuster results for clients.
○ I consistently do my 10 daily personal habits.
○ I am proud of myself as a human and as a professional.

I. Accountability and Profitability

Number of circles checked (10 max) _____
Part of having a practice is running a successful business. Accounting, taxes, and profitability are necessary for the professional to be his or her best, to have a future, and to enjoy the present.

- ○ Bank reconciliations are complete and up to date.
- ○ All income, sales, and property taxes are filed, paid, and current.
- ○ All bills are routinely paid on time.
- ○ The accounts payable ledger is current and includes all bills and purchase orders.
- ○ Accounting department is well run and/or I use a superb bookkeeping service and CPA.
- ○ I have a budget that I compare with my monthly financial statements, which are done by the 15th of the month.
- ○ All accounts receivable are being collected per standards (average collection period is less than 150 percent of customer payment policy).
- ○ The firm's profits are very, very high at a very conservative level of revenue.
- ○ No single customer accounts for more than 25 percent of total sales or receivables.
- ○ Services and products are packaged so that they produce a stream of income, not just a one-time sale.

J. What else do you need?

Number of circles checked (10 max) _____
Every practice is unique. What else do you need to be able to have a full, successful practice? Write these on the lines provided and then check each item off as you complete it.

- ○ _____
- ○ _____
- ○ _____
- ○ _____
- ○ _____
- ○ _____
- ○ _____
- ○ _____

Intellectual Property Notice

This material and these concepts are the intellectual property of Coach U, Inc. You may not repackage or resell this program without express written authorization and royalty payment. The exception is that you may deliver this program to single individuals without authorization or fee. If you lead a workshop or develop or deliver a program to a group or company based on or including this material or these concepts, authorization and fees are required. You may make as many copies of this program as you wish, as long as you make no changes or deletions of any kind.

New Business Start-Up Program

We've identified the 100 key factors and steps to help the person starting a new business, and grouped these into 10 distinct areas:

A. Right opportunity?
B. Business skills
C. The plan and strategy
D. Sales tools and effort
E. Policies and procedures
F. High profits now
G. Long-term success
H. The specific outcomes
I. Personal life
J. Key distinctions

Congratulations for taking this one!

Instructions

There are four steps to completing the **New Business Start-Up** program.

Step 1: Answer each question.

If the statement is true, check the circle. If not, leave it blank until you've done what it takes for it to be a full *yes*. Be rigorous; be a hard grader.

Step 2: Summarize each section.

Add up the number of checked circles for each of the 10 sections and write those amounts where indicated. Then add up all 10 sections and write the current total in the progress chart.

Step 3: Color in the checklist provided.

If you have five checks in the Right Opportunity? section, color in the bottom five boxes of column A, and so on. Always work from the bottom up. The goal is to have the entire chart filled in. This will indicate that you are managing your company well.

Step 4: Keep playing until all boxes are filled in.

This process may take 30 or 360 days, but you can do it. Use your coach or advisor to assist you.

Progress Chart

Date	Points (+/−)	Score

New Business Start-Up Program 100-Point Checklist

Sections										
#	A	B	C	D	E	F	G	H	I	J
10										
9										
8										
7										
6										
5										
4										
3										
2										
1										

Give yourself credit as you get points from the 100-point program. Fill in columns from the bottom up.

A. Right Opportunity?

Number of circles checked (10 max) _____

○ Even if this one fails, it will train me well and put me in touch with more opportunities.

○ I don't need this new business, either personally or financially. Instead, I want it very much.

○ I have at least one year of strong and successful experience in this field or industry.

○ This opportunity has very low overhead, so I'll have flexibility and be able to afford the learning curve.

○ My family, banker, attorney, CPA, and coach are supportive of this venture.

○ I have at least 6–12 months' worth of expenses (both personal and business) in the bank before starting.

○ I have experimented first for at least 90–180 days with the field or business so I have evidence that it works, not just a plan or gut sense.

○ People know what it is that I am selling; it is familiar. I don't need to spend hours educating them.

○ People want this product or service; they may also need it. (Don't sell castor oil.)

○ I have used this product or service, know its value firsthand, and totally believe in it.

B. Business Skills

Number of circles checked (10 max) _____

○ Leadership: I direct people and efforts easily and well.

○ Influence: I am not afraid of people (staff, prospects, and customers); I have no problem telling them what they should do.

○ Consistency: I have enough personal discipline to stick to this and carry it out. I self-manage and initiate. I don't need lots of support.

○ Eagerness to take risk: I am willing to constantly try new things, innovate, make it easier and better, go for it, and risk a portion of money I have.

○ Respect: I honor people and their unique contributions, and I include them in decisions. My staff members are my customers.

○ Emotional health and maturity: I don't get my needs met by staff or customers, I don't get angry or react, and I don't take things personally. This business is a game.

○ Adequate reserve: I always have more than I need of time, cash, space, skills, staff, sales, and opportunities.

○ Dedication: I am totally dedicated to being the best, making lots of money, and having the company be extraordinary.

○ Problem solving and prevention: I easily reduce a complex problem to bite-sized pieces and then take extra steps so that this type of problem never occurs again.

○ Managing: I manage the operation and am aware of the specific outcomes, factors, and early warning indicators that will make or break me.

C. The Plan and Strategy

Number of circles checked (10 max) _____

○ I've done a sales and expense pro forma (forecast) for the first 3, 6, 12, and 36 months of my business.

○ I have done a start-up cost budget, including equipment and/or capital expenditures, organizational expenses, and other expenses needed over the first three months.

○ I have outlined each person's job and how and how often they report to me. (Reporting form done, too.)

○ I have written out a step-by-step action plan with dozens or scores of steps, and I am working that list.

○ I know how much I am going to do and how much I am going to delegate.

○ I have hired an attorney, business consultant, coach, CPA, and other professionals that I need.

○ I have used well-sourced sales projections to establish inventory, personnel, and cash needs.

○ My top three goals are clear, written, visually displayed, tracked, and understood by all—including myself—as the priorities.

○ I am willing to rewrite, update, or even scrap my plan if the market dictates what I should sell and how I should sell it.

○ I track my action plan weekly to see if I am on course.

D. Sales Tools and Effort

Number of circles checked (10 max) _____

○ Only those who can really sell are selling, even if that means just me. I don't train weak ones.

○ The company has a daily sales quota, and I manage it.

○ I have the brochures I need to attract the customers to buy.

○ I have the sales script or selling points written out and memorized, and I am very polished in delivering them.

○ I know how to close people and get paid.

○ Every part of the company is designed to support the sales effort, from concept to quality control to delivery.

○ I have set up a great system to prompt word of mouth and referrals. I don't just rely on marketing or ads.

○ I have set up a system to fully comprehend what the customer or prospect really needs and wants and quickly make changes to sell them that. (This is relationship-based selling.)

○ On a percentage basis, my selling and marketing costs are very low, even if it means lost sales.

○ I have designed myself, my company, and my product or service to be very, very attractive (versus promotive or seductive) to my market.

E. Policies and Procedures

Number of circles checked (10 max) _____

○ I have a daily and weekly checklist of what must be done and by whom.

○ I have a similar monthly and quarterly checklist.

○ The accounting and bookkeeping is being done easily, accurately, and in a timely manner. I get frequent reports.

○ I have designed the company systems so that there is a minimum of paperwork and procedures.

○ I delegate many decisions down the line, even if it means that mistakes are made.

○ Staff meetings are creative, reportive, and training based versus chatty or confrontive.

○ The company has a policies and procedures manual.

○ My business is so well planned, controlled and insured that if my home or office were leveled this afternoon, I'd be back in business in the morning and/or have insurance money to help.

○ I have selected the best legal form of business.

F. High Profits Now

Number of circles checked (10 max) _____

○ I've set the company up to be more profit driven than growth driven.

○ I am naturally cheap, although I'm willing to invest cash in my business to make even more money.

○ My target market is well defined and can afford to buy, and I can access it easily with the contacts and tools I have.

○ I pay cash even for capital expenditures.

○ I let my clients tell me what they need or want to buy, and I create or sell them that instead of trying to come with what I think they want or should need. I am an extraordinary listener to the unspoken requests and needs my customers and prospects have.

○ There is a strong, profitable future in my field or industry. I am not selling buggy whips or hula hoops.

○ There is not much financial risk to me in the way I have set up my business. I can afford the mistakes that will be made.

○ I am not overleveraged or pushing to maximize every single opportunity. I have patience for the market to decide and buy.

○ I have future plans for additional products and revenue streams.

G. Long-Term Success

Number of circles checked (10 max) _____

○ My company's mission statement is authentic and reflects my feelings and thoughts perfectly; it doesn't just sound good.

○ The staff knows and backs the mission statement.

○ I have put together a savvy five-member board of advisors with whom I meet monthly and whose counsel I respond to.

○ I have implemented rigorous, but lucrative, incentive plans for all key employees.

○ My customers can easily articulate the benefits of my services or products—and do so.

○ I update my policies and procedures manual annually.

○ I continually upgrade all aspects of my operational systems for the highest possible productivity.

○ I know how to build a strong, positive reputation in my niche, and I do.

○ I continually add value to my product or service.

○ I don't just keep up with my competitors; I eclipse them by setting my targets higher and making them uniquely mine.

H. The Specific Outcomes

Number of circles checked (10 max) _____

○ I know what my gross profit margins are.

○ I know what my net profit needs to be.

○ I know what my reorder points are.

○ I know my cash flow needs.

○ I know my daily and weekly sales goals and results.

○ I know how quickly I collect my receivables.

○ I know my referral rate as a percentage of sales.

○ I know my sales costs percentage.

○ I know my current and aged receivables.

○ I know my _____.

I. Personal Life

Number of circles checked (10 max) _____

○ I have a right-hand person or executive assistant who handles every detail so that I have space.
○ I am adrenaline and addiction free.
○ I have a strong personal foundation.
○ My family loves and enjoys my company.
○ I am a model for other entrepreneurs or CEOs.
○ I take excellent care of my health.
○ I don't stress. Nothing is worth that.
○ I have plenty of personal funds.
○ I am proud of myself as I am. I don't have anything to prove, and I don't push myself hard. I know it is out of integrity to do so.
○ I have something better to do after work each day than work.

J. Key Distinctions

Number of circles checked (10 max) _____

○ Responsible versus in a position to react
○ Profitability versus growth or revenue
○ Minimum versus maximum work
○ Leadership versus management
○ Priorities versus agendas of others
○ Frugal versus penny-pinching
○ Risk or experimentation versus going for broke
○ It's a game versus a passion, cause, or need
○ Support versus control
○ Self versus ego

Intellectual Property Notice

Business Mission Statement

Ask Yourself

Why are we in this business?

_____

_____

Who do we serve?

_____

_____

What do we provide?

_____

_____

What makes us and our products special?

_____

_____

What are our goals?

_____

_____

How do we know we are succeeding?

_____

_____

Business Budget

Months	1	2	3	4	5	6	7	8	9	10	11	12
Sales												
Cost of sales												
Gross profit												
Variable expenses												
Salaries												
Payroll taxes												
Advertising												
Automobile												
Dues and subscriptions												
Legal and accounting												
Supplies												
Telephone												
Utilities												
Miscellaneous												
Total variable expenses												
Fixed expenses												
Depreciation												
Insurance												
Rent												
Taxes and licenses												
Interest only												
Total fixed expenses												
Total expenses												
Net profit (loss) before taxes												
Cumulative profit (loss)												

The Friday Checklist

What are the 25 personal and business tasks that would complete your week and prepare you for the upcoming week?

Write down the 25 items that you would need to do each week in order to feel totally organized, well maintained, completely done with the week gone by, and ready for the upcoming week. Include personal care items, business taskettes, housecleaning chores, and so on. As you complete each item, fill in one of the circles preceding it. (Thus, the form is good for one month.)

1. ○ ○ ○ ○ _____
2. ○ ○ ○ ○ _____
3. ○ ○ ○ ○ _____
4. ○ ○ ○ ○ _____
5. ○ ○ ○ ○ _____
6. ○ ○ ○ ○ _____
7. ○ ○ ○ ○ _____
8. ○ ○ ○ ○ _____
9. ○ ○ ○ ○ _____
10. ○ ○ ○ ○ _____
11. ○ ○ ○ ○ _____
12. ○ ○ ○ ○ _____
13. ○ ○ ○ ○ _____
14. ○ ○ ○ ○ _____
15. ○ ○ ○ ○ _____
16. ○ ○ ○ ○ _____
17. ○ ○ ○ ○ _____
18. ○ ○ ○ ○ _____
19. ○ ○ ○ ○ _____
20. ○ ○ ○ ○ _____
21. ○ ○ ○ ○ _____
22. ○ ○ ○ ○ _____
23. ○ ○ ○ ○ _____
24. ○ ○ ○ ○ _____
25. ○ ○ ○ ○ _____

Annual Goals Chart

Select 10 goals for this year and write each one at the bottom of the 10 bars on the chart. Then, each month, fill in the bar to the level that represents how close you are to completing each goal. Track your progress monthly toward your annual goals.

Name _____

											DEC
											NOV
											OCT
											SEP
											AUG
											JUL
											JUN
											MAY
											APR
											MAR
											FEB
											JAN

1   2   3   4   5   6   7   8   9   10

|___|___|___|___|___|___|___|___|___|___| GOALS

Internet Marketing 100

This section contains 100 ways to market yourself and your site on the Internet.

We've organized 100 specific items into 10 primary marketing strategies that you can use to become more successful on the Internet.

Be findable on search engines and directories.

- ○ I have inserted meta tags in my home page.
- ○ I have used the right words in the meta tags to attract the right visitors.
- ○ I have put meta tags on every page of my website.
- ○ I have used a descriptive title for each of my pages.
- ○ I have listed my site on the top 10 search engines.
- ○ I have listed my site on Yahoo.
- ○ I have tested how well my site ranks on the search engines.
- ○ I have listed my site on at least five directories related to my field or interests.
- ○ I have learned how search engines work and have adjusted my meta tags and format to attract more visitors.
- ○ I have listed myself on at least 25 relevant directories.

Arrange for crosslinks and increase your exposure.

- ○ I know how many links to my site there are.
- ○ There is a link from at least 10 other sites to my site.
- ○ I have a favorite links page with at least 20 listings on it.
- ○ I am part of a web ring or am hosting a web ring.
- ○ I have applied to get my site linked from the awards or cool sites.
- ○ I post to newsgroups.
- ○ Join/get on ICQ.
- ○ I offer a membership and give people a reason to link to my site from theirs.
- ○ I have contacted 50 colleagues and gotten them to link to my site (and have installed links to theirs).
- ○ I have listed my site on professional associations' directories.
- ○ I've approached writers or editors on 20 e-zines and asked them to put me on their quote contact list.

Provide valuable content at your site.

- ○ I have at least ten Top 10 lists that share my knowledge about my subject or field of expertise.
- ○ I have identified the top four types of people who will visit my site.
- ○ I offer a track for each of them to follow, or solutions to their concerns, at my site.
- ○ I have written and posted an e-book at my site that visitors can purchase or download for free.
- ○ I have included RealAudio files at my site containing valuable information.
- ○ I have created a self-test that visitors can take and score themselves.
- ○ I offer a FAQs/Q&A section to answer the most often asked questions about my product or service.
- ○ My site is a portal containing many links to other sites related to my profession or industry.
- ○ I have included a searchable index of my e-tips.
- ○ I offer situational advice to anyone visiting.

Offer a free e-newsletter or e-tip broadcast.

- ○ I have selected a topic for my e-news or e-tip.
- ○ I have chosen the format and frequency of my broadcast.
- ○ I have written three editions and sent them out to at least 100 people who I know.
- ○ I have used Scout to announce my e-news or e-tips.
- ○ I have listed my e-newsletter on five repositories.
- ○ I have automated the subscribe/unsubscribe process.
- ○ I encourage subscribers to pass along the e-news/e-tip broadcast to anyone they wish.
- ○ Subscribing and unsubscribing instructions are at the top or bottom of each broadcast.
- ○ I ask my subscribers for feedback, comments, and questions, and I respond to these.
- ○ I offer free stuff or sell stuff as a plug at the bottom of each broadcast.

Have a well-designed web site.

- ○ My site gives immediate access or answers to 90 percent of all visitors.
- ○ My site looks professional, not hobbyish.
- ○ The graphics are of a high quality.
- ○ I prompt visitors to subscribe to my newsletter.

○ I offer a bulletin board or discussion list where visitors can post comments and questions.
○ I've designed my site to lead people through it, step by step.
○ There is at least one free product or service that visitors can download or request at my site.
○ I've designed my site to lead people, step by step, to buy something.
○ I've got a photograph of myself on my site so people can get a sense of me.

Work with the media.

○ I've written a press release announcing my site, product, or service.
○ I've broadcasted or distributed this press release.
○ I am giving something away for free and have let the media know about this.
○ I have let everyone in my network know that I am available for media interviews on a particular subject.
○ I've written a book and had it published.
○ I've gotten mentioned or featured in someone else's book.
○ I've contacted 500 radio stations that do interviews and offered myself as a guest.
○ I've written a pitch letter to the local news media suggesting a story that relates to my work or site.
○ I've conducted a poll and released the results of the poll to the media.
○ I've sent a video of myself to the morning TV talk shows and suggested a topic.

Advertise and promote your site.

○ I've purchased banner ad space for at least 10,000 views.
○ I've arranged for owners of lists to let me plug my site, services, or products via their e-newsletter or e-tip.
○ I advertise in opt-in mailing lists.
○ I've purchased promotional items that feature my web address.
○ I've put my web and e-mail address on my business cards and letterhead.
○ I've sponsored a web site.
○ I've had at least one banner ad created.
○ I use an extensive signature on my e-mail announcing all that I offer.
○ I have purchased an opt-in mailing list (not spam).
○ I have run classified ads selling my product or service.

Become the host of a network.

○ Offer a tip broadcast or e-newsletter.
○ Offer a directory or portal.
○ Offer for-fee or free teleclasses.
○ Invite visitors to local meetings.
○ Host a discussion group.
○ Offer a certification program.
○ Become a formal or information association.
○ Launch a virtual university.
○ Run a contest.
○ Offer free support or advice.

Offer lots of free stuff and stuff for sale.

○ Products
○ Services
○ Programs
○ Classes
○ Reports/information
○ Books/tapes
○ Memberships
○ E-books
○ Agents/affiliate programs
○ Advice and consulting

Keep experimenting.

○ Create a web site that reflects or expresses what is most important to you.
○ Keep experimenting to see what draws people in.
○ Add more web sites, just for the fun of it.
○ Offer links from your site to cool or new resources that your visitors may want to know about.
○ Sponsor a brainstorming session once a month with your colleagues or friends.
○ Keep testing the ranking of your site on the search engines (and keep tweaking).
○ Spend an hour a month surfing related sites and using or adapting some of their ideas to improve your own site.
○ Identify a need that the public has and create a web site to serve or solve that need, even if it is unrelated to your current area of knowledge or expertise or to your service or product.
○ Take a teleclass or buy a book on internet marketing to see what's new.
○ Add RealVideo to your site for a stronger punch and more traffic.

Web Site 100: Design and Functional Elements of a Terrific Web Site

This checklist has been designed for service professionals, but it is also useful for anyone setting up a web site and/or perfecting their web site.

1. ## Design, Research, and Planning

   ○ I've selected a great domain name and have reserved it (http:rs.internic.net).

   ○ I have described or outlined the four things that the people coming to my web site will likely be looking for or wanting.

   ○ I've downloaded or purchased an HTML software program that I like (http://www.claris.com or http://www.microsoft.com).

   ○ I understand at least the very basics of raw HTML.

   ○ I have sketched out at least 10 of the pages of my site and how they link together.

   ○ I have found at least 10 well-designed sites of competitors or in related fields and have made a list of the 25 design elements I want on my site.

   ○ I've got a web hosting provider picked out and ready.

   ○ I've got someone I can call or e-mail when I get stuck on my web page.

   ○ I've obtained www.myname.com if available (http://www.netsol.com).

   ○ I know my financial and time budget for this web site.

2. ## Basic Web Design/HTML Skills

   ○ I know how to "view source" to see the raw HTML code from any web page.

   ○ I know how to set the background color of the web page.

   ○ I know how to choose the default font so my web pages look clean.

   ○ I know how to insert a graphic into a web page.

   ○ I've experimented with at least two on-line create-a-site systems (http://www.tripod.com).

   ○ I know how to open a graphics file, add text, and save it as a .jpg or .gif file.

   ○ I know how to transfer files (called FTP) from my web site to my Internet provider's computer.

   ○ I know to how link pages together.

   ○ I know how to create tables and do basic layout.

3. Include Important Details and Information

○ I use a graphically great company logo or name.

○ My toll-free and toll phone numbers and fax number are on each page.

○ A copyright notice is on each page.

○ The title matches each HTML page.

○ I provide the city and/or state where I/my company is located (address optional—if it is a residence, don't provide it for security reasons).

○ The "last updated" date is included on the home page and selected pages.

○ I've got a professional photo of myself on my site so people can relate to me.

○ I have included an FAQ section.

○ Each page has a consistent look and feel.

○ I have meta tags on each page, not just the home page.

4. Basic Content to Include

○ I explain who I am and what makes me special.

○ I explain the services I offer and how they work.

○ I clearly state how much my services or products cost and what one receives for this price.

○ I have a list of solutions that will appeal to most of my visitors.

○ I describe at least three benefits to people who use my service or product.

○ I offer several things or services for free at my site to get people started.

○ I have a page containing links that might interest the visitor.

○ The site is organized around what's important to the visitor, not just what's important to me.

○ I explain who visits my site and what I can do for them.

○ I've had someone read my site and help me remove all jargon.

5. Technical Details

○ The site is viewable on a 14" monitor with no scrolling needed.

○ I've viewed my site via other browsers to make sure it looks right.

○ I've made sure all of my links work (http://www.linkbot.com).

○ I have had my HTML validated.

○ I have verified my meta tags.

○ Whenever an e-mail address is included, it is hotlinked.

○ My average page is less than 30K text and 50K graphics.

○ My e-mail address uses the same domain name as my web site domain name.

○ I've compressed my graphics for fast downloading (http://www.gifwizard.com).

○ I am getting a traffic report from my web hosting company.

6. Graphic Design and Appeal

○ My site has a professional (not hobbyist) look.

○ My art (logos, illustrations) is clean and crisp, not scratchy looking (http://www.andyart.com).

○ My site looks distinct; it's not a cookie-cutter duplicate of other sites in my field.

○ I use only one or two different fonts per page.

○ I used interlaced .gif files (they appear more quickly).

○ I use ALT tags.

○ I use only colors that all browsers can display properly (http://www.lynda.com/hex.html).

○ I chose colors carefully and artfully, not jarringly or slapdashedly.

○ There is a theme to my site; it is an expression of me or my company.

○ The names I use for the links make sense even to the ignorant visitor.

7. Ease of Use and Navigation, Intuitive Feel

○ The average user is never more than three clicks away from what they'll need.

○ I don't give the user more than six options on any one page.

○ I offer a site index.

○ I use image maps for a clean, easy look.

○ The visitor is guided as to what to do, see or go to next.

○ There are forward, back, top of page, and home page buttons throughout the site.

○ There is a site search engine that is easy to find and that works well.

○ The visitor doesn't get stuck going down any blind alleys.

○ I've asked five people to visit my site and tell me what they didn't like about it or found wasn't clear or easy.

○ I have walked all through my site and it flows.

8. Selling Power and Ease of Buying

○ I give the buyer four ways to buy (e-mail, web, phone, fax).

○ I have packaged my services to make them intriguing and appealing.

○ I make ordering a simple, immediate online process.

○ I am using a secure server; clients can sign up online (http://www.verisign .com).

○ Credit card transactions are processed in real time (http://www.commercepay .com).

○ I include testimonials from others who have used my services.

○ I offer a guarantee of satisfaction.

○ I offer enough content to show that I know what I'm talking about.

○ I've established my credibility completely.

○ There is a mechanism test or questions for visitors to qualify or disqualify themselves as potential clients.

9. Marketing and Links

- ○ I have included properly used meta tags on all of my pages.
- ○ Visitors can recommend this site to a friend, right at the site.
- ○ I am listed at Yahoo and other search engines.
- ○ I offer a free newsletter or tip nugget, and people can sign up from the web site.
- ○ I am linked to at least 10 others in my field or industry, and they are linked to me.
- ○ I know where my site appears on the search engines (http://www .positionagent.com).
- ○ I am part of a web ring (http://www .webring.org).
- ○ I mention or refer people to my web site in my e-mail signature.
- ○ I include my web site URL in my stationery, brochures, and tangible marketing tools.
- ○ I am part of a professional or trade association that has a listing for me or links to my site.

10. Ways to Engage Visitors

- ○ I offer a free teleclass they can sign up for online.
- ○ I offer a free newsletter or tip broadcast they can subscribe to online.
- ○ I offer a free consultation or sample.
- ○ I offer a chat room at my site.
- ○ I offer a discussion board at my site.
- ○ I offer a free report (related to my subject or field) via auto-responder.
- ○ I offer a book or tape they can buy or get for free.
- ○ I offer visitors referrals to someone who can help them.
- ○ I offer visitors a list of links worth remembering that will help them continue their journey.
- ○ I offer visitors a chance to say hello to me personally.

E-Tip Broadcasting: 100 Steps to Setting Up a Successful E-News or E-Tip Broadcast

Want to broadcast an e-newsletter or daily tip? The following checklist should help.

1. Decision Making, Planning, and Preparation

- ○ Set first-year goals: How many subscribers do you want within 12 months?

- ○ Select a topic or theme for your broadcast that you will really enjoy writing about.

- ○ Figure out why you want to do this and what the benefits are to you.

- ○ Identify the 10 things you like about other tips or newsletters that you receive.

- ○ Start writing (your first issue or five tips or nuggets).

- ○ Schedule time to write your e-newsletter or nuggets each week.

- ○ Share your initial writings with 10 people and ask for improvements (not feedback).

- ○ Make sure your e-mail program can handle 200 e-mail addresses for broadcasting.

- ○ Set up a web site or web area at which to upload your writings and tips.

- ○ Decide the level of automation you want your broadcasting system to have.

2. E-Newsletter or Tip Design Elements—Group 1

- ○ Title (of tip, nugget, or newsletter).

- ○ Personal news.

- ○ Topical news.

- ○ Share feedback from readers with everyone.

- ○ Provide a situational solution or strategy.

- ○ Suggest a change in thinking or behavior.

- ○ Pose an interesting question.

- ○ Provide a statistic.

- ○ Recommend a URL or web site link.

- ○ Share your opinion.

3. E-Newsletter or Tip Design Elements—Group 2

○ Quote an expert or author.

_____

○ Include a powerful and fitting quote.

_____

○ Profile or review a book.

_____

○ Share a client's story or case study.

_____

○ Point out a trend and link it to your topic.

_____

○ Provide a self-test.

_____

○ Write a "100 Days to …" type of e-mail-based coaching program.

_____

○ Tell a story.

_____

○ Provide your signature (with contact info).

_____

○ Offer a discussion list for readers to join if they desire.

_____

4. Write Your E-Newsletter or Tip Well

○ Write snappy titles: They should be exact, simple, surprising, directive.

_____

○ Use metaphors and analogies.

_____

○ Make a distinction (A versus B).

_____

○ Speak in messages that direct or guide the reader.

_____

○ Provide a three-step progression.

_____

○ Speak personally or conversationally, not theoretically.

_____

○ Be jargon free (or else explain any jargon you use).

_____

○ Use very specific words rather than general, vague, or over-used ones.

_____

○ Ask yourself, "What do I want the reader to know most?"

_____

○ Ask for feedback from readers in order to improve your style.

_____

5. Marketing and Building Subscribers

○ E-mail your first issue to everyone you know.

○ Add a "how to subscribe" segment at the beginning or end.

○ Let visitors to your site subscribe from your site.

○ List your newsletter or tips at "mailing list websites."

○ Get your newsletter or tips announced via Scout.

○ Write provocative, rich, opinioned copy that gets passed around.

○ Offer liberal retransmittal and reproduction rights; encourage others to take advantage of them.

○ Swap announcements with other list owners.

○ Offer more than one tip or news broadcast (multiple markets).

○ Purchase opt-in subscriber lists and market to these.

6. Broadcast Management Systems and Features

○ After you reach 100 subscribers, automate the subscribe/unsubscribe process with Majordomo, ListServ, or LetterRip.

○ After you reach 500 subscribers, start offering a daily tip.

○ After you reach 500 subscribers, use a broadcast queuing or hopper system offered by Julnet.com or WebValence.com.

○ After you reach 1,000 subscribers, start queuing your plugs or marketing messages.

○ After you reach 1,000 subscribers, offer a second e-mail list using a single database.

○ After you reach 1,000 subscribers, add a system to autodelete bounced mail.

○ Let subscribers receive a single-e-mail digest of multiple tips or newsletters.

○ Add a feature that lets you send out sequential e-mails (for a step-by-step course).

○ After you reach 5,000 subscribers, hire a broadcast manager.

○ Have your tips or newsletters automatically posted to your web site.

7. Making Money with Your E-Newsletter or Tip Broadcast

○ Offer a distance, virtual, or teleclass version of your professional services.

○ Offer a book or audiotape or audiotape set.

○ Offer free teleclasses (10–20 percent will convert to pay classes).

○ Offer fee teleclasses (1 percent of subscribers will sign up).

○ Plug a colleague (and then he or she can plug you).

○ Sell other people's stuff (books, programs, diagnostic tools, products, services).

○ Convert your topic into a web or RealAudio course.

○ Sell advertising (if your list gets to 10,000 or more subscribers).

○ Create an online community and offer them branded products.

○ Help others write or package their content into nuggets or newsletters.

8. Key Success Strategies

○ Offer a daily tip instead of just a weekly newsletter.

○ Have more than just one tip or newsletter; expand to have 3–25.

○ If you can't write well, learn how or hire someone.

○ Create corresponding services that go with your tip or newsletter topic.

○ Keep experimenting with topics or subjects until you find one that people subscribe to in droves.

○ After you reach 1,000 subscribers, turn them into a community.

○ Don't give up; critical mass is at 5,000 subscribers.

○ Don't expect immediate revenue, but it will come.

○ Pick a topic that is what people want, not just what you think is interesting.

○ Target market segments or industry groups given the high referral rate.

9. Topics to Write About

- ○ Relationships (finding and improving)

- ○ Career (advancement and transition)

- ○ Small business (entrepreneurship and making money)

- ○ Professional success (marketing and practice management)

- ○ Skills (communication and technical)

- ○ Internet (marketing and cyber skills)

- ○ Personal development (self-improvement and spirituality)

- ○ Self-care (nutrition and balance)

- ○ Market segments (women, men, parents, etc.)

10. Turn Your Newsletter into a Community or Network

- ○ Come up with a community name (not just a newsletter name).

- ○ Provide a directory of all subscribers who wish to be listed.

- ○ Offer special get-togethers or free services to members.

- ○ Put members together via "I need X" listings in your newsletter.

- ○ Offer discussion groups for subgroups of your subscribers.

- ○ Offer special discounts to your subscribers.

- ○ Turn your readers into your research and development team for program development.

- ○ Offer prizes, gifts, or shirts for their input, help, or ideas.

- ○ Set up local meetings or chapters for subscribers to meet each other.

- ○ Find out what your community wants and then offer that to them.

Intellectual Property Notice

This material and these concepts are the intellectual property of Coach U, Inc. You may not repackage or resell this program without express written authorization and royalty payment. The exception is that you may deliver this program to single individuals without authorization or fee. If you lead a workshop or develop or deliver a program to a group or company based on or including this material or these concepts, authorization and fees are required. You may make as many copies of this program as you wish, as long as you make no changes or deletions of any kind.

Appendix

About the CD-Rom

Introduction

This appendix provides you with information on the contents of the CD that accompanies this book. For the latest and greatest information, please refer to the ReadMe file located at the root of the CD.

System Requirements

- A computer with a processor running at 120 Mhz or faster.
- At least 32 MB of total RAM installed on your computer, for best performance, 64 MB or more
- A CD-Rom drive

Note: Many popular word processing programs are capable of reading Microsoft Word files. However, users should be aware that a slight amount of formatting might be lost when using a program other than Microsoft Word.

Using the CD with Windows

To install the items from the CD to your hard drive, follow these steps:

1. Insert the CD into your computer's CD-Rom drive.
2. The CD-Rom interface will appear. The interface provides a simple point-and-click way to explore the contents of the CD.

If the opening screen of the CD-Rom does not appear automatically, follow these steps to access the CD:

1. Click the Start button on the left end of the taskbar and then choose Run from the menu that pops up.
2. In the dialog box that appears, type **d:\setup.exe** (If your CD-Rom drive is not drive D, fill in the appropriate letter in place of *d.*) This brings up the CD interface described in the preceding set of steps.

What's on the CD

The following sections provide a summary of the software and other materials you'll find on the CD.

Content

The CD includes files for each of the 171 forms from the book in Word and .pdf format. Word files are designed with open spaces so readers can record information and/or customize them. PDF files (or "programs") provide information and can only be printed out. All documentation is included in the folder named Content.

Applications

The following applications are on the CD.

Adobe Acrobat Reader
Adobe's Acrobat Reader is a freeware viewer that allows for viewing files in the Adobe Portable Document format.

Microsoft Word Viewer
Microsoft Word Viewer is a freeware viewer that allows you to view but not edit most Microsoft Word files. Certain features of Microsoft Word documents may not display as expected from within Word Viewer.

OpenOffice.org
OpenOffice.org is a free multiplatform office productivity suite. It is similar to Microsoft Office or Lotus SmartSuite, but OpenOffice.org is absolutely free. It includes word processing, spreadsheet, presentation, and drawing applications that enable you to create professional documents, newsletters, reports, and presentations. It supports most file formats of other office software. You should be able to edit and view any files created with other office solutions.

Shareware programs are fully functional, trial versions of copyrighted programs. If you like particular programs, register with their authors for a nominal fee and receive licenses, enhanced versions, and technical support.

Freeware programs are copyrighted games, applications, and utilities that are free for personal use. Unlike shareware, these programs do not require a fee or provide technical support.

GNU software is governed by its own license, which is included inside the folder of the GNU product. See the GNU license for more details.

Trial, demo, or evaluation versions are usually limited either by time or functionality (such as being unable to save projects). Some trial versions are very sensitive to system date changes. If you alter your computer's date, the programs will time out and no longer be functional.

User Assistance

If you have trouble with the CD-Rom, please call the Wiley Product Technical Support phone number at (800) 762-2974. Outside the United States, call 1(317) 572-3994. You can also contact Wiley Product Technical Support at **http://www.wiley.com/techsupport.** John Wiley & Sons will provide technical support only for installation and other general quality control items. For technical support on the applications themselves, consult the program's vendor or author.

To place additional orders or to request information about other Wiley products, please call (800) 225-5945.

Coach U, Inc. Intellectual Property Rights

The following are the intended guidelines as to what you may and may not do with the Coach U, Inc. created materials, concepts, tools, processes, and programs. We encourage you to use many of the Coach U, Inc. programs and materials in ways that benefit you, your coachees, and your business. We are committed to your satisfaction and support as someone who is interested in Coach training and the profession of Coaching, so please read these guidelines with that in mind. If you have further questions or need additional support, please email licensing@coachu.com with your question or request.

THE BASIC INTELLECTUAL PROPERTY RIGHTS:

As an original purchaser of this material you are granted a license to use, not ownership of, specific materials and programs that are a part of Intellectual Property of Coach U, Inc. A license grants permission to use the selected programs and materials in approved ways.

Individual Use:
Coaches may use/duplicate/share/teach all of the "Coachee Coaching Programs" to anyone, group or individual, in a TeleClass, onsite, live workshop or live presentation, with no royalty due to Coach U, Inc. or permission required. This includes programs such as the Clean Sweep, 25 Secrets, Personal and Professional Foundation, and Irresistible Attraction, etc. When using the material, the integrity of the material needs to remain intact and the creation/copyright/contact information for Coach U, Inc MUST be included in use of the material (sample: copyright, 2005 Coach U, Inc.com, all rights reserved. www.coachu.com).

Use for the Training of Coaches:
If it is your intention to use these materials as curriculum for the training of coaches we ask that you request permission from Coach U, Inc. as original authors of this intellectual property. Our intention in making this request is not to restrict the use of the materials in any way but to support you in creating training programs that maintain the integrity of our intellectual property. Such requests can be made by sending an email to licensing@coachu.com.

Interested in Learning More?

We primarily provide coach training to individuals wishing to become certified coaches. We also offer other coach training, personal development, and professional development programs to individuals and organizations in person and through distance learning using the internet and TeleClasses.

Interested in Bringing Coaching to Your Organization?

If you would like to learn more about creating a coaching culture within your organization or having us speak at one of your organization's events, we would be happy to discuss this with you. We are experienced in providing customized coach training programs, individual and group coaching services, and can also consult with you to develop other customized programs.

Interested in Hiring a Coach?

Our International Coach directory contains listings of hundreds of Coach U and Corporate Coach U trained coaches located throughout the world. For information on how to hire a coach or to view profiles of coaches complete with contact information, please visit www.findacoach.com.

Don't forget to request your complimentary copy of our book *Becoming A Coach*.

Contact Us Today

1-800-48COACH
admissions@coachinc.com
www.coachinc.com
www.ccui.com / www.coachu.com

CoachInc.com
P.O. Box 881595
Steamboat Springs, CO 80488-1595

We Want Your Feedback!

We appreciate the opportunity to act upon your feedback. Whether you would like to share a positive review, provide constructive criticism, offer suggestions, or would simply like to share how this publication has made an impact on you or your organization, we want to hear from you. Thank you in advance!

Jennifer Corbin
President of Coach U and Corporate Coach U
jennifer@coachinc.com
1-800-329-5655